THEORY AS RESISTANCE

CRITICAL PERSPECTIVES
A Guilford Series

Edited by
DOUGLAS KELLNER
University of Texas, Austin

Postmodern Theory: Critical Interrogations
Steven Best and Douglas Kellner

A Theory of Human Need
Len Doyal and Ian Gough

Psychoanalytic Politics, Second Edition:
Jacques Lacan and Freud's French Revolution
Sherry Turkle

Postnational Identity:
Critical Theory and Existential Philosophy
in Habermas, Kierkegaard, and Havel
Martin J. Matuštík

Theory as Resistance:
Politics and Culture after (Post)structuralism
Mas'ud Zavarzadeh and Donald Morton

Theory as Resistance

POLITICS AND CULTURE AFTER (POST)STRUCTURALISM

Mas'ud Zavarzadeh
Donald Morton

THE GUILFORD PRESS
New York   London

©1994 The Guilford Press
A Division of Guilford Publications, Inc.
72 Spring Street, New York, NY 10012

All rights reserved

No part of this book may be reproduced, stored in a retrieval
system, or transmitted, in any form or by any means, electronic,
mechanical, photocopying, microfilming, recording, or otherwise,
without written permission from the Publisher.

Printed in the United States of America

This book is printed on acid-free paper.

Last digit is print number: 9 8 7 6 5 4 3 2 1

Library of Congress cataloging-in-publication data is available from
the Publisher.

About the Authors

Mas'ud Zavarzadeh writes on Marxism and (post)modernity, critical theory, film, and pedagogy, and is now at work on *The Alphabetical Life of Mas'ud Zavarzadeh*—narratives of racism, political exclusion, and the suppression of his writings in the "first world." He is the author of *The Mythopoeic Reality: The Postwar American Nonfiction Novel, Seeing Films Politically,* and *Pun(k)deconstruction and the (Post)modern Political Imaginary;* coauthor of *Theory, (Post)modernity, Opposition: An "Other" Introduction to Literary and Cultural Theory;* and coeditor of *Theory/Pedagogy/Politics: Texts for Change.*

Donald Morton teaches at Syracuse University and writes on critical theory and cultural studies, (post)modernity, and materialist queer theory. His writings have appeared in such journals as *Cultural Critique, Journal of Urban and Cultural Studies, Genders, Social Text,* and *diacritics.* He is the author of *Vladimir Nabokov;* coauthor of *Theory, (Post)modernity, Opposition: An "Other" Introduction to Literary and Cultural Theory;* and coeditor of *Theory/Pedagogy/Politics: Texts for Change.* He has just completed an oppositional anthology, *Reading (Post)modern Sexualities: The Return of the "Queer."*

v

We wish to thank the following publishers for permission to reprint materials previously published (sometimes in different form):

In Chapter 1, from "(Post)Modern Critical Theory and the Articulations of Critical Pedagogies" by M. Zavarzadeh and D. Morton, 1990, *College Literature, 17*(2/3), 51–63. Copyright 1990 by West Chester University.

In Chapter 2, from "Theory as Resistance" by M. Zavarzadeh, 1989, *Rethinking Marxism, 2*(1), 50–70. Copyright 1989 by the Association for Economic and Social Analysis.

In Chapter 3, from "Theory Pedagogy Politics: The Crisis of 'the Subject' in the Humanities" by M. Zavarzadeh and D. Morton, 1986/1987, *boundary 2, 15*(1–2), 1–22. Copyright 1987 by *boundary 2*.

In Chapter 4, from "The Cultural Politics of the Fiction Workshop" by D. Morton and M. Zavarzadeh, 1988–89, *Cultural Critique, 11*, 155–173. Copyright 1989 by Oxford University Press, Inc.

In Chapter 6, from "A Very 'Good' Idea Indeed: The (Post)Modern Labor Force and Curricular Reform" by M. Zavarzadeh and D. Morton, 1993, in *Cultural Studies in the English Classroom*, edited by J. A. Berlin and M. Vivion, Portsmouth, NH: Boynton/Cook. Copyright 1993 by Boynton/Cook Publishers, Inc.

In Chapter 7, from "Signs of Knowledge in the (Post)Modern Academy" by M. Zavarzadeh and D. Morton, 1990, *The American Journal of Semiotics, 7*(4), 149–160. Copyright 1990 by *The American Journal of Semiotics*.

In Chapter 8, from "Texts to Limits, the Limits of Texts, and the Politics of Contemporary Critical Theory" by D. Morton, 1990, *diacritics, 20*(1), 57–75. Copyright 1990 by The Johns Hopkins University Press.

Contents

Introduction:
Theory Now

1 The most urgent task for theory now, in this increasingly antitheoretical age, is to conduct – as we have done here – what amounts to a daily hand-to-hand combat with the liberal pluralism that underlies today's resistance to theory. After its decline in the aftermath of the Vietnam War, liberal humanism has once more returned to the knowledge industries of the advanced capitalist democracies. This return of liberalism in a "new" form has been enabled by shifts in understanding produced by (post)structuralism and (post)modernism. It has furthermore been strengthened by what seems to be, to those preaching the "end of history," indisputable evidence that capitalism has had a final triumph over communism in eastern Europe. We recognize that in the current climate, there is a strong risk in undertaking the kind of writing we have produced in this book, the hand-to-hand combat with the antitheorists, who in effect run the knowledge industry on behalf of the elite classes of the North Atlantic community. The risk is that the criti(que)al knowledge that results from such combat will be ruled – almost by reflex – "out of bounds," "unreasonable," and most tellingly, "extremist."

In its "revitalized" form, liberalism today supports not only the most easily recognizable elements of the "old" academic establishment, but even such seemingly "progressive" wings of higher education as the recently formed organization called Teachers for

1

a Democratic Culture, headed by Gerald Graff. Among the many "points" of their manifesto, Graff and his collaborators make sure to highlight one fundamental distinction for the public in which they are so interested (this happens to be such "sectors" of the public as grant-providing corporations and academic hiring and search committees). They draw a clear and firm line between those who, like themselves, are safely "raising legitimate questions about the relations of culture and society" and those questioners whom they (and their target "public") regard to be "extremists." However, the "extremists" they have in mind turn out to be in fact those who produce critique-al knowledge of the social totality, that is, knowledge that points to the manner in which the seemingly "progressive" practices of the Teachers for a Democratic Culture are in fact shown to be complicit with the very structure of exploitation that lies at the heart of the relations between culture and society under capitalism. Liberalism has always worked to suppress the knowledge of social totality that will reveal liberalism's exploitative and oppressive character. In striving to support the liberal democratic state, the bourgeois academy has always relegated such combative and explanatory critiques as the ones undertaken in the following pages to the space of "extremism." In other words, it interprets them as "polemics," which is the dominant academy's name for "nonknowledge." "Polemic," in the liberal academy's view, is the "other" of scholarly knowledge; it is therefore automatically "illegitimate."

As we argue in this book, the dominant academy is ultimately nothing more than an extension of the regime of wage labor and capital that has divided all contemporary societies into classes of the exploited and the exploiter and thus has produced a form of (in)human life founded on the asymmetrical distribution of economic resources on a global level. As knowledge workers, academics provide the abstract concepts needed to justify existing social relations. In return for their efforts, they receive their share of the surplus value. To be sure, the newer form of (post)structuralist-inspired liberalism has indeed declared itself (like Teachers for a Democratic Culture) to be "progressive." But its progressiveness aims merely at a superficial (superstructuralist) change in the existing social order by promoting a "multicultural community," the legitimacy of which is grounded in questions of representation and signification and whose vision of "freedom" amounts finally to nothing more than "free speech." In order to resist such superficial reformism and construct a new just society founded on economic equality, new theoretical knowledge of the social totality is urgently needed. Today's resistance to theory is precisely a resistance to such an emerging global understanding of capitalism.

Much like the traditional form of liberal humanism, the resurgent (post)modern liberalism resists theory in the name of defending the mutliplicity and incommensurable variousness of the experiences of the world's unique subjects. However, in actuality, this resistance to theory is only a new form of pragmatism that serves in this crisis moment of (post)modern capitalism as an apparatus of crisis management. This (post)modern pragmatism teaches the subject of late capitalism how to "survive" (get through) the contradictions of her "daily" life by ignoring the "big picture" (because, we are told, nobody knows exactly what it is anyway) and by dwelling instead on the actual, empirical aspects of "community" life. This pragmatism therefore rejects "theory" (the knowledge of totality) and focuses instead on the "dailiness" of life, taking the various facets of life as separate, discrete and utterly disparate entities. The dominant academy's antitheory theorists, therefore, turn themselves (and their students) away from the "abstract" and toward the "concrete"—as if these dimensions could ever be separated. By contrast, those who defend and promote the need for a theory of the "big picture" insist at the same time on the need for "coherence"; that is to say, they insist on examining the relationships among various facets of contemporary life that the pragmatists present as separate and incommensurate. It is this "coherence"—in the light of which a "total" knowledge of social practices is developed and the contradictions of ruling property relations are revealed—that is erased by the resistance to theory.

The resistance to theory is being promoted today in dominant academic and intellectual circles by a large number of writers: (post)structualists like de Man, Derrida, Lyotard; pragmatists like Fish and Rorty; performativists like Jardine and Butler; old liberals like Graff and Henry Louis Gates; advocates of the cult of experience like bell hooks, Lawrence Grossberg, Constance Penley, Andrew Ross, and other cultural studies critics; and those post-Marxists like Spivak, Aronowitz, Mouffe, and Laclau, who have in fact legitmated most of the dominant theories. No matter from what quarter its support comes, this resistance to theory is in the end a strategy of crisis management, nothing more than an ideological alibi that substitutes "ethics" (knowledge of the contingent) for "politics" (knowledge of the necessary). Theory resisters regard "politics" to be an act of "totalizing" and therefore "totalitarian" – that is, theory is held to be unrespectful of the contingencies of the experiences of subjectivity. These contemporary resisters of theory and politics are, at the same time, ardent ethics promoters. From their perspective, "ethics" is a mode of knowing and judging without appeal to any grounded norms. In short, ethics is put forward as a pragmatic, case-by-case process for dealing with "experience." This kind of ethical "knowledge" is therefore an ideal mode of knowing for dealing with (that is, for "erasing") the contradictions of daily life in class societies. Why has "ethics" become the privileged practice in the dominant academy? Precisely because it legitimates a case-by-case meditation on "life" that localizes class contradictions and, in doing so, renders invisible the structure of exploitation and oppression that underlies all these localities in class societies. The resistance to theory has therefore, in its most recent form, "gone ethical" and has finally naturalized what Geertz calls "local knowledge" (Geertz, 1983). It is this "local and localizing knowledge" that the writings of this book combat in support of a global knowledge that is capable of making available to its readers the logic of exploitation that underlies all practices of class societies.

Today's antitheory (which is actually itself the most dominant form of "theory" in the ludic academy) is thus an ideological alibi used to defend that "varying" and multiple subject needed by capitalism's "free" market. The resistance to theory has become, in actuality, the rejection of all those explanatory critiques and radical forms of knowledge that have already demonstrated bourgeois democracy to be itself a cover for exploitation at the very point of production–at the site of the deployment of labor power–in capitalist social relations.

In their most popular form, these antiproductivist forms of knowledge are of course set forth in the theories of the writers we have already mentioned. By instituting the "ethical" (the care of the self) against the political, on the one hand, and exchange value against use value, on the other, these apologists for liberalism posit democracy as an unending chain of contingent, incommensurate signifiers without any "totality," without any point of anchoring (that is, no place to situate "the origin" or "cause" of exploitation). Just reading the "signifiers" itself, in the ludic regime of knowledge, becomes, in the words of J. Hillis Miller an "ethical" act. Ethical readers like Miller read to discover only the local effects and not the logic of totality that structures the regularity of those localities. Process not production, exchange not use, signifier not signified, irony not epistemology, reading justly not justice, multiculturalism not class . . . these concepts form the grid of intelligibilities through which today's dominant (post)modern ludic knowledge is disseminated under the sign of (liberal) antitheory theory.

2   From the perspective just articulated, this book attempts to locate and trace various forms of resistance to theory in the (post)modern academy. It is thus a multiple text; its combat with liberalism takes multiple forms: formal essay, letter, collage, transcript of tapes, and manifesto. In short, the book attempts to "un-limit" theory, that is to say, to indicate how all regions of the bourgeois academy are constructed not out of the unquestionable truth emanating from the "nature" of things but out of theoretical assumptions that justify the free market; the exploitation of labor; complicit subjectivities; descriptive, ludic knowledge; evasive pedagogies; and coalitionist politics. This text is then "un-limit-ing" in the sense of being transgressive: it attempts to work its way *beyond* the familiar boundaries of contemporary theory, beyond the question of the canon, beyond the established and familiar protocols of reading, beyond the reigning trope-ical contemporary thinking, beyond the psychoanalytical "ignorance" so widely feigned today, beyond the epistemological (anti)foundationalism now dominant in the contemporary academy, and beyond the project of ludic "ethics." We have not directly engaged questions of labor theory, except in part of a chapter, because our aim here has been to examine the outcome rather than the processes of exploitative labor relations. We have, however, attempted to place theory in spaces where it is not used to finding itself: particularly in the spaces of pedagogy (which we understand to be not only acts undertaken in the "classroom," but all acts of cultural [re]production) where theory is asked to address new and even outrageous questions about its own legitimacy, end(s), and deployment.

For quite some time now, as we argue throughout this book, contemporary theory (antitheory theory) has been the captive of professionals of ideology. These are persons who have made careers out of watching over theory's "purity" and promoting what they regard to be its "strict" and "proper" uses within the confines of bourgeois academic and intellectual institutions. Their efforts to keep theory "clean" are basically efforts to block any trangressive theoretical discourses from disturbing the peace (and bourgeois comfort) of dominant academic and intellectual circles. These institutional peace keepers have made a special point of trying to erase the thought that theory might in fact lead to a praxis that will change society and its institutions. In their hands theory has lost its radical, transformative power and become just one more institutional discourse among many others: a privileged discourse, perhaps, but one still framed within, and bounded by, already existing discourses. In other words, although at one time, theory constituted a stubborn and resistant "outside" to the academy, it has become an insider. What's more, it has indeed used most of its energy over the last two decades to make the outside collapse into the inside and to argue that there are no such distinctions as "outside/inside," "theory/experience," "idea/discourse." The move of collapsing the outside/inside distinction, we believe, supports the dominant ideology, which is constantly striving for the elimination of the threat posed by any "outside." The "resistance" of our title, therefore, also refers to this stubbornly struggling outside. We want to make it clear that we understand this outside not as an already "known," epistemologically constituted domain of oppressive "norms," but as a historically produced and situated site from which to ask the kinds of questions we have raised in this book—questions about the political economy of theory, its constitution, its dissemination, its status as a guide to praxis, and finally its claim to legitimacy in the (post)modern moment.

3 Throughout the chapters that follow, we have used the term "ludic (post)moderism" (which we have taken from Teresa L. Ebert). We have explained "ludic (post)modernism" in our book, *Theory, (Post)Modernity, Opposition* (1991, 105–128), but we think it requires annotation here. We use "ludic" (post)modernism to mean an understanding of (post)modernity that makes sense of it as a problematics of "representation" and, furthermore, conceives "representation" as merely a rhetorical issue, a matter of signification in which the very process of signification (the machinery of meaning production as such) articulates the signified. Knowledge of the "outside"—if one can mark such a zone of being—is, according to ludic theory, traversed by rifts, slippage, and alterity that are immanent in signifying practices and above all in language. Representation, in other words, is always incommensurate with the represented since it is subject to the law of *différance*. Ludic (post)modernism, therefore, posits the "real" as an instance of "simulation" and in no sense as the "origin" of a "truth" that can provide a ground for a political project. *Différance*, in ludic (post)modernism, is regarded to be the effect of the unending "playfulness" (thus the term "ludic") of the signifier in signifying practices. It can no longer acquire representational authority by anchoring itself in what Derrida has called the "transcendental signified" (*Writing and Difference* 1978, 20).

Contesting the understanding of *différance* as an effect of rhetoric, "resistance (post)modernism"—of which we see our book as a part—articulates difference as the effect of "labor," focusing on congealed and alienated labor as private property. Labor, not language, we believe, is the frame of intelligibility that determines the regime of signification and the ensuing "representation" of the real. Language, and all other semiotic processes, are articulated by the division of labor. Difference, in short, is a "materialist" praxis produced through class struggle and not a "rhetorical" effect.

The argument of our book, then, is that like all limits, the limits that "ludic (post)modernity" has placed on theory today are neither "natural" nor "inevitable," but a part of the politics of the contemporary moment of late capitalism: it is in order to demystify the "obviousness" of the boundaries drawn for theory *now* that we focus here on the politics we must overcome in our "resistance" operation.

We would like to thank Teresa Ebert; Douglas Kellner; Robert Merrill; Benjamin, Karen, and Samantha Morton; Scott Severance; and Peter Wissoker, who have supported us intellectually and offered advice for re-understanding our projects in a more productive manner. We would also like to thank Mary Ellen O'Connell for her editorial assistance.

CHAPTER 1

(Post)modern Critical Theory and the Articulations of Critical Pedagogies

Since the early 1970s there has been much talk in U.S. universities about the need to change literary studies, especially the study and teaching of English. These discussions have been prompted by the impact of the works of European philosophers, intellectual historians, anthropologists, and literary critics collectively known as structuralists and (post)structuralists. There was a strong resistance in the United States to these thinkers, not only because their ideas were so unfamiliar but also because they were delivered in a language unintelligible to the average American academic. Words and phrases like "aporia," "mise-en-abyme," "interpellation," "pleasure," "dissemination," "articulation," and "the subject" were part of a language so opaque that it seemed to parody the very idea of communication.

The most basic reaction of the American academics was to claim that what these thinkers offered was fake and fraudulent, nothing more than old ideas couched in arcane jargon. For example, the humanists (as their opponents, who came to be called theorists, called these traditional literary scholars) argued that "the subject" was merely a fancy term for "the individual" and that theorists were trading on a false newness by applying an unfamiliar term to a well-known idea. For their part, the theorists took the humanists' equation of the subject with the individual as a sign of the humanists' philosophical naiveté. Left-leaning theorists argued that resistance to the idea of "the subject" was not just philosophical simplicity but rather part of a hidden political agenda, a result of an unwillingness to give up the notion of the free, enterprising, independent "individual." For politically active critics and English professors, in fact, the question of "the subject" eventually became the rallying point for showing how the traditional English curriculum—and the humanities in general—prompts students to view themselves as free individuals, at the same time blocking any inquiry into the status of this freedom.

To outsiders, of course, all this sounds rather insignificant: the choice between "subject" and "individual" may seem like quibbling. These people see a liberal education as simply a matter of turning out skillful, well-rounded, and independent-minded students. Theorists, however, argue that the production of a well-rounded person is in fact the cornerstone of contemporary capitalism, which they believe is exploitative by definition. In their view, capitalism works by producing (Louis Althusser calls it "interpellating") individuals in such a way that they think of themselves as being in control of their own actions, as masters of their own destinies, as the source of their own social values—in short, as "sovereign subjects." Theorists maintain that capitalism needs people who are unaware that they are constituted by existing social arrangements (for instance, by class, race, or gender relations) and who instead see themselves as being the way they are "naturally."

The conflict between humanists and theorists, therefore, evolves around the understanding of the human person. Before developing our argument here, we must pause to discuss briefly the dynamics of social change that affect all aspects of social life, whether on the specific level of the curriculum or on more general levels of culture and politics. Social change is not caused voluntaristically. That is to say, it does not come about by people dreaming of an alternative and then putting forth that alternative as a way to transform social structures. Change comes about, as Marx explains in his 1859 "Preface," from the conflict between the productive forces and social relations that set boundaries or enable the movement of productive forces. The possibility of an alternative (change), as Marx argues, does not occur to the individual before the emergence of necessary historical conditions. "No social order is ever destroyed before all the productive forces for which it is sufficient have been developed, and new superior relations of production never replace older ones before the material conditions for their existence have matured within the framework of the old society" (Marx, 1981, 21). The humanists and the theorists who participated in the debate over the change of curriculum were therefore acting within the historical conditions of (post)modern capitalism, which demanded change since it no longer had any use for the older humanities. The older humanities had taught students to adhere to such historically obsolete notions as "the coherent subject," "the nuclear family," "realism," and "the hegemony of heterosexuality." Transnational capitalism demanded, among other "new" things, a more flexible and multifaceted subject that did not insist on "coherence." The contestation between the humanists and the theorists was part of the contestations to determine the priority of "emergent" (postmodern) or "residual" (modern) relations of production. "Mankind thus inevitably sets itself only such tasks as it is able to solve, since closer examination will always show that the problem itself arises only when the material conditions for its solution are already present or at least in the course of formation" (Marx, 1970, 21). The humanists, in other words, were attempting to maintain those residual relations of production which were more appropriate for the earlier stages of market capitalism, while the theorists were responding positively to the demands of newer forms of transnational capitalism.

This, of course, raises a further question: is a "positive" and uncritical response to emergent forms of social relations a progressive practice in itself? It was around this issue that fractures and contestations among the theorists themselves developed. Some accepted the emergent social relations as liberating, innovative, and boundary forms of consciousness, while others were highly critical of these newer forms of social relations which, they believed, simply extended the range of deployment of capital and provided more flexible and subtle ways for capitalism to strengthen its hold over the international labor foce. *Change* had become historically possible and indeed necessary, but the question remained, Change in which direction?

Those theorists who fetishized the interests of the ruling class embraced uncritically the emergent social relations and quickly proceeded to institutionalize theory and to represent (post)modern theory in and of itself as an emancipatory intervention in the traditional curriculum and the mode of Cartesian subjectivity it had propagated. At Carnegie-Mellon University, Duke University, and Syracuse University (as we explain later), theory was institutionalized by claiming that it would free students from the shackles of the old subjectivities.

Throughout this book, we take an oppositional view of theory. First, we do not approach theory as a metalanguage nor equate it with (post)modern theory (deconstruction, [post]structuralism, New Historicism, ludic feminism, . . .), but instead understand theory to be a critique of material intelligibilities and a producing of historical knowledge of the social totality. Second, we believe that the teaching of theory should be displayed by teaching theoretically, and furthermore that theory should always be a "criti(que)al" theory, that is to say, it should provide critical (not simply affirmative) knowledges of social totality for the student so that he or she sees his or her positionality in social collectivity: that is, in social relations and the political economy of labor.

To sum up, the early turmoil over the curriculum was (as we describe in detail in Chapter 6) the site for contestations over the training of the labor force in response to changes within capitalism of forces of production. Humanists, like nineteenth-century Luddites, attempted to hold onto the old relations of production while theorists were aware of the historicity of those relations and attempted to open up spaces in the curriculumm to register the consequences of newer forms of social relations. However, among theorists themselves there were those who simply embraced theory as an "avant-garde" form of consciousness, and those who insisted on a criti(que)al understanding of emerging social relations (in order to direct it in the interest of social collectivity) and the necessity of historical knowledge provided by theory of the positionality of the subject of learning in these new frames produced by history.

In the following pages, for the sake of brevity, we stage this debate as if it occurred between humanists and theorists without creating differences among theorists. As our discussion progresses in this book, we will make further distinctions among the theorists themselves.

To return to our earlier discussion: theorists argue that students who have been produced by liberal education to think of themselves as free subjects will then "freely" subject themselves to the economic needs of the capitalist system and thereby sell themselves, as the popular phrase goes, to the highest bidder. From their point of view, far from "educating" well-rounded, free individuals, liberal education actually constructs one-dimensional subjects to fit the economic needs of the ruling classes. In this process, English departments therefore work as the agents of the capitalist economic system: they teach students to read literary works (the classics) in terms of their moral values and with attention to their stylistic features, thus evading questions about their ideological and political functions. Accordingly, in order to change English departments, a new set of questions should be raised about such fundamental issues as "the subject" (the student as a structure of cultural and economic codings and practices that have political implications and consequences), reading lists (the established canon of "acceptable" and "relevant" readings), and the act of reading itself.

The debate over new modes of reading and whether and how much to dismantle the established canon has led ultimately to a larger battle over the curriculum. In this battle—which has, in the past decade or so, divided English departments nationwide into traditionalists and theorists—the real institutional power has been held, more or less, by liberals who occupy the political center. The "center" is a structured space of containment in bourgeois institutions; it is marked by a highly plastic formation. Its plasticity enables it to assimilate the most advanced dissenting ideas and conserve established practices by rearticulating them in the new languages of the dissenters. The political role of the center is thus superstructural: it obscures economic domination in constant ideological (rhetorical) adjustments. We shall have more to say about rhetoric and the reasons for its immense influence in the (post)modern academy in the following pages. Although they sympathize mainly with the traditionalists and with humanist conventions, liberals have had to acquire the theorists' vocabulary, if only to update their skills and obtain what has become a marketable (new) subjectivity in the (post)modern academy. This liberal group, which constitutes the numerical majority of professors and runs the universities by involvement in committee work and in the established system of awards/rewards, has grown more comfortable with theory in recent years, but is still unwilling to abandon the basic tenets of established humanities studies.

The result has been a curious rewriting of the literary studies curriculum in U.S. universities. The curriculum has indeed changed in a certain sense: not only graduate students but even undergraduates in English are being taught "theory" today. (Some departments and programs have even gone so far as to change their names, for example, from "English" to "textual studies.") However—and this is what disturbs many politically committed pedagogues—in spite of this "change," everything remains the same: the basic ideology of the curriculum remains as it was, and, in spite of the possibilities for change offered by "theory," English department faculties continue to recycle the old values and practices with new theoretical strategies.

The most visible recent examples of the use of a "new" curriculum to contain change are to be found at elite private universities like Duke and Carnegie-Mellon, for instance, which have revamped their traditional programs and are trying to enhance their academic prestige in the process. Carnegie-Mellon's program is called "Literary and Cultural Studies." Duke's well-publicized move to transform its literary studies programs illustrates how the curriculum can be changed without transforming the basic structure of English studies. At the same time it shows how the idea of change can be used to conduct a public relations blitz. In the following chapters, we shall come back to the crisis management strategies at Duke, Carnegie-Mellon, and other universities. Here, however, by way of a general overview, we would like to make a few observations on their tactics of normalization.

In 1987 Duke was the subject of a three-page feature article in *The Chronicle of Higher Education,* "A Constellation of Recently Hired Professors Illuminate the English Department at Duke" (Heller 1987). In the article, Frank Lentricchia, one of the academic stars at Duke, pointedly acknowledges the widespread expectation that, if the consequences are taken seriously, curricular change can be painful and disruptive to institutions. But he nevertheless claims with pride that Duke has miraculously escaped paying the price for serious change. Lentricchia is quoted as saying that in his department, where "a revolution" in English studies is taking place, there "ain't any [bloodshed]" (Heller 1987, 12). This is not surprising, since on closer inspection it becomes clear that the changes at Duke are liberal "reforms" aimed at saving the student as "free" subject of capitalism (by preserving the dominant "structures" of knowledge). Lentricchia's own "change"—from cultural radical to New Age mystic searching for relief by going on "retreat" ("En Route to Retreat," 1992)—is relevant here because it marks the philosophical and social assumptions of one of the architects of the Duke curriculum.

It is significant that the chairman of Duke's "changed" English department, Stanley Fish, is a leading U.S. exponent of the theoretical approach to literary studies called "reader response criticism." According to this theory, the reader does not merely, as in the traditional view, passively extract from the text the meaning the author has put into it or the text's own (objectively verifiable) meaning, but in fact puts into the text what he or she sees as its meaning. This theory, which serves as the ground for Fish's later antifoundationalist neopragmatism, has been enthusiastically received in the U.S. academy because it gives new legitimacy to the traditional idea of the free, enterprising, pragmatic individual. It endorses the popular notion of participation without ever forcing questions about the political and social "principles" or consequences of what one is participating in. To "disparticipate" (see

Chapter 6), from this point of view, is to be "inactive," not to reject politically the "entrepreneurial" practices *actually* celebrated in the guise of a theory of reading. Rather than asking "What are we reading for?" or "What's being legitimated in our reading?," Fish is interested in pragmatics: finding out what operations are involved in the act of reading and how what might look like a foundation (principles) for meaning is itself actually the effect of prior readings/meanings.

Similarly, Duke's so-called revolutionary curriculum purports to undermine the traditional notion of the canon by altering the relationship between major authors, minor authors, and authors completely beyond the pale. On this issue, the *Chronicle* emphasizes that another new member of the Duke faculty is working not on classic U.S. authors like Herman Melville, but on the popular fiction of Louis L'Amour, as if the "replacement" of a popular culture author for a high culture author means, in fact, the displacement of the idea of the canon itself. All it really suggests is that the canon (as the dominant pattern of literary knowledge) is being reformed according to superstructural adjustments in culture: either by inclusion in the existing canon of previously excluded authors or by formation of another (in this case, a popular culture) canon to parallel the traditional one.

Instead of adopting Duke's expensive approach of hiring star professors, Carnegie-Mellon has focused more directly on producing a fully worked-out plan to foreground the new theoretical language and ideas. This plan's principal advocate, the former English Department chair Gary Waller, has dubbed it—with evident satisfaction—"the first poststructuralist literary curriculum" in North America (Waller 1985b, 6). What this means, however, is that students at Carnegie-Mellon will be exposed to a wide range of ideas drawn from the various (post)modern theoretical strategies (Saussure and linguistics, Eco and semiotics, Lacan and psychoanalysis, Irigaray and textual feminism, Derrida and deconstruction, and so forth) side-by-side with conventional survey courses and courses on such standard literary figures as Shakespeare and company. Again, as at Duke, what is being offered is an updated and adjusted curriculum that includes theory within the existing institutional framework, a curriculum that professionalizes theory, robbing it of its political edge in order to ensure that business in the renovated academy will continue along the same old lines, reproducing the ideological effects necessary for the constitution of the subject required by late capitalism.

This "reformism"–changing some insignificant features in order to relegitimate the dominant structure–can be seen in many new curriculum plans. At Syracuse, for example, the "new" English curriculum reintroduces a politically oppressive form of eclectic pluralism by simply providing three levels of study: the political, the historical, and the theoretical (see Chapter 6). Once again (as in the traditional curriculum) the notion is that a liberal education should produce a well-rounded individual, one who knows, in a *balanced* way, history, theory, and politics–the tropes of contemporary discourses on knowledge. What better way to do so than to expose students to many modes of knowing? The more diverse their knowledge, the better educated they are.

Syracuse's new curriculum is similar to many other "new" curricula in that it is part of a concerted political effort by neoconservatives to contain change by recycling traditional educational ideas and practices through updating literary studies as the study of rhetoric. This revival of the concept of rhetoric (through the deployment of the strategies developed in the writings of Jacques Derrida, Paul de Man, and their annotators and followers) is basically formalist: its main concern is with *how* discourses are produced and received without any concern with *why* they are there to begin with. Some more politically relevant forms of rhetorical studies, following the later writings of Michel Foucault and Michel de Certeau, attempt to overcome the reactionary aspect of rhetoric by posing ethical (but not political) questions about the ways that a particular text or discourse or way of conducting everyday life is legitimated in a given moment. Yet there is a vast difference between examining how certain ideas get legitimated and asking radical questions about their legitimacy. In fact, by distracting the attention of students to the study of processes of legitimation, the study of rhetoric ends up representing all existing discourses as automatically legitimate simply by virtue of their existence and thus, by implication, as equal. A rhetorician–in the name of the liberal ideal of pluralistic truth and the freedom of objective inquiry–can be as interested in the rhetoric of the Ku Klux Klan as in the rhetoric of the uprising in Los Angeles in 1992: all social phenomena are occasions for cognitive inquiry. There are no "grounds," no priorities, because priorities are assumed by this liberal ethic to be motivated politically (nonobjectively). But of course the very erasure of priorities is a form of giving priority to the already prior–of perpetuating, in the name of equality, the inequality between people who are already established and powerful and those who are not. This, of course, fits right into the dominant picture of what the academy is and tries to continue to be: a place where *all* inquiries are objective and equally urgent.

Advocates of theory, who envision the radical reconstitution of the student into a "subject of intervention," have found their study trivialized. The liberal faculty majority, who, although it marches today under the banner of fundamental educational innovation in almost every U.S. university and college English department, has contrived to trade one set of studies for another, purposefully leaving intact the overall institutional system that constructs student–citizens as bourgeois subjects and willing servants of the status quo. Marx once wrote, "It is clear that the arm of criticism cannot replace the criticism of arms. Material force can only be overthrown by material force: but *theory itself becomes a material force when it has seized the masses*" (Marx *Early Writings*, 251, emphasis added). The question for radical pedagogy, then, is how to make "theory" a material force, in other words, how to oppose both the traditional humanistic curriculum that attempts merely to enlighten the student and the now flourishing conservative (post)modern curriculum that also attempts to enlighten the student but in a "new" and "different" way.

Both traditional pedagogy and the "new" conservative (post)modern pedagogy are versions of what we discuss in Chapter 2 and might be called the "pedagogy of pleasure," a ludic educational program that takes the student to be a "free," enterprising individual and tries merely to enhance (make more "pleasurable") the student's experience of that supposed autonomy. By contrast, radical pedagogy is a pedagogy of enablement, one that attempts to turn theory not into yet another professional topic but into a material force. To do this, one has to raise questions that are missing not only from the traditional curriculum but also from the "new" ones, for instance, the question of what kind of student do these various programs attempt to produce: a knowledgeable, enlightened, well-rounded person of experience or a critical subject who knows that knowledge is a social product with political consequences who will be willing to intervene in the way knowledge is produced, not only in the classroom, but in all other sites of culture?

Radical pedagogy enables the student to see that his or her understanding of all of culture's texts (from philosophical treatises to popular television shows) is a result of her or his situatedness in a complex network of gender, class, and race relations that provide the subject with certain concepts. Such a student will realize that reading (and meaning) changes depending on whether the reader is male or female, a Hispanic or white, working class or upper class, because their subjectivities are historical: they mark different economic limits and different levels of access to knowledge. A student who knows these things can then begin to make the necessary connections between how he or she reads *Great Expectations* and how he or she "reads" Nicaragua and the changes in Eastern Europe, between the "sublime" "aesthetic beauty" of a Shakespeare sonnet and the "mundane" question of the plight of single mothers in the ghettos of New York City. In radical pedagogy, not only are the boundaries between texts dissolved—as conservative (post)modernism advocates—but also the lines between fields of knowledge (literature, economics, sociology, urban planning, and so on). We must add here that there is a fundamental difference between the way in which ludic (post)modernism theorizes this breaking down of the boundaries of knowledge and our own view of transdisciplinarity. The ludic mixing of fields of knowledge (interdisciplinarity) is a strategy for relegitimating pluralism and eclecticism: fields of knowledge are de-disciplined so that there can be a pluralistic interactivity among them—a mode of dialogical knowing that Rorty and others call "knowledge as conversation." Transdisciplinarity, by contrast, is not the peaceful, interactive coexistence of fields of knowledge but a transgressive form of redrawing the map of learning in a fashion that opens up new space for rising radical and revolutionary subjectivities. It is, in other words, knowledge with priorities – not conversation but critique. The question in transdisciplinary modes of knowing is not, for example, one of forming an alternative canon, but of how a particular canon is used. One can use either Shakespeare and Dickens (as the traditional curriculum does) or Saussure and Derrida (as the "new" curriculum does) in order to legitimate the dominant social system and the labor relations it justifies. The minimal radical alternative to this is to "read" the dominant social system and its texts against itself, finding in the folds, seams, and faultlines of its ideologies spaces in which to actively oppose oppressive modes of social and economic domination. Anything less than this partisan form of knowing will be a trivialization of educational "change."

2 As we enter the 1990s, this struggle over pedagogical practices and the curriculum can no longer be dismissed as merely a matter of petty squabbles among academic factions. It has produced the far-reaching institutional reconfigurations mentioned above. These institutional changes result, as C. J. Worth has suggested, from the "new kinds of coherence" produced by the impact of theory (Worth 1980, 29). Even more significant, it has resulted in the formation of a new field of intellectual and academic inquiry that we shall refer to as "critical pedagogy."

Before the onslaught of theory, notions of the good college or university teacher tended to rely heavily either on an analysis of the qualities of the teacher in question (that is, on the humanist notion of the "essentialized" individual – an ahistorical and nonmaterial subject) or on the presumed quality of the institution of higher learning to which the teacher is attached (that is, on unquestioned assumptions of institutional rankings; the two, of course are inseparable: a teacher at Harvard is presumed to be better than a teacher at Outerville State College). In recent years, however, under the impact of (post)modern theory, a sizable body of work in critical pedagogy has been produced that puts pressure on received valuations. It not only makes the concept of the "individual" problematic but also makes inquiries into the role of educational institutions in the production of the power/knowledge relations of culture. It shows that the "prestige" of an institution (which is equated with the quality of its pedagogy) is in fact the complex effect of political and economic (and not simply knowledge) relations. The scope of interest in this new field of inquiry can be indicated in brief by calling attention to the following developments: (1) the existence of professional groups such as GRIP (Group for Research into the Institutionalization and Professionalization of Literary Studies, a kind of U.S. version of the French GREPH, Group for Educational Research in Philosophy), which carries on investigations of these issues through conferences and investigated them in the journal *Critical Exchange* in its earlier stage of formation, and (2) the frequent appearance of special issues or parts of issues of major journals devoted to pedagogical concerns. One example is the Winter 1990 issue of *South Atlantic Quarterly*, "The Politics of Liberal Education"; another is the special double issue of *College Literature* (1990), "The Politics of Teaching Literature." Yet another example is the substantial portion of the February 1990 issue of *The Women's Review of Books* called "Women's Studies Enters the 1990's: A Special Section on Feminism in (and out of) the Classroom." Critical and scholarly journals as well as strictly professional journals (such as the MLA's publication, *Profession*) have devoted their attention to such matters. Interest has also spread from research institutions proper into other levels of teaching, including community colleges and high schools (for instance, the National Council of Teachers of English has published a book, *Practicing Theory in Introductory College Literature Courses*, which tries to reach college teachers as well as high school teachers). A number of university presses are publishing so many books on these questions that they have come to constitute a de facto series. The University of Illinois Press has published the following: Cary Nelson (ed.), *Theory in the Classroom*

(1986); Bruce Henricksen and Thaïs Morgan (eds.), *Reorientations: Critical Theories and Pedagogies* (1990); Susan Gabriel and Isaiah Smithson (eds.), *Gender in the Classroom* (1990); Donald Morton and Mas'ud Zavarzadeh (eds.), *Theory/Pedagogy/Politics: Texts for Change* (1991). The University of Minnesota Press has recently launched a new series on critical pedagogy under the editorship of Henry Giroux, whose pioneering work in the field precedes the emergence of (post)modern pedagogies in humanities departments. Henry Giroux, Peter McLaren, Alfred Apple, Ira Shor—in different ways—have all been instrumental in opening up new discursive spaces in educational practices in the United States. Broadly speaking, their pedagogy aims at freeing students from oppressive cultural frames of knowing by providing them with new ways of reclaiming authority for their own experience. This is essentially an activist, anti-elist pedagogy that draws, for at least part of its theory, on the writings of Paulo Freire. Although we have not engaged their projects in this book, in our critique of experience, we address some of the historical limits of experiential pedagogy that some of the work of these thinkers has addressed. The major difference between our own theoretical work and that of Giroux and McLaren in particular can be seen in a comparative reading of our text, "The Crisis of 'the Subject' in the Humanities" (see Chapter 3) and their essay, "Radical Pedagogy as Cultural Politics: Beyond the Discourse of Critique and Anti-Utopianism" (in Morton and Zavarzadeh, *Theory/Pedagogy/Politics*). Our idea of "critique" and their desire to go "beyond critique" mark the boundaries between the pedagogy of concept, on the one hand, and the pedagogy of experience, on the other.

The burgeoning of this new field of inquiry—how it came into being and the differing and contesting approaches taken to it—can be traced in a set of articles published in the last two decades in critical and scholarly journals supported by the most widely respected academic presses in the United States.

One prominent strand of critical pedagogy has defined itself within a deconstructionist framework. Early in this effort in the United States Christopher Fynsk published his essay "A Decelebration of Philosophy" (1978). There he reviews the book *Qui a peur de la philosophie?* produced by GREPH, with which Derrida is associated. The book's title (*Who's Afraid of Philosophy?*) hints at the anxiety shown by those who occupy positions of privilege and power in the face of the de-author-izing and de-center-ing possibilities of speculative thought, which by definition moves beyond and disrupts culture's established "common sense." As Fynsk indicates, the whole point of GREPH's project was to understand—in response to specific historical conditions—the relation of knowledge dissemination practices to structures of power: "a critique of the French philosophical institution . . . as a response to a more or less systematic project of isolation and even suppression of the discipline of philosophy [by French educational institutions]" that had gained new impetus from various legislative reforms. It was GREPH's goal to defend "philosophy's current place in the lycée (the 'classe de philosophie') while instituting a systematic critique of that position and a demand for its transformation" (Fynsk 1978, 80). In other words, the GREPH project raises the possibility of a defense of philosophy that is not a celebration of it as it stands but a decelebration (a critique) that aims at its transformation. Fynsk's essay was followed—in the pages of *diacritics*—by a number of texts which began not only to further articulate the issues but to situate them with increasing specificity in relation to the American academy. Two such works are James Siegel's "Academic Work: The View from Cornell" (1981) and Derrida's response to Siegel, "The Principle of Reason: The University in the Eyes of Its Pupils" (1983).

The deconstructionist—broadly (post)structuralist—line of critical pedagogy was expanded and institutionally acknowledged in an issue of *Yale French Studies* edited by Barbara Johnson, "The Pedagogical Imperative: Teaching as Literary Genre" (1982). This collection (which includes a few contributions by European thinkers like Derrida and Lyotard, but the greater number by American critics like Paul de Man, Shoshana Felman, Neil Herz, Michael Ryan, Jane Gallop, Joan de Jean, and Johnson herself) constitutes a "Who's Who" of (post)structuralist critical practice in the United States. Johnson characterizes these essays as not only dramatizing "the problematics of teaching," but also as providing teachers with the opportunity "to reflect on the nature of their profession and to examine the dynamics of their own language—indeed of language itself—in relation both to the play of power and to the process of understanding" (Johnson 1982, iii). The deconstructionist and grammatological importance of the project is further indicated in the special stress placed on *literarity*. Johnson says she does "not mean to estheticize pedagogy into a form of art, but rather to attempt to analyze how and what the literarity of literature itself 'teaches' " (p. iii). Following an exemplary deconstructive analysis of "The Rime of the Ancient Mariner" in her introduction, Johnson concludes that what literarity teaches is in fact "the agony of teaching": it is the moment of confronting the aporia in the text and learning the lesson of the fundamental undecidability of meaning. Furthermore, in Johnson's assertion that there is "always a 'written' dimension to the learning process" (which is an implicit invocation of the Derridean notion of Writing as the agency of *différance* and self-division—the lack of that very *identity* that is the ground of humanist pedagogy), we begin to glimpse the trajectory of what was shortly to come in Gregory Ulmer's well-known study *Applied Grammatology: Post(e)-Pedagogy from Jacques Derrida to Joseph Beuys* (1985a) and his more recent *Teletheory: Grammatology in the Age of Video*. Together they represent the fullest statement to date of what Mas'ud Zavarzadeh has called "pun(k)deconstructive" (see Zavarzadeh 1992b) critical pedagogy, which Ulmer himself calls "applied grammatology" and treats as a species of anecdote ("mystory") as the site of theorizing. For Ulmer anecdote plays the same pedagogical role that Johnson attributes to literarity: they are both places in which one learns not a positive, certain, decidable knowledge but a new relationship (that of Lacanian "ignorance") to the "real." The practical results of Ulmer's pedagogical project can be seen in the textbook he wrote with Robert Scholes and Nancy R. Comley, *Text Book: An Introduction to Literary Language* (Scholes et al. 1988).

The traditional humanist response to the pressure of theory—particularly of (post)structuralist theory—is articulated in a line of new pedagogy exemplified in the special issue of *Critical Inquiry* edited by Robert von Hallberg and later published as the book

Canons (1984). The genealogy of this line of thought (its connection, for instance, to the practices of I. A. Richards, Erich Auerbach, and even Foucault) is traced, in part, in Paul Bové's *Intellectuals in Power: A Genealogy of Critical Humanism* (1986). In the Hallberg collection, the mainstream academy is characterized as making an effort to come to grips with the pressures of contemporary thought is placing on its own standard, normative, and self-evidently meaningful pedagogical and curricular practices. However, in the very act of making the effort, the project underwrites itself with the same presuppositions that have always informed traditional practices, that is, eschewing the theoretical consistency and rigor displayed by the Johnson collection. As such this one is frankly eclectic, its essays reflect what Hallberg says is "the range of current thinking about canon-formation" (Hallberg 1984, 1). To return to the distinctions introduced above, whereas the Johnson collection represents the interests of the theorists (who stress the value of speculative thought, the importance of theoretical rigor, the inseparability of theory from practice, the limitations of common sense, and so on), the Hallberg collection represents the interests of the humanists (who assume that theory is a metalanguage occupying a space distant from and barely related to their own concerns—the importance of practical and not speculative thought, the celebration of common sense, and so on). The distance between the two collections (their preoccupations and theoretical commitments) is evident in the different, if somewhat overlapping, conceptual series designated by each editor as fundamental to their projects: Johnson sees her collection as concerned with "authority, seduction, judgment, resistance, desire, mystification, narrative, ignorance, and the relations between the sexes" (Johnson 1992, iii), whereas Hallberg's is concerned with " 'politics,' 'economy,' 'social,' 'authority,' 'power' " (Hallberg 1984, 1). The difference is, in part, that the first discursive/conceptual series contains a reflexiveness (by which, for instance, authority is problematized through such notions as desire and seduction) that is absent in the second series. According to Hallberg, the *Canons* collection as a whole investigates three broad questions: "how artists determine canons by selecting certain styles and masters to emulate; how poet-critics and academic critics, through the institutions of literary study, construct canons; and how institutionalized canons effectively govern literary study and instruction" (1984, 1–2).

It must be noted that the discourses of Hallberg's "overview" have nothing to do with (post)modern theory, hardly give any evidence of reflexive thought; instead they draw heavily on the traditional category of the "individual," essentialize the human subject in a commonsensical fashion, and thus situate the Hallberg project as an effort by the traditional mainstream—that needs to show that it can indeed "look at itself and its practices" when pressured to do so—to respond to the challenge of theory. When Hallberg remarks that "the formation of canons is a measure of the strength of institutions devoted to the study of art" (Hallberg 1984, 1), he hints that his volume—whatever the critical intentions of some of its contributors—is a celebratory rather than a decelebratory project (to abandon canons would require abandonning the very premises of essentialism, eclecticism, and so on, on which the collection is based), that it represents business as usual in the academy where *criticism* rather than *critique* is the only intelligible and acceptable mode of operation. Furthermore, although Hallberg tries to locate the collection in an oppositional political space by noting that today's "intellectuals" (he is presumably referring to himself and his contributors) recognize their "adversarial role" "by consensus," he conflates intellectuals with academics and, in any case, goes on to trivialize their supposed oppositionality by suggesting that it is motivated simply by the fact that they are not getting their share of the wealth of the economy. In Hallberg's view, then, intellectuals/academics merely constitute one more "interest group" (upper middle class and professional rather than blue collar) like all the other interest groups that take as their social goal trying to get their "fair" slice of the U.S. economic pie.

As part of the same humanist, moral approach to pedagogy, Gerald Graff presents the notion of the pedagogy of conflict. In his "Teach the Conflicts" (Gless and Smith 1991, 57–73), Graff argues that mainstream pedagogy is essentially immoral because it hides from the learner the conflicts that are involved in the actual constitution of knowledge. The best pedagogy, then, according to Graff, is ethical: it rends the veil of concealment and exposes the student to the presence of conflicts. Graff's pedagogy of honesty, however, is his contribution to managing the current crisis of the capitalist knowledge industry because the main purpose in "teaching the conflicts" is to establish a "conversation" among the conflicting discourses and thus – by reasserting neopluralism – diffuse them. Graff's is thus a counterrevolutionary pedagogy with a slightly different articulation of the neopragmatic theories of Rorty and others who deploy "conversation" as a way of deferring reaching any conclusion about the political economy of knowledge. This, as we shall see, is the model behind all "new" curricular reforms. Syracuse University's "new" curriculum in "English and Textual Studies" – which has had a great influence on Graff's notion of teaching the conflicts – is based on the same maneuver.[1] The purpose of the new curriculum, according to "Not A Good Idea" (Syracuse University's explanation of its new curriculum) is to structure the curriculum itself as a "series of conflicting practices" (Cohen et al. 1988, 5) and thereby avoids the "reduction of those conflicts" (1988, 5) into a new answer.

The idea of learning as the acquisition of the ability to raise questions is, of course, an ancient one. The knowledgeable person, in all conservative theories, is the one who has questions and is emphatic about his "ignorance" of "answers." Only crude and reductive revolutionaries have "answers": the knowledgeable person is too subtle for answers. Avoiding answers is, of course, one way to avoid conclusions: to provide answers for such questions as "Why are things the way they are?" or "How can an end be put to class exploitation?" is to prepare the student to participate in social change. Graff is absolutely clear that he is *not* interested in deploying pedagogy for social change. He states that he finds "it tempting to try to turn the curriculum into an instrument of social transformation," but predictably he believes that the curriculum "should not become an extension of the politics of the left" (cited in Gless and Smith 1991, 70). Implicit in this view, of course, is the conviction that the current curricula are not extensions of the politics of the right. This assumption in Graff's theory therefore gives the right's position the status of the "natural" position. The ruling ideas (the dominant curriculum) are not the articulation of the ideas of the ruling classes, in Graff's view, but are in the curriculum because they are naturally the correct, mature, and subtle ideas. Only oppositional ideas are "extensions of left politics." Pedagogues such as Graff serve the ruling class in a most effective way by posing, as he says himself, as "leftists" (1991, 70). However, as we have indicated here, the views of these "leftists" are indistinguishable from those of the right. This is one reason for the immense popularity of such "leftists" and for their power in the (post)modern academy. Graff's ethical pedagogy is, it should be clear by now, aimed at erasing any knowledge with priorities. In his pedagogy priorities are immoral and unethical because they situate conflicts historically and aim beyond them toward a society without conflicts. Conflicts in the pedagogy of priorities are historical, that is, they are articulations of class conflicts. In other words, they are not permanent conditions of human life (as Graff believes), but are transitory features of life in class societies, especially in late capitalism. "Teaching the conflicts" is thus the pedagogy of late capitalism that through pluralism, dehistoricizes knowledge conflicts and fetishizes them as permanent and unavoidable conditions of knowing instead of seeing them as conflicts produced by class struggles and the class politics of knowledge— conflicts of knowledge, that is to say, in a particular phase of human history. Teaching conflicts historically (as conclusional contestations, that is, as controversies) is a radical issue we have dealt with elsewhere (see Zavarzadeh and Morton 1991, 1–6).

Whereas the (post)structuralist and the traditionalist perspectives have largely dominated the domain of critical pedagogy, others have begun to pressure both positions. For instance, the risk that focusing on the question of the canon may itself be a kind of business-as-usual way of trivializing the issues, has recently been pointed out by Hazel Carby, who writes that "debates about the canon are misleading debates" (Carby 1989, 36), if they really come down—as they have in the recent controversies over changes at Stanford and Duke— only to an argument about which texts should or should not be included in reading lists. The "hotly contested debates" about the canon are "absurd," she argues, because they "avoid the deeper problem" by forcing even people interested in "radical change . . . to act as if inclusions of the texts they favor" would take care of the problems of inequality (Carby 1989, 37). Carby points up the fact that both traditionalist critical pedagogy, which focuses on the surface questions of canonical inclusion/exclusion, and (post)structuralist critical pedagogy, which is preoccupied only with *representation, texts,* and *textuality,* are failing to reach the most significant levels of inquiry in pedagogical and curricular practices. Although Carby's observations must themselves be further examined, her remarks nevertheless hint at the complicity between these two presumably opposed forms of critical pedagogy that dominate the academic arena and collaborate to occlude more socially and politically productive modes of analysis. If (post)structuralist theory has introduced a dimension of self-reflexiveness lacking in humanist practices, it has nevertheless defined this self-reflexiveness more in textual, discursive, and significatory terms than in political terms. The implication to be drawn from remarks like Carby's is that we have reached a new stage in the debate over these issues, a stage at which the simplicities of a narrative that pits the humanists against the theorists must be pressured to reveal, as we argue in Chapter 2, Chapter 8, and in other places in this book, the overlapping political interests of the humanists with the dominant group of theorists, that is, (post)structuralists. These groups, once thought of as at war with each other, are now working together to maintain the academic status quo. (Post)structuralist theory has been thoroughly absorbed by the academy, and the language of *différance* does not seem to have made any difference in academic practices.[2]

From this perspective, what is urgently needed is a new critical pedagogy that reveals the merely localizing and reformist (not transformist) character both of traditional pedagogical practice (which defends the concept of the automonous and sovereign individual as its basic premise, sees signification as the effect of the individual, and conducts cultural politics as usual) and of (post)structuralist pedagogical practice (which though it displaces the notion of the individual in favor of the concept of the subect and sees the individual as the effect of signification, nevertheless limits cultural politics by situating it as a purely textualist and significatory activity, the aim being a supposedly oppositional act of delaying the connection of the signifier to the signified). What even the "political" approach of the latter ignores is a politics that aims at questions of the access of disenfranchised groups to the culture's bank of power/knowledge/resources. This is the "deeper problem" (not merely the superstructural character of oppressive and exploitative social relations) to which writers like Carby refer. Recently published texts that begin to probe this deeper problem tend to come from British academics who show a stronger awareness of inequalities in access to power and resources (i.e., of the problems of class structure) than do their U.S. counterparts. For example: Peter Widdowson (ed.), *Rereading English* (1982); Janet Batsleer et al. *Rewriting English: Cultural Politics of Gender and Class* (1985); and Frances Barker et al. (eds.), *Literature, Politics and Theory: Essays from the Essex Conferences 1976–84* (1986).

The preceding analysis raises a pressing question: if these competing and contesting understandings of teaching are indeed—as we claim—really decisively different, then how do they all form parts of something called critical pedagogy? This question has to be explored in terms of the different understandings of the word "critical" involved in the practices of each group. Contemporary humanists still tend to regard their pedagogy as "critical" in the sense that it involves "criticism," or the evaluation and judgment of the merits of various works of art and of those who teach them. That is, they still use "the critical" in the sense exemplified in works like Leavis's famous book, *Revaluations*. As for the other two groups, the term "critical" relates to the practice called "critique," that unlike criticism, must be understood as the investigation of the enabling conditions of production of meaning in culture. If this is the common ground of the latter two kinds of critical pedagogy, then what separates them? What is the difference between (post)structuralist "critique" and oppositional "critique"? How does the latter respond to the former's preoccupation with the significatory, the textual, the discursive? These are some of the issues that we shall take up in the following chapters as a part of a larger question: how to produce a "theory as resistance" in the sense of a theory whose main purpose is emancipatory.

CHAPTER 2

Theory as Resistance

. . . and your view of theory as an abstract apparatus of mastery – a metalanguage – leads you to the conclusion, for example, that poetry is, by nature, atheoretical. Poetry, in your discourse, however, stands for a structure of understanding: the specificity of the "aesthetic" experience in general. Paul de Man, in his discourses, regards this to be the particularity of the "rhetorical," but it operates as the strategy of a transhistorical general "literariness" that resists theory. I, on the other hand, understand theory to be what I call an "intelligibility effect" – a historical understanding of the material processes and contradictory relations through which the discourses of culture make sense. I therefore find it difficult to see how any cultural act that produces "meaning effects" could be outside such historical mediations and the workings of social intelligibilities and be atheoretical. To produce and to understand meaning effects is always already theoretical. Poetry is as much a theory of reality as any other discourse; it produces intelligibility and knowledge, and knowledge is always an effect of cultural and political institutions. To say, as you do, that poetry is by nature atheoretical amounts to saying that poetry is a transdiscursive act that is autointelligible – that it makes sense and is meaningful in and of itself outside all cultural mediations and without being entangled in the materiality of the signifying practices of society. Poetry, in short, is declared to be a transcendental moment of self-identity, panhistorical plenitude, and nonmaterial transparency.

To say that poetry is atheoretical is a partisan political statement and not, as you seem to think, a disinterested defense of the human imagination against the totalitarianism of theory, because what you are actually saying is that (poetry as the synecdoche of) desire is outside ideology. That this is a political program becomes clearer when you consider that it is aimed at, among other things, producing a particular type of subject. Reading poetry as an atheoretical and transhistorical discourse produces the reader as a nonconstrained, selfsame (speaking) subject who is marked by autonomy with direct, unmediated access to the plenitude of the imagination—a presence free from all social contradictions. This notion of the subject is necessary for the maintenance of existing exploitative social arrangements.

"Sense-full-ness," I believe, is the effect of cultural assumptions or frames of intelligibility and historical practices of knowing--in other words, a "theory." Such an understanding of theory makes it impossible for me to comprehend how anything could be anything by nature—poetry or nonpoetry. Things become "something" when they are used in a culturally senseful way, that is to say, when they are situated on a cultural grid of intelligibility in a social location. It is the process of such situating—the use of discourses to enunciate them—that produces a "thing" as (socially) "something." There are, of course, modes of representation that suppress the material processes involved in producing this cultural something and consequently attribute the "something" to the "thing itself" (that is to the "nature of things"), but this suppressing is itself a mode of cultural behavior and a consequence of the social situating of discourses. It is the effect of a theory of the real.

In short poetry is not "by nature" atheoretical; it is your "situating" of the discourse of poetry—its particular uses by you—that deems it atheoretical and "by nature" resistant to theory. In other words, the atheoreticality of poetry is the effect of your use of poetry. Because the site in which you produce poetry as atheoretical is your classroom, I would like to focus on the theory of pedagogy you use in the classroom.

1 In his writings on drama, Brecht speaks of a familiarizing drama and a familiarizing method of acting and, in contrast to them, proposes his own defamiliarizing drama and theory of acting. In the familiarizing drama, the "walls" of the theater are demolished and the experience on the stage is represented – following the codes of realism – as an alternative (imagined) form of life itself. The audience is removed from its habitual cultural situationality and is transported to a world other than the one in which it lives its routine life; consequently, for a short period of time, the audience is "liberated" from the drudgery of bourgeois life into a libidinal exuberance and autonomy.

The actor in this familiarizing drama also acts in a "transporting" manner: engaged in what Stanislavski called "method acting" (Stanislavski 1958, 36), she forgets herself (is liberated from her self) in the role assigned to her. Brecht thinks that familiarizing drama and acting lulls the audience into emotional submission and intellectual passivity. It is a drama that, in short, merely liberates the audience from their bourgeois lives, but fails, for ideological reasons, to emancipate them. His own theory of drama is based on the notion that the dramatic should not conceal itself, but, on the contrary, should mark itself as such: a constructed act, a social use of codes and language, a textual entity that never allows the audience to forget that it, too, is playing a cultural role (the role, that is, of audience), watching others (actors) play their own cultural role (producing an "aesthetic" experience). The purpose of such "marking" is to prevent the naturalization of social processes. "What is involved here," Brecht writes, "is . . . taking the human social incidents to be portrayed and labelling them as something striking, something that calls for explanation, not to be taken for granted, not just natural" (Brecht 1979, 125). The goal of this drama is to give the spectator the chance to "criticize" what it encounters "from a social point of view" (p. 86). The Brechtian actor involved in such dramatic performances has no urge for self-expression, for "making a part one's own," for a "spiritual experience" (pp. 22–29, 91–99). Rather than becoming one with his role, the actor stands outside it and points to his role and thus never allows the spectator to forget that he is watching an actor. For Brecht, this is necessarily a calculating actor, not a spontaneous one; she stands "between the spectator and the event" (p. 58). She has no use for the "artistic" marks popularized by the culture industry: improvisation, vision, originality, or the "mystic moment of creation" (p. 95) in the sense that the Stanislavskian "method actor" employs them in order to emphasize his or her own inner life. By foregrounding the actor's inner life social meaning evaporates. It is in the space between the actor and the role to which he gestures that the audience can intervene and begin its interrogation of the ideology and/or dramatic representation. Brechtian drama and acting are together a process of denaturalization – a theater with heavy, thick "walls" (of discursive practices), a theater firmly situated in the texts of history.

2 The site in which you construct poetry as atheoretical, namely your classroom, bears an uncanny resemblance to what Brecht describes as familiarizing drama. And like that drama, it produces certain ideological effects such as the panhistoricity of textuality (whether we call it "poetry," as you do, or generalize it into "literariness," as de Man does) that are necessary for the maintenance of dominant social arrangements. (By "your classroom" I mean the structure of pedagogy that you put forth as the ideal site for pedagogical activities.) As in the familiarizing drama, your classroom attempts to become one with reality itself and to liberate itself from its cultural situationality as a classroom. As in the familiarizing drama, it encourages its audience/participants to forget that they are being produced as subjects by their cultural positionality and thereby abandon not only their present but their past and future as well. This is the classroom without walls.

Despite their seeming differences, the dominant humanist and (post)structuralist pedagogies are alike in having always attempted to remove the "walls" of the classroom, because to remove the "walls" is to remove all traces of their own historical constructedness and their cultural limits and thus their political institutions. The hegemonic pedagogy is articulated by the prevailing relations of production that need their ideological effects for their own reproduction. But in order to operate effectively with the authority of (noninstitutionalized) "truth," hegemonic pedagogy represents itself as the autonomous search for knowledge, and attempts to erase all traces of its connections with the dominant economic practices that in fact determine what it will discover as "truth" and legitimate as "knowledge." The "walls" are markers of institutionality, that is to say, the ideological embeddedness of pedagogy (drama) in the ruling socioeconomic order. Bourgeois pedagogy has always made the eradication of these "walls" a professional priority for pedagogues. This project has been carried out at different historical moments according to varying strategies that are legitimated by historically convincing and up-to-date philosophical and theoretical discourses. Humanism is only one, although the most familiar, of these historical strategies for removing "walls" (denying the institutionality) of the classroom. It is so familiar in fact that, for many, humanist pedagogy is identical with bourgeois pedagogy itself. However, bourgeois pedagogy has many historical discourses and, as I have already hinted by drawing a parallel between your idea of "poetry" and Paul de Man's notion of "rhetoric," the most effective form of bourgeois pedagogy at this historical juncture is articulating itself in terms of (post)structuralist theory. (Post)structuralist theory/pedagogy, in other words, is the most recent updating of the processes and discourses through which the dominant ideology is reproduced.[1] In the familiar humanist pedagogy, the "walls" are removed by positioning the pedagogue and the student as sovereign subjects who originate meaning (just as the method actor creates a character through her "vision" and "originality") rather than as agents who produce meaning through the mediation of institutional arrangements that make certain "effects" intelligible as meaning. (Post)structuralist pedagogy removes the "walls" (the traces of the political) by offering textuality as a pan-historical truth that is considered to be beyond ideology, just as is the "truth" produced in humanist versions of bourgeois pedagogy. On the surface this may seem rather obscure because the whole point of "textuality," in the overt discourses of (post)structuralism, is to locate, with analytical precision, the markedness of truth in all texts of culture–including, presumably, the text of the classroom/the classroom as a text. But textuality in (post)structuralist pedagogy operates in such a manner as to place the classroom without walls (the classroom as text) beyond the reach of history and thus achieve the same ideological effects as those produced by other types of bourgeois pedagogy. The putative "war" between humanism and new theory, that is, (post)structuralism, is not a war between discourses that support and others that oppose bourgeois pedagogy. It is rather a family quarrel to determine which discourse represents the truth (of late capitalism) with authority and in an up-to-date and thus convincing fashion.

The real "foe" of bourgeois theory is "political" pedagogy/critique/theory against which humanism and (post)structuralism are in fact united. An even cursory look at the reconfiguration of the power structure of the academy will indicate how the "young Turks" of (post)structuralism (who have very quickly become "old") are now ruling the academy in a coalition with the traditional liberal conservatives (antitheorists) and the reactionary elements of creative writing programs in order to contain radical theory and pedagogy. This is the "foe" that Hazard Adams (the humanist editor of an anthology aimed at the wide dissemination of (post)structuralist theory) warns against. Mapping the quarrels on the scene of interpretation today, he concludes:

> The quarrel is sometimes seen as one between old style interpreters and the new style poststructuralist theorists known as deconstructionists. *But what I am concerned about here is a third force* . . . the triumph of a reborn sociology. So complete has this triumph been prophesied to be that the term "literary theory" is completely smothered by the term "critical theory," which in turn means only sociological analysis. Before this triumph has its way completely, we should ask what it represses. In the question we may yet rescue what must always be rescued from abstraction and generalization in order to maintain sanity: the unique and individual. (Adams "The Dizzi-

ness of Freedom; or Why I Read William Blake" 1986, 441, emphasis added)

It is in order to rescue the unique and individual (the subject of patriarchal capitalism) that resistance to theory has come about. Your "poetry" and de Man's "literariness" are all part of this discourse that attempts to project theory (concept) as the embodiment of a coercive totalitarianism so that it can demolish it and thereby rescue the unique, cellular, nomadic, and particular *experience* of the subject. By removing *theory as the critique of intelligibility* from the scene of "reading" texts of culture, experience is represented as the site of the real. By positing experience as the real, the resistance to theory actually protects the dominant ideology. However, there is no such thing as "experience" in culture; what is made sense of as "experience" is actually an "experience effect" that is constructed, by means of a theory of the real (legitimating the ruling social order), in the discourses of ideology. The politics of resistance to theory is one of collusion with the oppressive ruling social regime. The unity of the discourses of humanism and (post)structuralism in their resistance to theory and in their opposition to radical theory and its consequences does not, of course, mean that humanism and (post)structuralism do not distance themselves from each other. In fact, it is through various devices of distancing that bourgeois theory differentiates its diverse products (as in its production of consumer goods) and thus endows each of its manifestations with a seeming apartness and represents them as individual and unique theories in conflict with all the others. This represented difference gives each theory a local legitimacy by making it more responsive to specific regional demands on the conjunctural level, at the same time adding to the effectivity of bourgeois pedagogy–an ensemble of all differences, in its global operations. Diversity, in short, insures that the hegemonic pedagogy's agenda is reproduced in all sites of culture.

I shall call the ensemble of all the strategies that the diverse theories and discourses of bourgeois pedagogy use to deny the historicity of pedagogical practices and the politics of its truth– thereby reproducing the exploitative relations of production–"the pedagogy of pleasure." It does not matter whether the pedagogy of pleasure removes the "walls" of the classroom through the agency of the theories of Paul de Man, Jacques Lacan, Michel Foucault, Jean Baudrillard, Gilles Deleuze, Jacques Derrida, Hélène Cixous, Felix Guattari, and Jean-François Lyotard, or through those of Matthew Arnold, F. R. Leavis, Lionel Trilling, Stanley Fish, Richard Rorty, Clifford Geertz, Wayne Booth, Elaine Showalter, Sandra Gilbert, and Susan Gubar, since my concern is with the global political effects of theories and not with their local differences.

The pedagogy of pleasure aims at demolishing the "walls" of the classroom and promises spontaneity, originality, and vision. Then, by virtue of these qualities, it places the student in a position of intelligibility from which she believes she is an autonomous, unique, ethical being. The concern with ethics as a set of strategies of self-fashioning that produces the "freedom" of the subject is as much the concern of Leavis and Booth as it is the focus of attention in Lacan and Foucault. It operates in the discourses of both humanists and (post)structuralists as a means for containing the political. "Pleasure"–for all versions of bourgeois pedagogy–is an experience for attaining ethical goals and subverting the political.

In the classroom without walls all participants are liberated for a short period of time (as short in fact as the class lasts) from their cultural situationality (as students, teachers, members of a class, race, gender, etc.) into a libidinal unboundedness, into an "other" space without oppressive social roles, and into a playfulness that is at odds with the serious bourgeois workaday life. Their liberation is achieved, however, not through entanglements with the materiality of knowledge/knowing and the social order that underwrites it, but by suspending those involvements. What is at work in this classroom is not "imagination" but what Coleridge called "fancy." "Fancy" (as opposed to "imagination") is a "mode of Memory emancipated from the order of time and space and blended with, and modified by that empirical phenomenon of the will, which we express by the word CHOICE. But equally with the ordinary memory it must receive all its materials ready made from the law of association. . . . Fancy, [consequently, has] no other counters to play with but fixities and definites" (Coleridge

1983, 1:305). Like "fantasy" in Barthes (*A Barthes Reader* 1982, 477) and "desire" in Lacan (1977, 292–325), "fancy" is an instance of ceaseless slippage from one "fixity" to another "guided" only by tropes that establish associations, similarities, and coincidences among the "fixities" and thus conceal the social logic that makes them intelligible. The sliding of "fancy" from one "fixity" to another along the trace of tropes provides the subject in this classroom with the illusion of freedom and unboundedness, but what she or he experiences is more a liberation (a relief) than an emancipation: the outcome of an active intervention that transforms the existing social relations and thus situates the subject in a different set of relations. "Fancy," like "desire," does not intervene in the "fixities" and the social logic. All that "fancy" does is to temporarily displace the dominant logic with pleasure and put the subject of pleasure in a position of intelligibility from which he can momentarily suspend the "law of the Father" and all its injunctive rules, regulations, and institutions. As long as the class lasts, the unleashing of "fancy" produces a pedagogical space that is at odds with the institution of the classroom. In removing this institutionality, "fancy" provides a sense of "liberation" for the subject from the constraints and "seriousnesses" of bourgeois life and its rituals such as "education." The working of both "fancy" and Lacan's "desire" are markers of "loss"–that estrangement that is inscribed in the culture of capitalism and that both humanist pedagogy and Lacanian psychoanalysis attempt to sidestep. Humanist pedagogy posits "loss" not as the effect of social relations but as a lack in the individual, whereas Lacan posits it as the very condition of existence of the speaking subject and therefore as having little to do with the social.

One of the most significant political features of the pedagogy of pleasure is that it places power/knowledge relations fully in the background or completely conceals them. The power relations that always exist in a pedagogical (social) situation are treated as accidental, as false and unnecessary "extras" that can be thrown away. Thus freed from social constraints, the student and teacher can relate to each other on equal terms as if they were in a "lounge"–or, better still, in that privileged space in the bourgeois home, the living room (which is, of course, itself a culturally constructed site). Together on equal terms, they can continue what Richard Rorty tellingly calls "the conversation of the West" (Rorty 1979, 394). The suspension of power/knowledge relations in these "conversations" is the outcome of a locutionary strategy devised to protect exploitative social arrangements. This point becomes clearer in Roland Barthes's "Inaugural Lecture" to the Collège de France:

> What I hope to be able to renew . . . is the *manner* of presentation of the course or seminar, in short of "presenting" a discourse without imposing it: that would be the methodological stake, the *quaestio*, the point to be debated. *For what can be oppressive in our teaching is not, finally, the knowledge or the culture it conveys, but the discursive forms through which we propose them.* Since . . . this teaching has as its object discourse taken in the inevitability of power, method can really bear only on the means of loosening, baffling, or at the very least, of lightening this power. And I am increasingly convinced . . . that the fundamental operation of this loosening method is, if one writes, *fragmentation,* and, if one teaches, digression, or to put it in a preciously ambiguous word *excursion.* (*A Barthes Reader* 1982, 476, emphasis added)

"Power" is suspended in the discourses of the Barthesian classroom, and the classroom becomes, to use his privileged word, a space of pleasure, of playfulness, of "fancy," at the same time diverting attention from (and therefore shielding) the economics of social power that underwrite all present relations, including those in pedagogical institutions such as a course or a seminar. For Barthes (and bourgeois pedagogy in all its forms) it is not knowledge or culture that is oppressive but the manner of their representation! The "radicalness" of Barthes's pedagogy, like other modes of (post)structuralist theory, is therefore in the manner in which the student is situated toward knowledge (regardless of the content of knowledge)—that is to say, *how* the student comes to know. (Post)structuralist pedagogy inquires into the *how* of knowing, thereby distinguishing itself from the humanist version of bourgeois pedagogy that mostly concerns itself with *what*—the question of the canon, great books, and the like. (Post)structuralism regards its displacement of the *what* of knowing to be a pedagogically radical move. However, this staging of the discussion between *how* and *what* rigorously avoids the question of the *why* of representation – the politics of representation: *why* a particular representation at a given historical moment is acceptable as a representation of "something" to the members of a particular group of people with historically determined class/gender/race relations.

The initial difference between (post)structuralist and humanist inquiry embodied in the varied focuses on the *how* and *what* of representation eventually vanishes because the humanist preoccupation with *what* finally turns out to be a species of aesthetics: *how* to know *what* (*how* to grasp *what* through the rhetoric of its particularity and uniqueness). Both humanist and (post)structuralist pedagogy, as Adams points out, regard abstraction (concept) to be an instance of pedagogical falsehood. What is preserved in the rejection of abstraction (theory) is the uniqueness of the individual and the irreplaceable nature of experience – the site of operation of the dominant ideology.

Barthes's focus on the *how* of representation, therefore, is not an eccentric feature of his pedagogy but an integral part of bourgeois pedagogy that aims at concealing its embeddedness in the economics of power. By focusing attention on *how*, dominant pedagogy eventually achieves its main goal, which is to replace intervention with "textualization." "Textualization" is thus a new form of politics.

By forgetting and suppressing the "authority" of the knowledgeable, such a pedagogical situation proposes that knowing (knowledge) is itself a nonpolitical act – the outcome of the encounter between an object of knowledge and a natural subject (in other words, empiricism) – rather than the effect of the contesting discourses of culture and the structures of power inscribed in them. The view of knowledge as contestation, on the other hand, inevitably leads to the sites of these contestations, which are social class, gender, race, and labor relations. In bracketing the power relations involved in the production of knowledge in the classroom, the liberationist, familiarizing classroom achieves a significant ideological function: it erases the awareness of meaning as conflict by substituting "difference" for contestation and replacing conflict with pluralism. Through this erasure it rejects the notion of history as the struggle between classes and denies that knowledge is an apparatus of political power. It is in this conflict-free, pluralistic classroom of the pedagogy of pleasure that poetry is pronounced atheoretical, and atheoreticity is in fact the ideologically necessary discursive condition for securing hegemonic social relations.

The pedagogy of pleasure uses a number of strategies to remove social struggle from the classroom and liberate its participants from the dailiness (the historicity) of their lives. Chief among these is the realization of libidinal liberation through laughter, parody, pastiche, and play. In other words, it brings to the foreground an ironic stance that safeguards the integrity and wholeness of the subject and guarantees disengagement. "Laughter" is a mode of deliverance from the mundane and the routine, and the only way that politically conservative pedagogy knows how to place itself at odds with the "other" (engaged) pedagogy. In (post)structuralist theory, laughter, parody, irony, and pastiche are regarded to be apparatuses of subversion and devices for radically decentering the bourgeois worldview upon which other practices of the social are based. Through "laughter" (and other decentering means), (post)structuralism deconstructs the "serious" in bourgeois life by textualizing its solemnities–demonstrating, in short, that the "serious" is the effect of "concept" (that is to say, an instance of illusory selfsameness and presence) which is itself a language construct. Thus the strategic uses of parody, pastiche, and similar devices expose the solemn beliefs of the bourgeois (and all the practices that are based upon them) as moments of textuality, sites of slippage, and aporia. The solemn, in other words, is subject to the laws of *différance* and as such is at variance with itself. "Laughter" textualizes the "serious" and shows how what it takes to be a self-identical idea/concept/belief is in fact reversible–both inherently unstable and without access to a grounding logic. Without such a logic, the "serious" loses the protection of "reason" and becomes hopelessly ridiculous.

This deconstructive move that deprives bourgeois beliefs of their authority is what (post)structuralist theory and pedagogy regard as their contribution to radical change. In fact it provides the foundation for a new definition of politics in (post)structuralism. Politics, as far as contemporary (post)structuralism is concerned, is not discourses and practices of power and economics, for example, but a set of reading strategies through which the easy access of the signifier to the signified is blocked and thus the traffic of meaning in culture is deferred through its *différance*. This deferring and *différance* is the locus of radical politics for (post)structuralism. Laughter, parody, and pastiche are some of the devices that make this problematization of "meaning" possible, and as such they are essentially political and subversive devices. (Post)structuralist pedagogy—the classroom without walls—is the site of the joys of reversibility: the deconstruction of the serious in bourgeois life and the libidinal liberation of the student in relation to serious "knowledge."

The institutionalization of "laughter" in conservative (post)modern pedagogy is now well under way, as demonstrated in Gregory Ulmer's notion of "lec(ri)ture." Ulmer's writings synthesize (post)structuralist theories of pedagogy in an effective and imaginative way. He deploys "laughter" as his inaugural strategy for overcoming the "seriousness" of traditional teaching, thus realizing the ethical goals of (post)modern pedagogy. He calls the space within which he sets up his program a "textshop," a site in which pedagogy as a process is itself textualized (*Applied Grammatology* 1985a, 52). The pedagogy of pleasure is always anxious to get out of the "classroom"; therefore it often calls the space of its operation by such other names as "textshop" or "humanities laboratory" (mostly by [post]structuralists) and "studio" or "workshop" (by humanist pedagogues). The main apparatus of subversive laughter in the textshop is what Ulmer calls "lec(ri)ture": a portmanteau joining "lecture" and *écriture* (in the Derridean sense of inscription and textuality). What interests him in this macaronic punning is the foregrounding of "ri" that makes the new word echo with laughter (*rire:* to laugh, laughter). Lecriture, then, is a lecture that is textualized and thus decentered from within because now—its "seriousness" gone—it is a discursive space within which "happy knowledge" is born. "Lecture as texts," Ulmer writes, "is a certain kind of placing or spacing, the point being to refocus our attention, as composers or auditors, to the taking place of this place. At issue in these lectures is the extent to which the *performance* aspect of the lectures (the scene of lecturing, rather than the referential scene, the 'diegesis' of the lecture) is foregrounded, violating the students' expectation of information as message or content" (*Applied Grammatology* 1985, 43). Lecriture as a pedagogical apparatus "operates by means of a *dramatic,* rather than epistemological, orientation to knowledge" (p. 38). Lecriture is an anticonceptual mode of knowing that situates the student in the experience of knowing and attempts to change her contact with knowledge. What is at stake here is not knowledge as content but knowledge as relation, and this "radical" pedagogical act—the change of relation—is brought about by "laughter."

(Post)structuralism's claim that laughter and similar devices are radical strategies demonstrating the "undecidability" of bourgeois beliefs—by displaying them as instances of textual "excess," as slippages within the system of representation—and that such an operation is therefore a means for change is itself an example of (post)structuralism's collusion with the status quo. The reversal of concepts/ideas through parody, satire, jokes, and other textualizing means, far from being strategies of decentering, are in fact the most common strategies for conserving (through renewal) the prevailing common sense. Common sense uses parody, pastiche, and similar strategies to reassert itself whenever its limits are transgressed by oppositional discourses. It not only parodies the intruding discourses but, at its most radical moment, in fact directs the parody at itself in order to jettison those elements in its knowledge repertoire that have become historically unviable. In other words by reflexive parody, autopastiche, and self-mocking, the common sense conserves itself through these tactics of renewal. "Laughter" then is far from being "radical"; it is a very conservative device. Overthrowing bourgeois solemnities when they have become historically and politically counterproductive is in fact one of the pastimes of the bourgeoisie. Jettisoning the "serious" is one of the most conventional modes of rescuing the authority of an imperiled common sense.

For instance, upon his election to the presidency, George Bush – who is keenly aware of the limits of his own seriousness and the transgressive potentials of seriousness to undermine the laissez-faire politics of conservative common sense – decided to subject the "serious" to the "excesses" of parody and to "reverse" the solemnities of the presidency itself: deconstructive practices that made another pillar of common sense, the *New York Times,* proclaim, "Bush Stands up for Impish and Will Veto the Imperial" (5 December 1988, A1). The "imperial" is, of course, totalizing and repressive "seriousness," the "solemn." The "impish" is the general name for all deconstructive reading strategies and, in this case, Bush's tactics for debunking the "official": eating popcorn and watching *My Stepmother Is an Alien.* His "funny" rewriting of the presidency and authority and Derrida's witty puns and parodies in his disrespectful readings of the presiding texts of Western philosophy both reverse and reinscribe the dominant. But these reversals do not transform the asymmetrical power relations in which they are involved. In fact, the unserious, the funny, and the parodic secure those relations in a more ecumenical, casual, democratic, and noncoercive (hegemonic) manner. Parody is a discursive detour for achieving consensus by building a "community" of the laughing and the amused. "Laughter" does not intervene in the reigning social relations; it merely subverts them and thus purges them of their unproductive elements. "Laughter," in other words, is a strategy of containment and is complicit with (not oppositional to) common sense. Contrary to the (post)structuralist claim that "laughter" (the carnivalesque) dismantles the dominant, "laughter" in fact renews the dominant and gives it a new lease on life.

This becomes even clearer if we briefly examine Bakhtin's idea of the "carnivalesque" which in fact lies behind some of the poststructuralist theories of pedagogy. In *Rabelais and His World,* Bakhtin theorizes the "carnival" in a manner that clearly "justifies" the existing social contradictions by postulating a politics of laughter. As with the (post)structuralist theory of politics as parody, the "carnivalesque" simply textualizes social contradictions, arguing that social contradictions are textual constructs and thus unstable and other than what they seem to be; they are not contradictions but instances of *différance*. The carnival in Bakhtin is a moment of up-roarious laughter in which "the entire world is seen in its droll aspect, in its gay relativity" (Bakhtin 1968, 11), and this for Bak-htin is a subversive act. Laughter in the carnival, however, does not change the system and structures of domination; it merely changes, for a short time, the relation of terms within the system–it brings about a passing "reform." The system reemerges in full power after the carnival is over. However, the incoherence of Bakhtin's notion of the carnival begins to surface when he goes on to claim in the same text that laughter, which only temporarily suspends the operation of the system, produces "the utopian realm of com-munity, freedom, equality, and abundance" (p. 9). For laughter to be effective it must maintain the terms of the system, yet for change to take place (utopia), these very terms must be overthrown! It is only through a change without transformation that the car-nival/laughter can function, and that is exactly what makes the notion of laughter/parody/pastiche so appealing to contemporary (post)structuralism. Like (post)structuralist "immanent critique," laughter/carnival conserves the system within which it operates. Instead of contesting the ruling system and its structures of domi-nation, the carnival, through laughter, merely builds, in Bakhtin's own words, "a second world and a second life outside officialdom" (p. 6). So, through laughter, parody, and pastiche, Bakhtin and (post)structuralist pedagogy provide the illusion of change by retreating into a "second" world, while the first world (the dominant one) goes on.

In the same manner, Ulmer's "textshop" constructs a "second world," a parapedagogy, that simply jettisons the obsolete elements of traditional pedagogy only to renew its ideological effects. Through "laughter" the textshop merely rearticulates conventional pedagogy so that it can carry on its ideological role in a new lan-guage and in a new setting. The pedagogy of "lec(ri)ture" becomes the pedagogy of evasion (parapedagogy) rather than a pedagogy of "practice": praxis means forming, grasping, and changing one-self and a historical world through collective productive work that mediates between the object and the subject. Parapedagogy focuses on the relation of the subject to the discourses of knowledge and quietly brackets the subject's relations to social practices. It thus separates itself from the division of bourgeois life into playtime and work time by turning the work time into playtime. In doing so it leaves work time outside the intervention of the subject of pedagogy; in other words, it establishes a Bakhtinian "second world." The division of life into play and labor is part of the practices that prepare "the enormous majority" to "act as a machine" under late capitalism. Ulmer's program simply ignores the political economy of this division and turns the classroom into a place for restaging the imaginary, a place in which students and teachers dream the (fusional) dreams of André Breton that are not dreamable in the course of the daily life of the bourgeois. Ulmer's "solution" of dissolving work into play is a repetition that becomes, this time around, a "farcical" (to use Marx's word) repetition of the Fourierist program in which "textshop" takes the place of "phalanstery" and, by a regress to the "imaginary" in a haze of idealism, suspends the social division of labor.

Transforming the labor/play distinction will come about only when the social division of labor as practiced in late capitalism is abolished by class struggle, not by delivering "lec(ri)ture" to desire-full fancy-ing students. The classroom that Ulmer proposes is the trivial space that Robert Bork articulated in his fall 1987 Senate testimony. "In a classroom," Bork told his audience, "nobody gets hurt." But in real life–in the courtroom–"someone always gets hurt" (*New York Times,* 16 September 1987, A27). The fact is people do get hurt in the classroom, because it is there that they are recruited into those subject positions that are necessary for maintaining existing social relations. It is to divert attention away from this ideological role of the classroom that Bork plainly declares its vacuity and Ulmer turns it into a ludic space of difference, thus suppressing its "conflicts." The "other" pedagogy–the pedagogy of enablement–uses the classroom with walls as a space of contestation and a site in which emancipatory knowledge of the reproduction of social subjectivities and its politics is constructed through theory as the critique of intelligibilities.

The regress to the imaginary is the condition of possibility in the classroom of pleasure, the classroom without walls. There is, of course, a variety of classrooms without walls. Again, the difference between, for example, the traditional humanist and the new deconstructionist pedagogy is one of strategy. Both are founded on the notion that learning (like watching a play) should at all times be "fun," that is to say, a deconstruction of the "dull," structured reality. Neither, therefore, interrogates that structure, but merely brackets it, thereby protecting it from the inspection and intervention of critical pedagogy. An interventionist pedagogy, as far as humanists and deconstructionists are concerned, is "propaganda" (the name that the bourgeois endows on the political practice that aims at dismantling bourgeois, ideologically secured beliefs).

3   In contrast to this familiarizing classroom in which the real loses its strangeness and acquires a nonthreatening sameness and familiar look, there is the defamiliarizing classroom in which social difference is recovered. This classroom—in opposition to the familiarizing classroom where the discourses of culture are produced as instances of transparency—is the classroom that aims at making itself opaque, "strange," "different" from the world outside. In the words of Brecht's devoted reader, Roland Barthes, this classroom is "a mask which points to itself" (*Critical Essays* 1972, 98) and, in so doing, problematizes itself as a cultural (that is, a political) situation. In contrast to the situation in the familiarizing classroom, the power/knowledge relation between the teacher and student and among the students in this classroom is fully foregrounded and made visible; student and teacher know at all times that they are in contestation over the "interestedness" (cultural significance) of the knowledge that is being produced, and that at various times during the class the power will shift from center to center but at no time will it be absent. This classroom recognizes the fact that authority and power are always present in social situations. The question for this classroom is not then to essentialize and thus conceal the existence of authority by "lec(ri)ture" and other bourgeois pedagogical devices but to mark it, to put it forth for interrogation in terms of the historicity of its uses. This classroom understands that the question is not the existence/nonexistence of authority, as (post)structuralist pedagogy proposes, but the uses of authority. In order to occlude contestations of authority and to contain issues on political legitimacy, (post)structuralism essentializes authority, it places authority outside the history of its uses. Authority, removed from the specificity of its uses in the Paris Commune or in fascist Italy, thus becomes one and the same. The question, however, is whether authority is used to oppress or to enable. It is only through such an inquiry that it becomes clear how pernicious are the uses of authority in the ludic classroom without walls in which authority makes itself invisible in the ideological haze it generates.

The participants in the defamiliarizing classroom are produced socially by their work, by their practice, in the sense I proposed (the production of discourses that construct knowledge); those who are not enabled to work (to produce discourse) will not have knowledge, they will remain powerless. This is a classroom with thick walls constituted by social codes, political constraints, and cultural and ideological practices. This thick-walled classroom is always at variance with the "real world," and it is in its variance—in the space it deliberately, and in full recognition of the world, places between itself and that world—that it interrogates the practices of that world and produces (theoretical) knowledge about it. It is through such knowledge that a critique of the constituents of experience is produced. It is precisely because of its function as a critique of experience that "theory," as I have suggested, is attacked by both humanists and (post)structuralists. This classroom, in short, is a very unnatural place, a highly constructed time and space, a very coded stage.

I have already mentioned Barthes's idea of the "mask" that points to itself and thus recognizes itself as a construct, but I would like to develop some of the political implications of that notion a little further here. To be in such an uncanny "masked" classroom is similar to reading some of the (nonrealistic) fictions of a (post)modern writer such as Vladimir Nabokov. In reading *Pale*

Fire, for example, it is impossible to forget that one is reading "fiction"; in being constantly reminded of this fact one is made aware of one's situationality as a "reader," made aware of the cultural role one is given to play. For instance, by being denied the pleasures of "method acting," the Brechtian actor is placed in a post of intelligibility from which he sees the distance between the *subject* and the *subject position.* Furthermore, he realizes that the subject position is a highly political locus constituted by an ongoing social struggle over the meanings of signs of culture and the consequent definition of the real. The reader of *Pale Fire* as well as the participant in the self-situating classroom with walls are also denied the pleasure of mimesis and the self-sameness of their subject positions, whether the self-identity of realism (the identification of "method acting") or the simulation of *realia* of the ludic textshop. They become aware of the way they are the sites through which structures of social conflicts produce meanings. Conscious of this cultural role, the reader knows she is playing the role of the reader and is not a natural discoverer of meanings. She becomes an interrogator of the ways that cultural practices turn the "actual" into the "real" and make the world intelligible. She, in short, becomes a "theorist" (in the sense that I suggested earlier) and is consequently empowered as an instance of resistance: resistance to the social classes that put forth the reality of their class as the universal reality of all classes by concealing the codes of intelligibility involved in constructing the(ir) "real."

The idea of theory as resistance that informs the defamiliarizing classroom is, of course, radically different from the founding notion of the familiarizing classroom: "the resistance to theory." The "resistance to theory" in contemporary pedagogy takes a number of forms from de Manian deconstruction to the various types of contemporary humanism. All these positions, however, have certain cognitive views in common: all, for example, oppose "theory" to "criticism," privilege the "local" and the cellular over the "global," and reject "concept" in the name of the "particular" (experience). More importantly, they also hold a common political agenda that is rooted in an ecumenical liberalism that restricts political struggles for social transformation by replacing conflict with difference, thus naturalizing pluralism and coalitionism. Humanism and deconstruction defend the same canon and the same eclectic interdisciplinary practices as opposed to a radical, committed transdisciplinarity. Contrary to commonsense discourses, deconstruction does not dismantle humanism or its liberal pluralism and ethics of self-fashioning; rather, deconstruction perpetuates this regime of truth by renovating it through new technological devices (that is, new methods of reading and interpretation and novel ways of organizing texts along interdisciplinary lines). The humanistic notion, for example, that poetry is atheoretical is not only supported by deconstruction but developed into a hermeneutic principle. Poetry in deconstruction, as I have said earlier, possesses an inescapable literariness (a configuration of tropes) that always resists theory (the "concept" in argument). "Resistance to theory" is the effect of the aporia between the "figure" and "argument." Humanist discourse and the discourse of deconstruction support the same political regime, thereby making the institutional "center" of literary and cultural studies a coalition of humanists and deconstructionists.

The Brechtian classroom reunderstands "theory" itself, a reunderstanding that is different from both the traditional notion of theory and the deconstructive view. Humanism's resistance to theory is conducted in the name of the uniqueness of the autonomous subject; deconstruction's "resistance" to theory, as I have suggested, is based on its own hermeneutic proposal that holds that theory is a coercive totalization violating the rhetorical particular. As a language construct, theory is, in the last analysis for deconstructionists, not an instance of "truth" but the site of tropological playfulness. The "argument" of theory, in other words, is always already "resisted" by the literariness of its own discourse. Again, such a resistance to theory is a defense of dominant ideology. It is based on an idealistic view of signification, a view that regards "tropes" to be inherently meaningful regardless of the frames of historical practices of intelligibility through which they are read. According to this approach, a "metaphor" is always panhistorically a "metaphor"—an instance of "excess" that disturbs representation by turning its identity into *différance,* thus subverting the argument of the text in which it occurs. But "tropes" acquire their tropicity (their recognition as metaphors and so on) only within a given historical and cultural frame of intelligibility: metaphors can cease to be metaphors and literal entities can lose their literalness and acquire metaphorical density. Similarly, "excess" is always made intelligible as "excess" within the historical limits of a system of representation. Tropicity, then, is not a natural, inherent attribute of certain linguistic entities, but the historical effect of their *uses*.

The question is what metaphors *mean* within a particular historical/social discourse, not whether they are metaphors. Sense-fullness (in this case, the sense of a linguistic construct as a "metaphor") is the outcome of cultural and historical assumptions and practices of cognition, that is, according to a theory of intelligibility. The *différance* that (post)structuralism locates in textuality is thus not panhistorical (inherent in textuality itself) but is in fact historical and political. Language/textuality is the instance of *différance*, slippage, and aporia not because textemes are unstable in and of themselves—outside their systems of social representation—but because they are the objects of class struggle and social contestation. In *Marxism and the Philosophy of Language* Voloshinov situates *différance* in the social:

> Existence reflected in the sign is not merely reflected but *refracted*. How is this refraction of existence in the ideological sign determined? By an intersecting of differently oriented social interests within one and the same sign community, i.e. *by the class struggle*.
>
> Class does not coincide with the sign community, i.e. with the community which is the totality of users of the same set of signs for ideological communication. Thus various different classes will use one and the same language. As a result, differently oriented accents intersect in every ideological sign. Sign becomes an arena of the class struggle. (Voloshinov 1986, 23)

Difference, in short, is historical and material. Nothing (neither metaphor nor anything else) is, in and of itself or by nature, always already anything. Things become "somethings" when they are used in a culturally senseful way, as when they are situated in a social location by struggle and have become part of social relations. It is the process of such situating that (socially) produces a thing as "something." The uses of a linguistic construct make it senseful as metaphor and endow it with the subversive power of *différance* that it acquires in contesting the argument of theory. This contestation is itself historically specific, because it is enabled only within the historically determined frames of understanding in which a particular linguistic entity is designated as a trope and thus seen as an antiargument—an antiargument that, by the way, is a mode of argument nonetheless. The force of the trope, in short, is part of its historicity: in a given historical moment the trope is endowed with subversive power that is (as a consequence of social struggles) a forceful argument against the *other* argument offered by those linguistic items of a text that are historically specified (as part of the same social struggle) as nontropic.

Inquiry into processes of sense making is an inquiry into the ways things (metaphors, tropes, and other cultural artifacts) make sense and become comprehensible. An understanding of this comprehension-effect inquiry is what I proposed "theory" to be at the opening of this chapter. Theory, then, is not—as humanists and deconstructive critics alike characterize it—an abstract apparatus of mastery, but an inquiry into the grids of social intelligibilities produced by the discursive activities of a culture. Theory is a critique of intelligibility. As a result of such a critique, readers in a culture become aware of the ways in which signifiers are always organized so that through them the world is produced in such a manner that its "reality" supports the "reality" of the interests of state power, gender, race, and the dominant classes. Through such a recognition, theory enables readers to historicize the "reality" of the ruling class that is presented in cultural texts as being the universal reality of all classes and thus to engage in ideological struggle. Theory, as Gramsci has suggested (Gramsci 1976, 323–472), is an ally in political and ideological struggle: theory as resistance, not the resistance to theory, is what marks radical pedagogy and distinguishes it from the hegemonic pedagogy of "lec(ri)ture."

The defamiliarizing classroom intervenes in the reproduction of dominant cultural meanings that lend support to the continuation of existing social relations. Radical pedagogy thus goes "beyond" the humanism of common sense and the undecidability of deconstruction. This going "beyond" involves, among other things, a reunderstanding of "the subject" of knowledge as not merely the cognitive one "who is supposed to know" but as one situated in the grid of class, race, and gender relations, and who is "critical." But this going "beyond" is prohibited in almost all the discourses of contemporary theory. The discourse of humanism posits common sense as the limit beyond which pedagogy should not move. For Derrida a going "beyond"—striving for a "post" state—is merely an expression of a desire, an illusion of progress, a logocentric wish to get ever closer to truth (presence). It is, of course, highly instructive that Derrida's injunction against going beyond has not deterred him from undertaking a rather violent move beyond. In recent pronouncements about his nonopposition to presence he has revealed a side of his work that accepts mysticism as a mode of authentic knowing (Sturrock 769). In this he has indeed gone "beyond" and in a manner similar to that of Julia Kristeva, Philippe Sollers, and other *Tel Quel* intellectuals of his generation who are embracing mysticism (through a new reading of Martin Heidegger) as the region of unbounded (ethical) knowledge and libidinal freedom: a region free from the rancor of the political.

In contrast, the going "beyond" of radical pedagogy is not undertaken to acquire transdiscursive (mystical) knowledge, nor to foster the illusion that cultural meanings are somehow authorized by a panhistorical truth. The "beyond" or "post" of radical pedagogy is not so much the site proximate to truth as it is the space of opposition to the reigning "truth." It is in this space that the radical classroom intervenes in readings of the texts of culture by inscribing opposition and conflict in the production of meanings. The apparatus of such an intervention is theory as critique, a practice that, as Marx explained, does not "dogmatically anticipate the world, but wants to find the new world through a critique of the old" (Marx and Engels 1975, 142). It is in this sense that theory, to quote Marx again (*Early Writings* 1975, 251), becomes a "material force". . .

CHAPTER 3

The Crisis of "the Subject" in the Humanities

The contest over the structure and contents of the humanities curriculum has always been a struggle among various social classes and economic and political groups over the meaning of the social signs that intersect to form codes out of which the "individual" is constructed. It is the meaning of the "individual" in culture that is what is at stake in the humanities curriculum. The fact that almost all existing humanities programs will deny and reject the theory of the individual implied in our opening sentence is itself a mark of this contestation. The traditional humanities curriculum is based on the idea that the individual is the cause and not the effect of social meanings: he is the origin of signification. In fact theoreticians of the traditionalist curriculum remind us constantly that the liberal arts program derives its authority from the two components of the concept inscribed in the term "liberal," from the Latin *liber(us)* – "free" and "man." The goal of the humanities program, the humanists believe, is to educate this "free" "man." However, they take both of these concepts to be self-evident and beyond the contingencies of history. "Free" and "man" are, in the traditionalists' theories, timeless essences on which the humanities curriculum is founded. The outcome of such an education is equally

55

timeless and ahistorical; that outcome is, in the words of O. B. Hardison, Jr.: "Wisdom . . . a combination of self-confidence and humility" (1985, 576). Over and against this transcendentalism stands the genealogy of both "free" and "man" as historically specific terms: the modern history of the humanities curriculum since the late eighteenth century has been the history of contestation over the meaning of these two concepts. The rise of the modern humanities in the eighteenth century and their institutionalization in the nineteenth century are directly related to the rise of the bourgeoisie in the West, having won the battle with the old aristocracy over the meaning of "free man" redefined in the context of competition in the marketplace by free agents.

Today under new economic and political forces the concept of individuality is once more under pressure, but this time the pressure is so radical that the idea has been decentered to the extent that the term "individual" that has dominated the Western notion of selfhood since the Renaissance, has itself been rendered historically obsolete. We no longer talk about the individual, but about the subject. The effect of this fundamental reunderstanding of the subject in (post)modern critical theory[1] has been so far-reaching that the very function of the humanities curriculum itself has been displaced. In *The Savage Mind* Lévi-Strauss remarks that "the ultimate goal of the human sciences is not to constitute but to dissolve man" (1983, 247). This new crisis of the subject has forced to the surface the enormous contradictions and ideological incoherences of the traditional humanities curriculum. As the current proliferation of proposals for curricular reform attests, the present curriculum is in fact collapsing under the force of these contradictions, for it is no longer capable of dealing with the new power/knowledge relations that shape the subject. As implied before, the contradictions of the curriculum are themselves the result of previous power/knowledge relations deriving from the historical struggles of various social groups over signification and the constitution and circulation of the "real" meaning of the subject in culture. These historical struggles, the effects of which coexist in the dominant curriculum, have given it a layered and residual character. The curriculum's bourgeois moralism, for instance, clashes with its aristocratic aestheticism, and both of these elements conflict with its feudal historicism. Furthermore, all of the elements just mentioned oppose the curriculum's new middle-class postindustrial careerism, which is presently manifested in the concern for "basic skills."

The dominant curriculum constructs the subject in such a manner that it can be readily inserted into the existing social order. This says that the dominant curriculum is an ideological operation, the purpose of which is to maintain the existing system by producing subjects who will not only see it as acceptable, but perceive it "precisely as the way things are, ought to be, and will be" (Coward and Ellis 1980, 68). Our purpose here is not to survey the various views on the subject or theories of subjectivity (that task has been undertaken by Coward and Ellis, Julian Henriques, Kaja Silverman, among others) but to consider the implications of contemporary interrogations of the subject for a reunderstanding of the humanities curriculum. The subject (or more precisely, the individual) conceived and educated in the dominant curriculum is marked above all by his having an independent and private "consciousness" that endows him with plentitude and presence. It is through his consciousness that the individual not only understands himself, but also brings meaning to the world. As we have already suggested, in the dominant curriculum the subject is the origin and source of meaning. It is through his consciousness that the individual achieves not only privacy, in the sense of autonomy, but stability and above all unitariness. Consciousness provides a principle of cohesion and union for the individual throughout his life; and it is by the agency of his consciousness that the individual, in spite of all his fragmentary and diverse experiences, remains single, self-identical, and–of course by virtue of such continuity of self–legally accountable. The ideological function of consciousness is, as Coward and Ellis put it, to provide coherency for the "subject in the face of contradictions which make up society" (p. 68).

Cohering consciousness provides the individual with a sense of stability in her relationships with the social order–a stability that she will attempt to preserve so that the very principle of her self-intelligibility is protected. The dominant curriculum regards the individual and her consciousness as manifestations of a human essence that is timeless, ahistorical, transcultural, and not determined by the circumstances of social and economic life. The individual, in other words, is free. The only limits to this freedom come in recognition of a higher authority, whether this authority is conceptualized in theological terms (the authority of God) or in secular terms (the authority of the state, the boss, or market forces). The humanities curriculum, as we shall suggest, through its practice of textual interpretation inculcates obedience to authority in the free subject. In theorizing the individual as "free" and yet at the same time subjected to the "authority" of a higher power—whether text, author, or tradition—the dominant curriculum responds to the call of ideology. It preserves the notion of the free person who can enter into transactions with other free persons in the free market but who is, at the same time, obedient to the values of the free market that legitimate the existing political order. The conflict of these two contradictory notions (freedom and subjection) leads in the humanities program to a transcendental resolution: a going beyond the contingencies of history to resolve the contradictions that are not resolvable in capitalist society. The humanities curriculum's major role is to provide the means for transcending the contradictions by initiating the individual into the realm of the aesthetic. Art, music, literature, and religion are all means by which the individual can purify his worldly and contradictory existence into a contradiction free moment of lucidity, transparency, and presence. This moment of plenitude is beyond any interrogation: all one can do is "analyze" it in order to appreciate it more deeply. We shall discuss the ideological function of "analysis" in the dominant curriculum later, but it is important to note here that this injunction against interrogating the transcendental aesthetic moment reveals the antiintellectualism of the dominant curriculum. In this curriculum, professionalism (analysis) and not intellectual inquiry (interrogation) is the privileged mode of activity.

The subject of the dominant curriculum not only possesses a private consciousness that endows the subject with a coherency and unity but also rationality. In the humanities curriculum reason (like consciousness) is conceived of as a timeless essence through which the subject has access to the "truth," which is also seen as pancultural and beyond the limitations of the socioeconomic order. Foucault and many other contemporary historians of ideas have demonstrated how the idea of reason and the rational, far from being purely cognitive, stable, and transhistorical, varies from one epistemic community to another. Each community produces reason, the rational, and the true differently because it needs different discursive practices in order to represent its version of the real as the most natural and thus inevitable "truth." However, having decided what constitutes "eternal" truth, the dominant curriculum moves on to designate what it regards to be timelessly "right" and "wrong." The moralism of the humanities curriculum is thus an extension of its politics.

In contrast to the dominant notion, (post)modern critical theory does not conceptualize the subject as a stable entity but argues that the parameters of the subject vary according to the discursive practices that are current at a given historical moment. In this view, the human does not have a timeless essence, a nature or a consciousness that places him beyond historical and political practices, but rather is considered to be produced by these practices or as an effect of these discourses. In a famous passage in *The Order of Things,* Michael Foucault seems to articulate this idea when he states that "Man is only a recent invention, a figure not yet two centuries old, a new wrinkle in our knowledge, and he will disappear again as soon as the knowledge has discovered a new form" (1973, xxiii). The "disappearance" of man is the disappearance of discourses that enable his being in its present mode, a point that Foucault emphasizes in *The Archaeology of Knowledge:* "The researches of psychoanalysis, linguistics, and ethnology have decentered the subject in relation to the laws of his desire, the forms of his language, the rules of his actions, or the games of his mythical or fabulous discourse" (1972, 13).

The linguistic dimension of the subject's discursivity and thus of its variable and shifting character is the focus of the work of Emile Benveniste, who in his seminal essay, "Subjectivity in Language," states: "It is in and through language that man constitutes himself as a *subject,* because language alone establishes the concept of 'ego,' in reality, in *its* reality which is that of the being." He goes on to clarify, " 'Ego' is he who *says* 'ego.' That is where we see the foundation of 'subjectivity,' which is determined by the linguistic status of 'person' " (1971, 224). In Benveniste's work the subject is constantly displaced: "Consciousness of self is only possible, . . . if it is experienced by contrast. I use *I* only when I am speaking to someone who will be a *you* in my address. It is this condition of dialogue that is constitutive of *person,* for it implies that reciprocally *I* becomes *you* in the address of the one who is his turn designates himself as *I*" (pp. 224–225).

This notion of the subject in constant displacement is further radicalized in the work of Jacques Lacan, who pointedly rejects the attribution of consciousness to the subject: "The promotion of consciousness as being essential to the subject in the historical after-effects of the Cartesian *cogito* is for me the deceptive accentuation of the transparency of the *I* in action at the expense of the opacity of the signifier that determines the *I*" (1977, 307). Lacan sees the subject as produced by its entry into language (or the symbolic order) and postulates that this entry results in the "splitting" of the subject, a theory that deconstructs the unitary subject. The subject's discursivity and its production through such a system of signification as language dissolve private consciousness into a set of signs that are generated by various signifying practices. Consequently, what is seen in the humanities curriculum as the transcendental human essence is unveiled as a collectivity of conventions. In the (post)modern view, man emerges not as the instigator of meaning but rather as the effect of intersections of meaning generating signs: he is the result of cultural overdetermination rather than a free agent. The signifying activities that constitute the subject are historically specific and unconscious. Whereas the humanities curriculum places a great deal of emphasis on the unitary and cohesive nature of man's identity, (post)modern theories of the subject regard this unitariness and cohesiveness as the outcome not of the timelessness of man's nature, but—as Lacan has argued—as the effect of a trope (a metaphor). By establishing a bewildering network of connections and significations the type brings about the sense of continuity in the subject. The enabling condition of the vast network of connections established by metaphors is, in Lacan's view, the state of loss he names "desire," which must be distinguished from "need" and "demand." Thus, the "identity" and "cohesion" of the subject, far from constituting instances of plenitude, are effects of signification, absence, and nonrationality. Lévi-Strauss, Benveniste, Foucault, and Lacan, among other (post)modern thinkers, have decentered the subject by inquiring into the discursive practices that constitute her. In the works of Louis Althusser the political formation of the subject is foregrounded through the investigation of the process that he calls "interpellation" or "hailing" (calling upon the individual as a singular totality and a selfsame social identity). It is by addressing the individual as a unified and coherent person who is the sovereign author of her acts that the dominant social order recruits her and assigns her a place in its labor scheme. The insertion of the subject into the social formation provides the individual with a post of intelligibility from which, as a "mother," a "successful woman," a "learned scholar," a "skillful surgeon," and the like, she can *see* the world in a manner supportive of the dominant social relations. Consequently, she consents to the proposition that the existing order is not only the way things are, but the way they ought to be. The subject, in Althusser's view, is the set of relations through which the social order of late capitalism reproduces itself.

The dominant curriculum carries out its ideological program through specific practices and strategies that, in various ways, reproduce its underlying values. The current curriculum in literary studies, for instance, inscribes the contradictory ideas of freedom and obedience to authority in students through its most privileged pedagogical apparatus, namely the "interpretive essay." The interpretive essay is based on the assumption that the subject, in her rationality, can, in the privacy of her consciousness, discover the truth of the text. But the interpretive essay also allows for the fact that, because each subject is endowed with a different consciousness, there will be variety in the readings of a text, thus it tolerates differences in interpretation. However, the interpretive essay firmly asserts that in spite of all the differences, there is a core truth in the text itself and the ultimate goal of interpretation is access to this truth, put there by another consciousness (the author). By allowing for individual variation but insisting on the central truth of the text, humanistic pedagogy reifies the subject as free but at the same time obedient to the authority of the great mind of the author. The author, needless to say, not only inscribes the idea of the subject in the project of interpretation but also stands for the authority of the social order that is itself organized by the prevailing class. What is taught in the interpretive essay is the proper mode of situating oneself in regard to authority.

The author constucts the notion of the subject by deploying social codes; all authors do this, although the humanist authors insist that whatever they do is the effect of their "genius." As Heidegger states, it is the "language" that speaks the subject and not the subject that speaks the language. The act of speaking/writing is, therefore, constitutive of subjectivity.

The interpretive essay therefore effectively blocks an interrogation of the concept of the unitary rational subject upon which the notion of authority and obedience is based. In order to undertake such an interrogation, contemporary critical theory intervenes in the traditional humanities program and pressures the "interpretive essay" into becoming a "critique." A critique (not to be confused with criticism) is an investigation of the enabling conditions of discursive practices. It subjects the grounds of the seemingly self-evident discourse to an inspection and reveals that what appears to be natural and universal is actually a situated discourse. It is a construct positioned in the historical coordinates of a cultural institution, even though in blindness to its situationality, it presents itself as a panhistorical practice. The function of the (post)modern critique, therefore, contrary to that of the interpretive essay, is to demystify "authority" (that of the author and of those who he represents in the symbolic order of culture). In undertaking a critique rather than writing an interpretive essay, the learner also discovers that the text is not inherently meaningful but rather that meaning is an effect of the signifying practices and codes with which he is familiar. Thus, the critique is not a means through which meaning is excavated and extracted from the text, but a process through which the learner realizes that making sense of a text depends on frames of intelligibility, that it is therefore impersonal (nonsubjective), and that at any given historical juncture frames of intelligibility (meanings that are allowable) are closely associated with the economic and political order. Meaning consequently emerges not as the result of certain stylistic maneuvers (as the aestheticism of the humanistic curriculum implies) but as a mode of cultural and political behaviour. It is in the semantic space opened by the demystifying critique that the learner further recognizes that there are close affinities between the way she reads a Shakespearean sonnet (the so-called aesthetic experience) and the manner in which she "reads" and understands the events that take place in South Africa or Nicaragua or her domestic life. A critique relocates "reading" in the humanities curriculum and problematizes it by indicating that it is not the outcome of a simple connection between two independent consciousnesses (author and reader) but a mode of producing significations, of making the world intelligible.

In humanistic pedagogy, right and wrong are pregiven; values and ideas are considered to be determined outside discursive practices, and language is therefore treated as an aesthetic category and not as an epistemological ensemble through which reality and values are produced. If values are not constructed, but are transcendental and simply conveyed through language, what else is there to do but examine the elegance with which those values are expressed? Style thus becomes the privileged topic of study, and stylistics, whether in its technical linguistic mode or in a more general appreciative mode, dominates literary studies in the classroom. (Post)modern critical theory understands language not as a simple tool—a transparent means through which already formulated meanings are transmitted—but as a system of differentiation that constructs the world in the sense that it provides a grid of intelligibility for it. The stability/naturalness of language (that lies at the core of the dominant humanities program) disappears and instead its arbitrariness is foregrounded. The arbitrariness of signifying activities–demonstrated by the differential character of language–more clearly points out the ultimate constructedness of the meaning and the values that the traditional curriculum offers as natural and given. Meaning is shown to be an effect of the frames of intelligibility that are themselves the boundaries of ideology. These limits of ideology and boundaries of allowable meaning are constantly contested by various classes in society through the types of writings they put forth as being most significant. The humanistic curriculum always places the texts that are written from within these boundaries (namely, realistic texts) at the heart of its prescribed reading. In order to demystify the dominant curriculum's acts of naturalization, (post)modern critical theory intervenes by introducing texts that test the limits of intelligibility and thus challenge the hegemony of the dominant ideology. These texts, which might be called "innovative" or in Barthes's term "writerly," oppose realism and unveil it as the accomplice of the reigning political order. By interrogating realism, the close affinity between this mode of writing–this organization of cultural codes–and other dominant patterns of organizing social codes (racism, sexism, heterosexism) becomes clear. In other words, the innovative text is a critique of realism (that reifies the subject as character), and the demystifying power of its critique helps to produce new subject positions for the reader.

The central device used in writing the interpretive essay and in stylistic studies is "analysis." As we have already hinted, analysis in the dominant curriculum is essentially an anti-intellectual activity that is taught in order to divert attention from a genuine interrogation of textuality. Analysis is aimed at extracting meaning from the text, and accepts as pregiven the existence of an already formulated meaning in the text. Analysis does not question the political and epistemological status of the text, but merely attempts to open it up, as it is, and, by opening it up, make it possible for the reader to appreciate it. The activity of appreciation is the dominant curriculum's way of concealing its commodification of sensations and aesthetic experience. Through teaching analysis the dominant curriculum inculcates acceptance of what already exists and is therefore inevitable; it directs the focus of inquiry onto its elements and away from its mode of being. Analysis often proceeds by what is commonly known as "close reading"—an attentive seme-by-seme examination of a text that quietly inscribes empiricism (as an ally of historicism and humanism) in the dominant curriculum. (Post)modern critical theory rejects this empiricism and argues that details are appropriated by different readers through various frames of intelligibility at diverse cultural junctures to form different meanings. Details in themselves are not sites of meaning, and so to emphasize them as units of intelligibility is an ideological decision privileging the subject that interprets them and not a reflection of the "natural" way of reading all texts. By questioning the status of "close reading" as a means of reaching the true meaning of a text, (post)modern theory also problematizes the notion of a "faithful" reading and argues instead for a "strong" reading.

The unity and coherence with which the dominant curriculum invests the subject is reflected in the reading list prepared for a literary studies class. The texts are almost always organized around the unifying concept of "literariness," the idea that there are inherent textual properties that distinguish the literary from the nonliterary. As a concession to the present pressure for theoretical inquiry, this homogenized reading list sometimes includes a text or two dealing with media, popular culture, or other "secondary" texts, but even then it remains distinctly "literary." The notion that literature is a discourse that is inherently different from other discourses of culture—because of its internal properties (textual opacity, metaphoric density, and fictivity)—is part of those centering ideologies that attempt to represent all phenomena (consciousness/self/gender/political order) as timelessly and inherently significant: it is, in other words, a strategy of essentialization. Contemporary theory argues that literariness is an effect of systems of signification at any moment in history. "Written texts," Tony Bennett writes, "do not organize themselves into 'literary' and 'non-literary.' They are so organized only by the operation of criticism upon them" (1979, 7). This is another way of saying that the "literary" and the "nonliterary" are produced by the reader as an ensemble of codes whose production of meaning, as we have already indicated, is itself determined by frames of intelligibility situated in ideology.

A critique of literariness produces a mixed reading list composed of many discourses deriving from many cultural sites. This heterogeneous reading list, furthermore, is long, because it aims to bring to the pedagogical situation as many frames of understanding as possible in order to problematize the subject. If the traditional literature class uses "literariness" to read texts according to the established frames of intelligibility institutionalized by "English departments" and to provide cognitive closure, the new reading list tests those limits and, through such testing, puts in question the institutional boundaries of those "English departments." The new, long heterogeneous reading list is an implicit move toward (post)modern transdisciplinarity. In the humanistic program, especially in recent years, a few books concerning the media or other "nonprimary" texts are often included in the reading list in order to give the curriculum an air of "interdisciplinarity." However, we think that the "interdisciplinarity" of the dominant curriculum is a version of the "great books" teaching model and as such it is in fact a mode of "varidisciplinarity": a reinscription of "pluralism" in the reigning curriculum. Both varidisciplinary and interdisciplinary models (like political pluralism) are modes of eclecticism—forms of (ac)knowledgment: accumulating knowledge without having to confront the ideology of the production of knowledge.

Transdisciplinarity, on the other hand, is aware of the status of knowledge as one of the modes of the ideological construction of reality in any given discipline. Through its self-reflexivity it attempts not simply to accumulate knowledge but to ask what constitutes knowledge, why and how, and by whose authority, certain modes of understanding are certified as knowledge and others as paraknowledge or nonknowledge. Thus, the dominant notion of the "interdisciplinary" as the space of liberal, pluralistic negotiations among fields of knowledge is radically different from the "transdisciplinary"—as the locus of a politics of knowing and the site of interrogation—of the power/knowledge relations of culture. Transdisciplinarity is a "*trans*gressive" space in which configurations of knowledge are displayed as ultimately power related. This space is not the quiet "*inter*active" realm where Marx and Hegel and Protagoras can live in peaceful coexistence. The unsaid of the dominant notion of the interdisciplinary is grounded in the concept of discipline as a coherent (i.e., theoretical) articulation of a subject. In other words, institutionalized interdisciplinarity presupposes a "logical" configuration of a field and then places itself at odds with it. But disciplines are not logical; discourses of ideology merely represent them as such. Our theory of the transdisciplinary, on the other hand, emphasizes rather the institutional arrangements of knowledge—"discipline" is historico-political rather than merely logical.

In addition to problematizing "literariness" and the question of "discipline," the new, conflictual reading list also puts the established canon under erasure. The closure that the traditional program brings to the curriculum by the notion of "literariness" is further enhanced by the way literary works are hierarchized according to the notion of what is "major" and what is "minor." (Post)modern theory points up the arbitrariness of such an organization and, by foregrounding changes that have taken place in the established canon, indicates that there is nothing inherently natural about the canon itself or about its "major" and "minor" categories. "Major" is not major because of some given property of texts/ideas/emotions, but because frames of intelligibility at a given historical moment allow those texts/ideas/emotions to operate as models of coherence and sensemaking that the dominant ideology needs in order to reproduce the existing practices in the economic and political sphere.

We would like to end our inventory of the pedagogical practices that underlie the production of the unitary subject in the dominant curriculum as a well-rounded, educated person who is prepared to occupy her position in the existing economic order by discussing the role of teaching in this mode of learning. The humanist curriculum privileges what is widely known as the Socratic mode: the teacher as midwife of truth. In this curriculum it is assumed that the student already contains knowledge and that the function of the teacher is to help bring that knowledge into life. A teacher who violates this code is usually regarded as insensitive to the processes through which knowledge is born in the mind of the student. The ideological function of this theory of teaching is, of course, to represent the values that are actively advocated by the dominant curriculum in the classroom as the values that the student himself brings there. The curriculum manages to hide the constructedness of its values and its political assumptions with the midwife/teacher as an ideological "secret agent." Concealing the constructedness of the values embodied in the curriculum enables the dominant pattern of teaching to offer its own presuppositions about truth, knowledge, and the subject as natural, given, and thus unalterable. (Post)modern theory reveals the Socratic method to be a mode of inscribing the unitary, rational, and unconstructed subject in the curriculum. The (post)modern teacher, by assuming a specific ideological position in the classroom, makes it possible for the student to become aware of his position, of his own relations to power/knowledge formations. Such a teacher often has an adversarial role in relation to the student: the teacher is a deconstructor and not a mere supporter in the traditional sense of the word "teacher." She helps to reveal the student to himself by showing him how his ideas and positions are the effects of larger discourses (of class, race, and gender, for example) rather than simple, natural manifestations of his consciousness or mind.

The outcome of the (post)modern teacher's adversarial relation to the student is to develop in him a critical opposition to the dominant order. The subject of such a (post)modern pedagogy then is a partisan subject: one who—far form being "well-rounded"—self-reflexively acknowledges his own partiality, in the sense both of incompleteness and committedness. Acknowledging his "partial" (that is, split) nature, this subject knows that he is constituted by a set of contradictory, indeed incoherent, subject positions produced by various discourses of culture. Having de-naturalized himself, such a partisan subject will see the arbitrariness of all the seemingly natural meanings and cultural organizations based on them. The false closure that is imposed on history by the notion of the timeless natural subject endowed with a private consciousness is thus placed under erasure for him. The space of culture is opened up for different organizations of the real that are contrary to those put in place by the hegemonic concept of the subject.

(Post)modern critical theory's contestation of the concept of the unitary subject has created tremendous pressures – originating from both inside and outside the academy – to change the humanities curriculum. The aim of the resulting moves toward change is to reorient the existing curriculum so that it can survive contemporary theory's radical challenge to the curriculum's enabling notion: the subject. These attempts at change then work to preserve the ideological assumptions of the dominant curriculum in a new, more up-to-date form. They ensure that the education of the subject as a unitary, rational, individual willing to participate in the established systems of signification that legitimate the dominant power/knowledge structure and its underlying economic order can continue. The desire for change, in other words, is the desire to save the subject.

If we put aside the most deeply fundamentalist of these calls for reform – those from religious radicals who are so convinced of the traditional curriculum's inability to survive decentering theory that they have consequently established their own colleges and curricula to inscribe the subject-as-theist in culture – the most persistent pressures for change from outside the academy come from political neoconservatives. Their efforts to save the subject take the form of an eagerness to return to traditional educational norms; a demand made in the name of the enduring classics and of standards of taste and refinement. In predictable fashion, this resurgent neoconservatism justifies itself by commonsensically appealing to the notion of the "free man" as a set of self-evident concepts. Like all projects based on self-evident truths, this neoconservatism – which is most clearly articulated in a publication by the National Endowment for the Humanities, *To Reclaim a Legacy* (1984) – has a hidden ideological agenda. The agenda's immediate goal is to end the "open curriculum" that was the answer of the 1960s to the contradictions of the curriculum and its attempt to save the subject as a liberal person. In that decade the efforts to save the subject from the onslaught of new radical theories led to an expansion of the traditional curriculum with new courses that were, in their contents, socially relevant. They resituated the subject in opposition to the public sphere, yet the pedagogical programs of the 1960s were theoretically too weak to cope with the incoherencies and contradictions of the humanities curriculum surfacing in the face of the new view of the subject. In the spirit of liberalism, educational institutions of the 1960s simply evaded the philosophical and political issues involved in decentering the humanist subject and grafted onto the existing pedagogical discourses a new set of discourses, thus adding fresh contradictions to the curriculum by tolerating the old side by side with the new. So enormous was the need for a new understanding of the subject that for a brief period the new courses overshadowed the traditional ones and the core curriculum was more or less abandoned. The neoconservatives of the 1980s wished to restore the core curriculum and purge it of such extraneous elements as women's studies, black studies, and other similar programs.

Whereas the neoconservatives' surface argument for returning to tradition is an Arnoldian one, their covert agenda is a political one directly related to the idea of the subject as an economic being with a role in the competition of world markets and thus in the struggles of the superpowers. Concealed in the neoconservative argument is the view that the subject should be a free entrepreneur in the world arena without constraints or limitations. As articulated in the NEH document and in such neoconservative organs as *Commentary, The New Criterion,* and *The Public Interest,* the function of humanistic study is to teach the learner how to live free, and think freely. However, to think freely, the argument goes, one must live in a society that recognizes freedom as a human right. Such recognition, it is assumed, is badly neglected by the current liberalist pedagogy. The liberalist curriculum takes the freedom of the free world (that is, the United States) for granted, organizes courses "critically" rather than historically, and consequently attacks the fundamental institutions of the West. What neoconservatives wish to see presented in university and college curricula are the concepts of individual enterprise, free market competition, and a simple moral binarism that divides the world into the good and the bad. This is, of course, essentially a "cold war" curriculum, aimed primarily at securing world markets but concealing this aim under advocacy of the values of living and thinking freely.

The pressures from within the academy are exerted by both students and faculty. Today's students demand career and vocational training, a desire manifested by growing enrollment in courses in expository, technical, and professional writing, which are seen as the basic "communication" skills. If neoconservatives demand that their children be taught traditional texts and values to guard the "free" economy of the United States, the children themselves demand that the curriculum prepare them to take their rightful place in that economy. In order to accomplish this goal, the humanities curriculum must include a carefully planned and packaged series of writing and skills courses that will secure for the student the job he "deserves." The other internal pressure for shifting the paradigms of knowledge and teaching, a pressure exercised mostly by the faculty, stems from new developments in the humanities. To understand this shift, we must first consider the recent history of the humanities as disciplines of knowledge. Since the mid-1960s, as we have already indicated, there has been a major change in the humanities, a change inaugurated by the configuration of a mode of knowing commonly referred to as "critical theory," "literary theory," or simply as "theory." Theory aims at interrogating the foundations upon which inquiries in the humanities are based and the principles involved in their dissemination through various pedagogical practices in institutions. Essentially, theory calls into question the founding notions of the traditional humanist curriculum and puts under erasure its idea of the free subject and its various means of indoctrinating that subject. In its most sophisticated form, theory is a reunderstanding of the political and cognitive conditions of possibility in the dominant knowledge/power relations of the contemporary situation—a radical regrounding of the study of the humanities.

Theory's questioning of the foundations of the traditional humanities program has been unsettling to many faculty members who are demanding change in the curriculum in order to stop the trend toward a radical theoretical and political interrogation of the humanities. The efforts of these faculty members have taken two distinct forms. Tradition-oriented faculty members have attempted to save the subject by appealing to established norms in the humanities (the free subject, the canon, moralism, and aestheticism, for example) and by striving to recommit the curriculum to empiricism, historicism, and humanism. The clearest defense of the traditional humanist position is presented in W. Jackson Bate's "The Crisis in English Studies" (1982). The ideological project of the humanists is very similar to that of their neoconservative allies outside the academy, and their strategies have evolved around renewed emphasis on certain kinds of courses and the use of established institutional and bureaucratic channels to block radical change in the academy.

The courses privileged by the humanists are mostly courses in "writing," whether in the form of technical writing and composition ("basic skills") or "creative writing." Writing courses (in fact, the entire Freshman English Programs of many colleges and universities) have become the last bastion of defense for traditional humanism against radical (post)modern critical theory. At a time when theory has questioned the grounds of conventional literary training, writing courses have been enthusiastically embraced by humanists as being happily beyond the contestation of theory: they are firmly grounded in the "self" of the writer–student. Regardless of their specific model and method, most writing courses are based on the notion of the subject as a rational, coherent, and unitary individual. The writer–student is assumed to have direct access to the "raw materials" of writing through his sensations, perceptions, and cognitions. The function of the teacher is to enable him to "discover" them and articulate them in a clear manner and in an unobtrusive language (language being a "means," or a "vehicle," for the "expression" of ideas that the subject has already formed extradiscursively). In the model of the traditionalists, the writings of great authors are thought to be the agency for such a discovery. By studying and emulating the texts of genius writers, the student "discovers" the ideas inside himself and consequently learns to articulate them. William Smart, in his *Eight Modern Essayists,* which is an exemplary text advocating this model, doubly inscribes the subject in the writing project: he presents the essays of contemporary writers as manifestations of the "great mind" (the independent consciousness of the author) and encourages the student to immerse herself in this consciousness as a way of discovering her own. In more recent models of teaching writing, the emphasis is placed on the "process" of writing. The process model also essentializes the subject. The philosophy of this model can be either a residual phenomenological theory of self–such as the one used by Jeff Rackham, who believes it is "the process, not the product" of writing that holds the "secret" (1980, 1) to the act of writing and employs an unproblematic notion of "perception" ("a sensory act," 1980, 2)–or the psychologically oriented cognitive model used by educators, such as Linda Flower and John Hayes, who postulate the subject as the originary site of knowledge. In Flower and Hayes's problem-solving approach to writing, both the writer and her reader (audience) are posited as self-present subjects. Flower and Hayes's own research into writing is partly based on "protocols": autobiographical accounts by writers of the ways in which a writer builds or creates new concepts out of the "raw material of experience" (1980, 22–23). The inscription of the self-identical subject in the dominant humanistic pedagogy through autobiographical narratives has become one of the most popular strategies in composition, as well as in traditional literature, courses where the coherent subject is retained by appeal to the writing self. Students in these classes are asked to keep journals/workbooks/notes on their own (implicity unique) encounters with the assigned texts–for discussion and in order to generate their own "protocols."

Donald Hall articulates the underlying assumptions of the contemporary pedagogy of writing when he says, "By learning to write well, we learn methods of self-discovery and techniques for self-examination" (1979, 6). The "self" ultimately is the cognitive domain upon which the practice of writing (and by extension, the study of literature) is grounded. The self that is justified and reinforced in this perception of writing, derives its legitimacy and authority from consumer society. It is a self that is transparent, thinks straightforwardly, writes clearly, and acts efficiently. It adheres to a set of unambiguous (businesslike) moral values and is organized by the pragmatic logic of managed capitalism. The various practical devices used in order to reinscribe the subject in the curriculum through "writing" are given further support by recent work by theorists of written composition. The work of Kenneth Bruffee is perhaps an interesting instance of such reification of the subject. Bruffee's notion of knowledge as socially justified belief (the cornerstone of his "theory"), for instance, is nothing more than an elaboration of Richard Rorty's native pragmatism. In other words, there is in Bruffee no sense of the politics of cognition that organizes this socially constructed knowledge. Society and the social for him (as for Rorty) are cognitive domains—areas in which "knowledge" somehow appears by means of such apparatuses as agreement and convention and so forth. As a result of such a conservative (cognitive) theory of knowledge both in Rorty (following Dewey) and in Bruffee, the subject is presented as an uncontested category different from the way it is formulated in mainstream idealistic theories, but it is nevertheless privileged ground and characterized by coherence, unitariness, and rationality). Bruffee's "collaborative learning/teaching" is, in other words, the latest reproduction of the "management" of the subject and the latest effort to save it through "collaborative learning and the *conversation of mankind*" (1982, 96). The teacher in this model is the manager of the classroom—an agent of social coalescence. We ourselves are interested, by contrast, in a notion of knowledge that can account for the relations of production in the social formation—to put it another way, in the materiality and not the mere conventionality of knowledge.

Under pressure to offer new grounds for their practices, many well-known professors of literature, including some theoreticians who find the radical insights of (post)modern theory dangerous to the ideals of traditional humanism, have responded to the call for "writing as a university discipline." The names of E.D. Hirsch, J. Hillis Miller, Wayne Booth, Frederick Crews, and Robert Scholes head this list.

Opponents of theory also make strategic use of creative writing courses that privilege the human subject by their heavy emphasis on aesthetic experience, on style (as the signature of the subject) and on such notions as "genius," "inspiration," "intuition," "author," and "authority." The prevalent antiintellectualism and conservatism of these courses give them a retrograde role in most of the humanities programs in the United States. Emphasis on "realism" in these programs, for example, is a means of reifying the status quo, because, as we have already indicated, realism is a mode of encoding the cultural "reality" that is located inside the familiar frames of intelligibility and that is thus respectful of the limits of understanding set by the dominant ideology. It is inside these limits that realism represents such cultural practices as racism, sexism, and heterosexism as the "way things are" and, by such a representational move, legitimates the prevailing economic order. In depicting the arbitrary organization of the cultural codes that constitute the "real" as the natural reality, realism posits a coherent, causal, stable, and senseful world (necessary for the steady accumulation of capital) that is inhabited by noncontradictory and unitary subjects who are always present to themselves and thus gifted with introspective consciousnesses. The pedagogy of creative writing programs rejects all modes of innovative writing that put pressure on culture's boundaries of intelligibility and that defamiliarize its given as nonserious; in this way these programs construct realism as the only mature form of art, the only form in which the moral problems of adult life can be explored. The difficulties of middle-class life in late capitalism are therefore universalized as the timeless problems of humankind the world over, and the desire for transcending history and its contradictions is quietly written into the mimetic text.

In addition to writing courses, traditional humanists have placed new emphasis on courses on Shakespeare and other "great authors" because, as with the writing course, they too are self-evidently part of humanities studies and do not need a theoretical accounting: such courses are the embodiment of "literature." A course on Shakespeare not only inscribes the notion of author/authority/genius in the curriculum, but also quietly revives the category of literature (by appeal to "literariness").

The other strategy used by academic humanists to save the subject is to manipulate bureaucratic institutional apparatuses in order to contain radical theory's pressure for fundamental change. Through such strategies traditionalists attempt to forestall a radical shift by substituting a program of reform (that is, change on a trivial and insignificant scale that will not disturb existing power/knowledge relations). In one English department with which we are fairly familiar, for instance, a committee established to review the curriculum and make recommendations for possible changes began its investigation by surveying the faculty in individual interviews. As a mode of knowing, the interview technique is an exemplary strategy of traditional humanism because it inscribes fundamental humanist values (that is, liberal pluralism, unmediated knowledge, participatory democracy, consensus among free subjects) in the very practices it claims to be studying. By framing the committee's interpretations of the curriculum in face-to-face contact, the interview technique gave those interpretations the objectivity of "hard data" and thus represented its ideological readings as the consensus of the community. But in fact this "consensus" was determined at the very moment when the committee made the decision to use the interview technique: various views tend to cancel one another out in a diverse community and leave an intellectual vacuum in which the status quo is revalidated. The inclusion of all faculty members in this opinion-gathering process further legitimated it as democratic, open, and above all, nonpolitical. The focus of the interviews (unitary, sovereign subjects) reaffirmed the belief that people contain knowledge (they are self-present subjects) and all that one has to do to have access to that knowledge is to engage in "free" and "unconstrained" discussions—a notion that is ideologically related to the dominant curriculum's understanding and use of Socratic pedagogy in the classroom. Thus, legitimated by the human contacts involved in interviews, the committee could mask its own conservative views regarding the curriculum and its ideological program for saving the subject as the "natural" consensus of the community. The interview technique is, of course, an exemplary instance of what Derrida has called the desire for presence, which is an effect of the dominant logocentrism in the academy.

To further frame its actions in commonsensical modes of intelligibility, the committee sent out a memorandum to the faculty, asking them to write "a narrative about our curriculum" and urging them to include in their narratives answers to such questions as these: "How do we see what we do in courses in relation to scholarship in the field?" and "How do you see the courses you teach connecting with other courses in the department?" Obviously such questions constantly point back to existing practices and frame the issues in the dominant ideology, thus protecting those issues from a demystifying inquiry. The questions ask about the relation between an individual faculty member's practices and those of others rather than the grounds upon which each faculty member justifies his own pedagogical undertaking. Such a set of questions, of course, has another ideological function: to privatize the curriculum. These questions focus on the connections between individuals and their practices and not on the connection between the curriculum and existing power/knowledge relations. The committee's memorandum shows special concern for the humanist valorization of continuity. It inquires: "With respect to 200-level courses, . . . what do we want students to bring to them from levels 101–102?" The same question is raised about 300-, 400-, and 500-level courses. Finally this line of questions is summed up this way: "Is there perceptible tier-building from 100- to 400-level courses?" The theory of learning behind such questions is of course a developmental one; and such a developmental view projects a line of continuity and gradualism into the activity of knowing that protects the subject from any disruptive intrusion of modes of knowing that have not yet been prepared for. The subject is conceived as Piagetian child whose growth takes place in a series of causal stages: A form of neogeneticism is quietly introduced in the framing of questions, and the subject as a living, developing entity (rather than a set of subject positions in discursive practices) is reinstated in the discussion of the curriculum. The most significant of all questions, in terms of the committee's attempt to save the subject, is this: "What are the competencies . . . we want/expect our students to have/learn at each level?" To formulate the question in terms of "competencies" is to assume a built-in subjectivity, a point of origin: the individual. The same English department's catalog description of its graduate programs ends by reasserting that those programs "offer a unique opportunity for . . . self-discovery . . . "

Opposed to the traditionalists' way of going about saving the subject, but sharing their philosophical and ideological desire to reinscribe the subject in the humanities curriculum, are those faculty members who have not rejected theory but have assimilated it in order to forestall its radical dismantling of the subject. The domestication of theory and its use to contain the interrogation of the subject has taken place on both the level of criticism and scholarship and on the practical and pedagogical levels. As far as criticism and scholarship are concerned, many contemporary literary critics and theoreticians have appropriated (post)modern theory in order to reproduce the philosophical and ideological presuppositions of the dominant mode of literary knowledge in new modified forms that still retain the subject. Because our main focus in this essay is on the consequences of (post)modern theory and the crisis that it has engendered for pedagogical practices, we confine our discussion of the assimilation of radical theory to one important group: the Yale Critics, whose philosophical and critical practice seems on the surface to be far removed from the humanism of the traditionalists.[2] Revising Derrida and other contemporary theorists, each of the Yale Critics has in his own writing preserved the subject from the demystifying interrogation of radical theory. Geoffrey Hartman, for instance, has produced in his criticism a new version of the subject as stylist in whose consciousness literature, as an aesthetic act, unfolds as a moment of plenitude and presence. In a rather telling phrase, Hartman inscribes his book, *Saving the Text,* "For the Subject." Even if the "subject" is the subject of his discourse (à la Derrida), the inscription is nevertheless an indication of his desire to bring back the human to literary studies. The writings of J. Hillis Miller revive the existential subject, who—confronted with the insurmountable aporia of literary signification—is in eternal despair. Rather than realizing that the aporia is the effect not of the text but of the historical situation in which the text is made intelligible, Miller regards it as a purely cognitive matter—a matter of knowing through reading. Paul de Man's attempts to save the subject take the form of his invention of the subject as tropologist: the reader in whose unitary consciousness tropes of the text are the real sites of cognition. The critic's task is therefore the construction of a world in which the subject's consciousness can expand in the realm of aesthetics through the "tropological displacements of logic" (de Man, *Resistance to Theory* 1986, 111). The Yale Critics thus approach theory as a purely cognitive matter. This cognitivism also informs the work of those faculty members who have tried to save the subject by introducing new curricular plans based on contemporary theory in order to prevent the total eclipse of the subject under the pressure of radical interrogation.

An interesting example of such an appropriation of theory for constructing a new humanities curriculum can be found in Gary F. Waller's proposals for what he calls—in language well-suited to consumer society and its rational efficiency—"the first poststructuralist literary curriculum" (1985a, 6). Waller does attempt to reunderstand and repattern the traditional humanities curriculum, but his ideological commitment to the unitary, sovereign subject reduces his project to merely introducing new ideas to the curriculum; as in any reformist program, the controlling structure remains intact. It is in fact through maintaining this traditional humanistic master structure that Waller is able to inscribe the subject in the curriculum. For example, whereas in individual courses the texts of Lacan, Derrida, and Foucault place the notion of the subject under erasure, the unitary subject in its plenitude and presence is reinstated in the curriculum through its organizing structure, which incorporates courses on "major authors": "In our curriculum," Waller reassures his liberal audience, "there is even a (seemingly) privileged place for the author whom we have most often valorized, Shakespeare" (1985a, 11). (The parenthetical "seemingly" shows the eclectic self-consciousness with which this operation of resurrecting the subject has taken place.) In another reformist move that adds to the incoherencies of his curriculum, Waller attempts to question the theoretical justification for organizing literary and cultural studies in terms of mere chronology that passes as "history" in the academy, but at the same time he embraces "survey" courses constructed along those very lines (which Althusser has demystified as "historicist") and makes these courses mandatory for all undergraduates (1985b, 9).

These contradictions, as we have already suggested, are caused by the ideological imperative of the curriculum to retain the subject, an urgency that in turn has lead to an uninterrogated eclecticism. This eclectic project is marked by philosophical and political naiveté and, for the most part, is put forth in a set of ad hoc ideas rather than theoretically grounded concepts. Waller's program, for instance, is founded on an unproblematic notion of history ("the texts of our past," 1985a, 8); an uninspected and merely descriptive view of "culture" ("the particular cultural juncture in which we live," 1985a, 8) and a functionalist model of intelligibility that aims at maintaining and justifying the existing ideological, economic, and political order. By his own admission (1985a, 1), Waller's plan is a mere "application" of (post)modern critical theory to the curriculum. This means (and here is another moment of theoretical confusion in this eclectic curriculum) that he, in a profoundly un-(post)structuralist manner, posits a "metalanguage," a master discourse that from the "outside" authorizes and orders the pedagogical activities of the "inside."

The ideological solidarity between Waller and the neoconservative advocates of change in the curriculum becomes clearer when one notices how eager he is to inscribe vocational training in the humanities curriculum. "There is also great emphasis," he guarantees, "on that other basic skill, writing, and the opportunity to explore the possibilities of computer-aided instruction in reading and writing" (1985b, 7). As befits his technocratic audience, Waller's rhetoric is that of an efficient manager concerned with the "application" of ideas (produced by others), and with "dovetailing" their various parts in the curriculum so that he can achieve a "breakthrough" and thus produce the first (post)structuralist curriculum for (consumption in) the profession. The outcome of such a technocratic approach is that Waller's proposed curriculum is purely and safely cognitive; the students are taught to "understand" but not to "intervene." Although, according to him, they will "understand" the whole culture in his curriculum (1985b, 3), there is no indication at all that such knowing ever leads to an engagement in the affairs of the culture that they now supposedly know. The dominant power/knowledge relations are non-negotiable in Waller's program: Students may learn all about the codes through which reality is constructed, but they are not placed in an oppositional subject position through which they can interrogate that reality and consequently intervene in its reconstitution.

Unwilling–and from his position clearly unable–to acknowledge the political conservatism and intellectual quietism of his curricular proposals, Waller tries desperately to shield them from inspection by those occupying an oppositional position. Appealing to Foucault, he insists that in order to "speak meaningfully to and within a dominant discourse, we must be inserted within it" (1985a, 11). "Deliberately choosing," he says, to be situated on an interrogative margin is a "kind of masochism, the root of martyrdom." ("Not that martyrs aren't occasionally useful," he adds for the amusement of his commonsensical audience, 1985a, 11.) According to him, any critique form the margin is merely "prophetic diatribe" (1985a, 1). Those on the margin should give up their hopeless ideas and locate themselves in a middle discourse, in what he calls the "compromise of debate and praxis" (1985a, 1). In his privileging of "compromise," as in his valorizing of the "application" (rather than the interrogation) of ideas, Waller's fundamentally anti-intellectual professionalism is in alliance with the agenda of the neoconservative technocrats of the center. His proposals, in short, transform (post)modern critical theory–a weapon for bringing about social change by intervening in the educational apparatus–into a mere tool for private enterprise: a device for reproducing the exiting relations of production under a new set of names and terms.

(Post)modern critical theory has decentered the humanist regime of truth and engendered a crisis in the philosophy and practice of its pedagogy. The crisis is too fundamental to be contained by such new humanist programs as those articulated by a reformist (post)structuralism or its seeming opposite, a nostalgic neoconservatism. Such intellectual improvisations aim at saving the subject by modifying the curriculum, but the serious question is no longer how to save the subject by changing the courses studying it, but how to change study itself. The (post)modern pedagogue now must consider a subjectless humanities program: one that does not evolve around the production of a unitary, rational subject ready to be inserted into the dominant social formation but one that situates itself in the interstices of diverse subject positions produced by the social apparatuses (family, church, labour union, media, school, political parties) and the processes of signification that enable them.

CHAPTER 4

The Cultural Politics
of the Fiction Workshop

1 The dominant form of the fiction workshop in creative writing programs of contemporary U.S. literature departments is founded upon a set of assumptions that have been put in question by (post)modern critical theory and oppositional pedagogy. These assumptions include the idea of the free "subject," the integrity of "experience," the sharp separation of "reading" from "writing," the individual "voice," the "authority" of the author, uniqueness of "style," the obedience of the reader, "originality," and "intuition." Although the (post)modern critique of these and related issues in the fiction workshop is partial, limited, and, as we shall argue, ultimately ideologically complicit with the dominant power/knowledge relations in the academy, it is nonetheless a pedagogically useful beginning for interrogating the dominant practices in the fiction workshop. By problematizing the assumptions about writing in the fiction workshop, such a critique foregrounds the constructedness of the notions that the workshop treats as self-evident and consequently opens up possibilities for a more historical reunderstanding of creative writing programs in general. The most effective aspect of such a (post)modern critique is derived from the early work of Derrida, Foucault, Lyotard, and others in their deconstruction of the Western subject. However, as the work of these (post)modern philosophers (in response to the historical situation in the West) moves away from rigorous conceptual analysis and dissolves into a ludic, anticonceptual "literariness," their effectivity for the critique of the cultural politics of late capitalism rapidly diminishes. In the later writings of Foucault, Derrida, and others, what we in fact witness is the rebirth of the subject and the return to some of the very practices that they had critiqued in their earlier writings. Those earlier writings are put aside by some of their followers who today celebrate their later ludic writings (an exemplary instance is Gayatri Spivak, in her "On the Politics of the Subaltern") in order to discredit the practice of ideology critique.

In her essay, " 'Homeward Ho!': Silicon Valley Pushkin," Marjorie Perloff concludes that the "battle" now under way between contemporary creative writing practices and (post)modern critical theory in the U.S. academy is specifically "being fought between the Creative Writing Workshop and the Graduate Seminar in Theory" (1986, 45). "The A Team," she says, "accuses the B Team of writing impenetrable jargon and pseudo-Marxist double-talk: in return, the B Team accuses the A of being 'soft and naive,' and of failing to understand that all language is mediated. . . . A wants poetry to be more what it has always been; B insists that 'you can't say it that way any more' " (1986, 45). Perloff's account "trivializes" the theoretical, aesthetic, pedagogical, institutional, and cultural implications of what is, in the last analysis, nothing less than a battle over subjectivities in culture. The contestation between (post)modern theory and the creative writing workshop is in fact most clearly articulated in their respective theories of reading/writing texts of culture.[1]

(Post)modern critical theory in all its various forms argues that acts of reading/writing the texts of culture, which shape the "meaning" of (cultural) reality, are not a matter of the reader/writer's "private taste," "intuition," "sensitivity," "vision," or "originality." They are, in other words, not "natural" acts, but complex social practices that are acquired by the people of a culture in the process of being socialized through education—in the inclusive sense of the word, in schools, churches, families, sports, and so on. Education in all of its forms is itself, of course, a social institution and

as such is always the effect of struggles among various social classes that attempt to shape it according to their own political agenda. (This political agenda is never put forth as overtly political but
is always defended under the guise of "moral," "intellectual,"
"professional" imperatives.) It is through the implementation of
its educational agenda, a program for teaching how to read/write
the texts of culture that is itself affected by specific economic and
ideological interests, that the socially dominant class has the final
say in the designation of what is "real" (what "makes sense," a
"good" story) and what is "nonreal" (what is "nonsense," an unacceptable narrative) in a society. There is, in short, a politics and
economics to the "meaning" of the texts of culture, because meaning is produced by a culturally situated reader who reads/writes
only by means of reading/writing strategies that are historically (in
terms of class, race, gender, and other social factors) available to
her. There actually is no singular, fixed, or uncontested (that is,
no transhistorically "stable") meaning in the text: what seems to
be the text's "uncontested" meaning is the one that is made to
make the most "sense" by the dominant class's ideological apparatuses, which naturalize the boundaries of intelligibilities.

The dominant fiction workshop, on the other hand, adheres
to a theory of reading/writing that regards the text's meaning to
be not so much "produced" by cultural and historical factors as
by the imagination of the author as reflected in the "text itself."
According to this humanist notion of meaning, a text (like language) acquires its meaning because of the reality that is located
outside of it and to which it faithfully "refers." The author is the
"authority" who situates the text in relation to "reality," and his
verbal skills and craftsmanship in making the text "correspond"
with reality are, in the last analysis, acts of a sovereign imagination –
unaccountable and unanalyzable moments of intuition, originality, and inventiveness. Because, from the traditional point of view,
the text is given its meaning by the reality "out there" (in the real
world as mirrored in the mind of the author), it is always already
"full" – it is determined and, as such, is an uncontestable entity.
This is not to say that all readers presumably get a uniform meaning from the text – because of course this view of reading/writing

allows the text to be interpreted in diverse and multiple ways—but that the parameters of these interpretations (boundaries of intelligibilities) are already set by the contours of nontextual reality; the text is, in other words, a secondary phenomenon. The supreme mark of artistry is to make this "secondariness" invisible and to produce an identity between the "world" and the "word." In its fullness, the text is an instance of presence and plenitude, designated by the writing workshop as the organic unity of the text and protected by the workshop from any historical interventions that reveal "trace"-as-absence to be the condition of possibility of this seeming presence by exposing the text's "lacunae" (its points of social–political and representational vulnerability). A full text is seen as already occupied by the real and thus comes to the reader as a coherent, independent, and meaningful totality. This is the text of "consensus" from which the contestations of dissenting classes are systematically removed. The function of the reader in the dominant fiction workshop is therefore also predetermined: to recover the consensus that is located in the text by its originary agent, the author. The conventional mode of straightforward aesthetic reading, then, is a monological model that sees the writer talking while the reader listens; the talk is about the reality outside the text, and the medium of this communication is a transparent language that does not in itself produce any dissenting disturbances, but represents the meaning of the world as unobtrusively as possible. The "clear," "concise," and "lean" style of the author makes sure that there is no intrusion by language itself: that is to say, no marks of class contestations over the meanings of the sign are allowed to distract from the aesthetic act. The politics of such a theory of text, language, reader, author, and their relation to reality is that reading/writing is a merely textual excuse for reader and author to relate to each other as two independent consciousnesses outside all constraints of history—outside language and other interruptions of history. In an ideologically significant sense, then, in this traditional view, the acts of "writing" and "reading" (which are material) completely disappear from the scene of reading/writing and are replaced by two sovereign selves—writer and reader—who communicate directly and thus ideologically affirm their separateness and uniqueness and, in short, their unique individuality. The unsaid of such a view of "reading" as receiving (to be distinguished from "producing") meaning is the sharp separation of "reading" from "writing." The writer is always the creative producer whereas the reader is the passive consumer. The political value of such a theory of reading for the dominant class is that in the name of "reading" the reader is taught how to "obey" "authority"—how, in other words, to "follow" the instructions of the writer, who stands for authority and controls meaning. But, as Barthes, Derrida, Macherey, and others have already shown, reading is nothing less than a rewriting, and all writing is a reading. Writing is an interpretation and thus a political contestation over the significance of the signs of culture; that is to say, like reading it is a discursive and political practice and not an effect of the private and direct intuition of a genius: that is, of a floating transhistorical consciousness. The valorization of "writing" as the immediate act of intuiting reality and the relegation of "reading" to the secondary status of the rediscovery of original meanings "intended" by the writer are so prevalent that Tess Gallagher goes so far as to completely separate the "literature" program (in which people simply "read") from the "creative writing" program (in which people "write"). Responding to an interviewer on the occasion of the publication of her book of short stories, *The Lover of Horses,* Gallagher remarks that she was part of such an active creative writing program, in which "there are no professional readers . . . only writers" (Tom Dial 1986, 13).

2   This violent separation of "reading" from "writing" is part of the division of labor in the contemporary academy that is in fact inscribed in the dominant power/knowledge relations, and that divides (and on a higher ideological level unites) the departments of literature into "readers" (scholars, critics, editors) and "writers." The scholars/critics/editors not only accept but indeed enthusiastically define themselves as the subjects of reading (as "subtle readers" or what Gallagher calls "professional readers"), whereas the creative writers posit themselves as the subjects of writing. The two, in other words, reproduce in the academy and in the literature department–which is one of the most effective and powerful sites for the circulation of the ruling ideology and the education of the labor force–the social division of labor that is the cornerstone of modern capitalism. This separation of "readers" from "writers" interpellates them as different "experts," "professionals" whose unique expertise cannot possibly be undertaken by "others." The "subject" of reading is thus distanced from the "subject" of writing, and consequently the two expert subjects of expertise are preserved as selfsame, unique, and unmixed. (Post)modern critical theory deprofessionalizes reading/writing and indicates that what is represented as "expertise" is in fact a reification of social practices, such as the division of labor, which are necessary for producing and maintaining the subjectivities upon which the labor force of late capitalism depends.

In its efforts to keep intact the legitimacy of bourgeois values embodied in such undertakings as the "professionalization" of social practices, the ideological arm of the dominant economic regime in the academy has engaged in a new mode of institutional politics, the purpose of which is to build up a new coalition of all those academic "experts" and "professionals" who acquire their own cultural authority from the ruling social order.

It is part of this coalitionism that in English departments all across the United States at the present moment a political rapprochement is being negotiated between traditional humanist scholar–critics and creative writers. It is historically significant that humanist scholars, who are now seeking a political alliance with creative writers, are the very people who a decade or so ago were opposed to establishing creative writing programs in their departments. Creative writing programs, the traditionalists used to argue, were intellectually "soft," and their existence in any department would inevitably lead to a "lowering of academic standards," because they enabled students to obtain degrees in English without having been subjected to the rigors of historical scholarship and other critical training. Under the pressure of radical critical theory, that argument has now lost its ideological usefulness, and instead, in a new political move, humanist scholars and critics are embracing creative writing programs as the genuine site of creativity and imagination, the space of a transhistorical "literary." The celebration of the "creative writing" program as the unique (institutional) articulation of the "literary," relates these programs not just to traditional humanist practices in the academy but also to the more recent developments in (post)structualism, to what Zavarzadeh calls "pun(k)deconstruction." Pun(k)deconstruction deconceptualizes theory by "performing" what Paul de Man and other classic deconstructionists call the "literary." In a book such as Derrida's *The Post Card*, "the literary" is deployed to perform the undecidable. This performance of the literary (what Gallagher calls "writing") has always constituted the "identity" of the fiction workshop and its main principle for resistance to theory. The crisis of the bourgeois knowledge industry in the late 1980s and early 1990s reached such a magnitude that all formerly invisible lines of alliance among bourgeois knowledge professionals became visible. It turned out that what seemed to be "bloody" battles among theorists and humanists, humanists and creative writers, creative writers and deconstructionists, . . . were all internal petty squabbles. Faced with the radical challenge of revolutionary Marxism (see our discussion of Hazard Adams's defense of the cult of uniqueness in Chapter 2 of *Theory, (Post)Modernity, Opposition*), a new coalition has been established among the creative writers, deconstructionists, and traditional humanists, the purpose of which is to contain Marxism in all sites of the academy. The principle of this coalition is the concept of the "literary"–the ideological alibi through which the bourgeois academy naturalizes an ahistorical "aesthetic" as the space of democratic unique self-expression of the difference of creativity (entrepreneurship). It is in the boundaries of such new cultural and academic coalitions that the historical limits of ludic (post)modern theory become more clear. Ludic theory inaugurates some necessary moves to foreground and mark the metaphysics of creativity and the cult of individuality in the bourgeois academy–in the fiction workshop, for instance. However, the main purpose in such a deconstruction of metaphysics is to get rid of those historical practices that are no longer useful for legitimating the continuation of the regime of capital and its knowledge industry in more effective ways in late capitalism. Only a radical Marxist critique of these institutions can lead to a revolutionary, rather than a reformist, conclusion. The institutional politics of this new coalition of traditional scholars and creative writers legitimates itself as a purely "aesthetic" act and is articulated in the representation of realism in the dominant academy as the privileged mode of reading/writing texts of culture. Common perception to the contrary, deconstruction is *not* against "realism." As Zavarzadeh demonstrates in *Pun(k)deconstruction* (1992b) the Derridean project is not antirealist or antimimetic. It does not oppose the actual practice of realism and mimesis, but only the way in which its logic is understood. In *Positions,* Derrida clearly indicates that his quarrel with mimesis is that it represents itself as a "deterministic" mode of writing. The relation between the signifer and the signified, as far as Derrida is concerned, can indeed be one of mimesis but not of determinism: the signifer and signifed are always coupled through the logic not of "necessity" (determinism) but of the "alea" (chance). This mode of nondeterministic realism he calls "mimesis" and rejects the deterministic form of realism as "mimetological" (*Positions* 1981, 70). It is this very nondeterministic realism that has become the basis of miminalism in the writings of Raymond Carver and more recently the principle of "experimental realism" that informs a work such as *Mao II* by Don Delillo, the new "literary" hero of the (post)modern academy.

Realism, however, is not just an aesthetic category, a mode or style of writing, but a regime of signification that aims at saving the fundamental ideological series necessary for the justification, and thus the unproblematic reproduction, of the existing social relations upon which the dominant social arrangements and class relations of contemporary bourgeois life and its economic organization are founded. At the "heart" of bourgeois life (what thus makes realism politically necessary) is the theory of the sovereign subject: the free, independent, and enterprising individual. The political agenda of realism (and thus its urgency for humanist critics and writers) is to save the bourgeois subject from the onslaught of radical theories of subjectivity that restructure the social "otherwise."

The subject, in short, is the vehicle by which the individual is situated in prevailing social and economic arrangements. In bourgeois ideology the subject is proposed as an independent, unitary, rational, and self-cohering individual who is free to initiate actions and take control of her life and is thus the source of all cultural and social "meaning." She reads the texts of culture and "describes" their "inherent" meaning (put there by an equally free subject, namely the author) in the privacy of her consciousness, aided by her creative imagination and personal taste. Such a subject is necessary for the reproduction of social relations in capitalism, and the support of this subject by dominant literature and writing programs is in fact a collaboration with the reigning political and economic order based on capitalist exploitation. Realism is the mode of signification through which this notion of the unitary and free subject, as we argued in Chapter 3, is preserved. The guarding of the subject is such a "natural" and "essential" part of the practices of the academy's professionals of ideology that no critique of it is tolerated. For instance, after the publication of an earlier version of this essay in *Cultural Critique,* Harold Fromm, in his book, *Academic Capitalism and Literary Value,* attacked our views on realism and our reading of Gordimer as "revolutionary blather" (Fromm 1991, 246) and labeled our text as a "madcap exercise" (228). Typically, Fromm did not offer any "reasons" why realism should be regarded as an enabling mode of reading/writing because he did not need to: Realism is part of the common sense of the dominant understanding of the world—it is an "obviousness" that does not need to be "argued." He counts, therefore, on an unthoughtful acceptance of realism on the part of many readers. This very "obviousness" is, of course, what we believe needs to be demystified: realism is not a "natural" form of understanding but a political construct that legitimates the subjectivites needed for the efficient operation of capitalism.

The fiction workshop is not a "neutral" place where insights are developed, ideas/advice freely exchanged, and skills honed. It is a site of ideology: a place in which a particular view of reading/

writing texts is put forth and, through this view, support is given to the dominant social order. By regarding writing as "craft" and proposing realism as the mode of writing, the fiction workshop fulfills its ideological role in the dominant academy by preserving the subject as "independent" and "free." In the fiction workshop the writer is postulated to be an independent person who discovers the secret of writing and the meaning of the world through the discovery of her unique "self." The main cultural purpose of the dominant fiction workshop in the present pedagogical regime is in fact to teach the student how to discover the "self." The cultural politics of this self-discovery, as we have indicated, is to construct a subject who perceives herself as self-constituted and free, so that she can then "freely" collaborate with the existing social system, a collaboration that assures the continuation of patriarchal capitalism.

The discovery of the self in the fiction workshop is achieved through a fairly complex and elaborate process. In her description of one of the most famous fiction workshops in the United States, Amy Hempel provides a clear account of the construction of the free subject in the contemporary writing workshop. Hempel's description begins in fact with the process through which the student is affirmed as a unique and ineluctable entity in possession of something so private that no one else has access to it—a "thing" that, like private property, sets the owner apart from the non-owner and thus not only gives her a mark of distinction, but of security as well by anchoring her in the truly unique and irreplaceable. "We are telling our terrible secrets," Hempel remarks in opening her narrative of Gordon Lish's very well-known workshop, "saying the unsayable to strangers in a room" (1984, 91). The secret establishes the singularity of the individual, saves him from mass anonymity, and also affirms his freedom because he is saying the unsayable as an act of free will and not under coercion. The production of the student as a free subject in the workshop takes a complex form: he is not simply established as a free subject but is affirmed as an "ego," directly by the act of confessing secrets. Having first established that the individual student is unique as a free subject in owning something special (a "secret"), the workshop then proceeds to point out that, although this is a necessary element, it is not sufficient. Lish says startlingly: "the best secrets are those that dismantle your sense of yourself" (Hempel 1984, 91). "Self," in other words, cannot be found easily, directly, and effortlessly (this would deny the privileged position of "hard work" in bourgeois ethics); the route to the true self is oblique and contrary. The process of arriving at one's "geniune" self by dismantling the superficial, worldly self, however, has a long tradition in Western mysticism. One dismantles one's ephemeral self on the level of the mundane and the voluntary only to find it on a higher plane of reality—and permanently. Hempel's account makes this quite clear: "You will fare better than some in this class," she continues, "if you are willing to undergo a kind of ego death" (1984, 93). And why? Again, she provides the answer: " 'Don't glorify yourself,' [Lish] says, 'convict yourself. And the wonderful paradox is that it's how you make yourself angelic' " (1984, 126). It is this making oneself "angelic," becoming a dematerialized subject who has access to his consciousness beyond all the mediations of culture, history, and politics, that is the outcome of a successful fiction workshop.

In the workshop, the discovery of the "free" self is what is regarded to be the mark of one's "creativity." It is through one's "creativity" (the quality that is the basis of entrepreneurship in capitalism) that one is able to "write." In his *A Theory of Literary Production,* Pierre Macherey inquires into this bourgeois myth of creativity and comments that "the proposition that the writer or artist is a creator belongs to a humanist ideology. In this ideology man is released from his function in an order external to himself, restored to his so-called powers. Circumscribed only by the resources of his own nature he becomes the maker of his own laws" (1978, 66). As a writer, "you are," in Lish's words, "God" (Hempel 1984, 126). "Creativity," in other words, is the ability to transcend the political, the economic, and in short the "material" conditions of writing (transcending the "order external to" oneself) as a social person and arrive at a transdiscursive space. It is in this unbounded space, free of all political, social, economic, and linguistic constraints, that the creative person is able to penetrate

the opacities of culture and experience reality in its absolute plenitude. Experience, the uninterpreted, unmediated, and direct, in-
tuitive knowing of the body of the world is the ultimate test of
truthfulness and authenticity in the fiction workshop. Readers "understand," that is to say, whereas writers "experience," that is, have
a direct awareness of reality. The prevalent theory of knowledge
in the workshop is that only the experienced is true and only those
who have had experience speak the truth. Experience, however,
as Althusser has effectively argued is not the site of truth, but the
space of ideology. "Lived experience," he writes, "is not *given*, given
by a pure 'reality,' but the spontaneous 'lived experience' of ideology in its peculiar relationship to the real" (*Lenin and Philosophy
and Other Essays* 1971, 223). It is through this privileging of "experience" that radical theory is attacked in the workshop, and by
humanist critics and such deconstructionists as Paul de Man. For
de Man *the* experience is the experience of the "literary," of verbal
sensuousness. Empiricism and its accompanying ideology of
experience-as-truth propose the world as the site of knowledge and
thus oppose the notion that "world" and "reality" are in fact economic and political constructs so produced as to legitimate the
interests of the ruling social arrangements. By this maneuver, radical critical theory, which is an inquiry into this construction of
intelligibility in culture, is pushed to the fringes of culture.

The mark of the arrival of the creative person at the domain
of the translucent experience of truth is having a "voice." The quest
to find a "voice" and the freedom of the subject that it marks is,
paradoxically, one of the efforts in which the interests of humanists,
creative writiers, and ludic deconstructionists overlap. This is "para-
doxical" because, to many contemporary readers, the opposition
to "voice" (as part of phonophallocentrism) is a hallmark of
(post)modern theory. However, the later experiments of Derrida
in such works as *The Post Card,* like the playfulness of Avital Ronell
in her *Telephone Book,* bear witness to the ideological necessity of
"voice" in the writings both of the mainstream writers in the fiction workshop and the deconstructionists. In fact, in Ronell, the
"tele-phone" (like the "post card" in Derrida) becomes the trope
of the elusiveness of the personal-as-literariness—the marker of un-

decidability, of the immediacy and distance of the "voice" of the speaking subject. The telephone, the postcard, and other means of "personal" communication become, in ludic (post) modernism, means for bringing back the subject, which was buried in earlier (post)structuralist writings. To find and develop one's "voice" is the unquestionable sign of creativity, and in turn is–as we have argued–itself a sign of irreplaceable "selfhood." Hempel's description of Lish's workshop makes clear that, although the class teaches "writing," its goal is really what lies beyond the act of writing, beyond the materiality of writing as a historical product and process. Lish's conviction about writing is that what counts "isn't what happens to people on a page–it's what happens to a reader in his heart and mind" (Hempel 1984, 92). In other words, it is by means of the extrahistorical (dematerialized) effects of writing (the assertion of the subject through the power of the creative writer whose unique "voice" commands and transcends the medium) that the writer makes his mark on the reader. In this way, as we have argued before, the writer and the reader relate to each other beyond the material confines of the "page." The immediate, extradiscursive connection between the reader and the writer, according to Lish, is a "conspiracy . . . the conspiracy is: It's us–smart people–talking to each other" (Hempel 1984, 126). The transcending of writing and arriving at speech (talking to the reader) is enabled by the "voice" of the writer–his "unimpeachable authority" through which the writer "persuades" you "that if you don't listen he'll die, and if you listen he'll save your life, and if you don't listen you'll die a lot harder" (Hempel 1984, 92).

The "voice," which is taken to be the sign that the writer has achieved transparency of self, is the mark of what Derrida calls "presence"–the immediate access of self to its inner truths, which are void of difference and identical with themselves. In his early writings Derrida has demonstrated (most powerfully in *Of Grammatology*) that in order to offer a representation of the world that is amenable to the existing order, Western philosophy has proposed as the goal of understanding, meaning, and signification the achievement of a state of being that is self-situating, self-explaining, nondifferential, and self-identical. He calls that state of being (bliss) "presence" and further argues that the state of presence is privileged in texts of Western literature and philosophy by denigrating "difference" and valorizing "identity," moves that, in the field of textuality, correspond to the denigration of "writing" and the valorization of "speech."

Derrida's investigation of writing requires elaboration. The traditional notion of writing, he observes, participates in what he calls "logocentrism," a term he employs to point to the complex of enabling conditions that undergird Western thought, one of the chief among them being the effort to find the "reality" behind the "appearance" of things. The quest for this hidden reality becomes particularly acute for philosophers, because they regard themselves to be the arbiters and guardians of "truth" in Western culture, but of course it is no less crucial an issue for all readers/writers. Logocentrism assumes that, because the "surface appearance" of things is not "reality," but merely a derivative of it, to acquire truth one must reach beyond this surface to the (founding) reality itself—reach beyond things in order to grasp the originative center lying behind them. Derrida's critique of logocentrism is, however, not only incomplete but is in fact complicitous with the ruling ideology. In his critique, Derrida attends mainly to the cognitive desire for identity. In other words, he denies the alienation of the "real"—the fact that, as Marx has argued, there is, in class-based societies, always a distance between the "appearance" and the "real," between *what is* empirically and *what is* structurally. Through his notion of representation as always being misrepresentation (because the medium of representation—language—is itself subject to the laws of *différance*), Derrida posits this gap as ahistorical and eternal, as part of the human condition as such. In his view, the gap between the appearance and the real is the effect of representation, and any attempt to overcome it is simply a manifestation of a totalitarian desire for harmony, unity, and identity. However, contrary to what Derrida "says" in *Of Grammatology* and what he later "performs" in *Glas,* this distance is not the ahistorical effect of representation as such, but the distance of alienated labor, the distance that is filled by ideology. Ideology covers the distance between the appearance and the real so that the world that empirically exists is perceived as the only world possible. The seeming inevitability of what exists is necessary for the continuation of capitalist class relations, because the opening of the gap makes visible the way in which the existing social relations are founded on the extraction of surplus labor. Ideology is not simply a logocentric desire for identity, but a systematic, material practice that justifies the processes that conceal the way surplus labor is extracted from the proletariat. In *Glas* and elsewhere, Derrida inaugurates a critique of the dominant practices, but then quickly transforms that critique into a purely cognitive reunderstanding of the issues involved and, by doing so, blocks any economic and political critique.

Derrida also accounts for the relation of speech to writing in terms of the Western imperative for finding the ground or foundation of things. The two communicative acts, he argues, are hierarchically situated, speech being seen as a form of "immediate" expression (involving the "actual" presence of those communicating), whereas writing is merely a form of secondary, "mediated" expression (operating through distance and deferral and allowing the absence of those communicating). Thus writing is seen as just a "weak" and "inauthentic" substitute for speech. In speech the signifier and the speaker acquire an evanescence: language disappears as soon as it is uttered, leaving behind the transparent "idea" and the transparent speaker (at one with the idea itself). In writing, by contrast, the signifier and the speaker retain their opacity: language cannot disappear, but instead its very materiality is foregrounded, and the "difference" between the writer and what she says is evident. By regarding "voice" as the mark of the true writer, the creative writing workshop becomes the accomplice of the metaphysics of presence, of logocentrism and its accompanying phonocentrism, which is the underlying theory of sense making in patriarchy and in capitalism.

The cultural politics of nurturing the "voice" in the fiction workshop develops out of a hegemonic mode ("voice") of writing and the consequent monopolization of publishing outlets. To focus on Gordon Lish's practices outside the classroom, he was not only (as an editor for Knopf and other publishing houses) responsible for cultivating the voice that led to the hegemonic dominance of "minimalist" fiction in U.S. fiction of the 1980s, but also introduced a journal, *Quarterly*, which published only those who spoke in this "voice." The political contradictions of what is supposed to be uniquely "individualistic" (the personal voice) become clear in this journal and in what Lish edits at Knopf. Far from being "singular," the voice is in fact a "construct"—a politically needed cultural product developed by professionals of ideology such as Lish and other writers who direct fiction workshops across the country. The commodification of "voice" and of individuality in the fiction workshop is in fact the major political role played by creative writing programs.[2]

The visible and external mark of the unique "voice" of the singular writer is his "style." The cultural paradox of the fiction workshop—a manifestation of its ideological contradictions—is that as the workshop focuses on style, which is the materiality of writing, it in fact is bent on eliminating it. The double move—both establishment and elimination—of style takes place through the theory of style that reigns in the contemporary workshop. The style of the writer is supposed to be so translucent as to be nonexistent. Style, in other words, establishes the uniqueness of the individual, but its transparency immediately enables the individual to transcend "writing" and "difference" (the materiality of labor) and reach a transhistorical space in which the writer can, in his absolute imaginative freedom, communicate with equally unfettered readers. "I want my fiction," writes Tess Gallagher, "to be transparent. I want it to involve the character and experiences, but I don't want the language to be visible" (Tom Dial 1986, 13). When the writer's language is visible (its materiality evident), it is an indication that the writer has not freed himself from his medium—in Macherey's words, from "the order external to himself" (1978, 64). The writer remains a social and political being entangled with the opacity of language and with what Bakhtin and Voloshinov have shown to be the space of class struggle.[3] He has not succeeded in becoming a "free" person in touch with the reality of "heart and mind" outside the language series of culture. It is this eternal, free individual who is the "subject" of interpellation in the capitalist order, and it is by causing persons to perceive themselves as "free" that the reigning regime continues its domination. The fiction workshop is the place in which this indoctrination is made to seem "natural," and capitalism's exploitation is an integral but invisible part of the workshop's operation. The translucent style leads the reader "directly" to the "meaning" of the text. "Meaning" in the writing workshop, as we have indicated, is itself explained by the theory of reference: meaning is the emergence of significance at the time when writing becomes one with the extraverbal reality to which it refers. In realism the referent is "the world out there." In a sense, then, the free subject, who has discovered his identity by developing a unique voice, discovers that what is out there – the existing social arrangements in the world – is the ground of his identity and consequently, in order to keep his identity unharmed, he consents to this existing world. In reading fiction, the reader learns how to discover the real meaning of the world (that is, of the familiar and existing world) through models of identity provided by characters in realist fiction.

As a quality second only to its reification of style as transparency, realistic fiction celebrates (even fetishizes) "character." Character (the model for the free subject) is depicted as a unitary and coherent individual who is always unique and, in his most authentic mode, solitary – like an entrepreneur, he works all by himself. Through individual characters realistically portrayed, the reader discovers his own subjectivity. The valorization of character in the fiction workshop, in other words, is part of its cultural politics in legitimating the ruling values of capitalism.

Writers/teachers who direct workshops will argue that, far from being a monolithic place with an ideological agenda, the workshop is in fact a "pluralistic" space where each individual thinks differently and where her talent is developed differently. The very idea of "individual talent," however, is an ideological construct, for, as we have argued, it is part of the interpellation of the individual as a free subject who will freely consent to the existing social order. Furthermore, the "pluralism" on which the workshop prides itself is one of the most powerful political strategies of containment that bourgeois democracy uses in order to conceal the dominant hierarchy of hegemonic power and exploitation in culture – by positing the various sites of power as "equal." This "equality" is, however, a legal fiction mystifying the relations of exploitation in society. It is through "pluralism" that, for example, the real (economic) difference between a banker and a janitor is occluded in the name of the supposed equality of their individual "voices."

All modes of writing other than realism, that is, those that are subversive of this regime of reading/writing texts of culture are banished from the workshop. In fact, realism is not only the name of a mode of writing but a regime of administration: a way of legitimating the distribution of financial and knowledge resources. Jack Leggett, the director of the Iowa fiction workshop, articulates this quite clearly when he says: "In judging the poems and stories of applicants, the selection committee avoids extremes, steering clear of experimental work" (Maureen Howard 1986, 47). The distance that is placed between "experimental" writing and the workshop serves a political need of the academy: Experimental texts are subversive texts; they put a culture's signifying practices in question and ask whether the real as constituted in the works of mainstream writers is not an ideological organization of the real that supports the political and economic status quo, and legitimates the exploitative social relations in culture. The innovative text not only foregrounds the materiality of the sign and thus opposes the theory of "presence" and semantic consensus, but dismantles the cherished concepts and practices of realism: "transparent style" as individualized "character," causal plot, and so on. Furthermore, and more important, as a consequence of this displacement of "style," "character," "plot," and other fetishes of the dominant fiction workshop, innovative writing intervenes in the discursive practices of culture and demonstrates that what is offered as natural/unchangeable/real is in fact an "unnatural" construct that can be changed. The practitioners of the realist workshop and mimeticist critics find this politics of shifts, changes, and transgressions so threatening that they are determined to keep it out of the classroom/workshop. The workshop is the site of eternity, stability, and the lasting values of the bourgeois. However, since realist writers are essentially catering to the dominant taste and image of the times, they are "popular," and their popularity constitutes a power base for them in the institution where, in running the fiction workshop, they "naturalize" hegemonic values under the guise of offering realism as an aesthetic practice. It is this power that is so highly attractive to traditional humanist critics. Humanist scholar–critics, who not so long ago were so contemptuous of creative writing programs because they degraded literary scholarship, have come today to rely on the institutional power of creative writers (realists who are on the bestseller lists and are therefore popular/powerful in universities) to help rescue them from the onslaught of radical theory. Among the political consequences of such a power play has been this: the university, which often represents itself as the site of an oppositional force in culture where commonly held values are interrogated, has been colonized by the mass media. Cultural representations that sell in the marketplace, such as realist fiction, dominate university humanities programs and through this domination provide realist writers with an institutional power base from which they attack the radical modes of cultural inquiry enabled by critical theory.

The institutional politics of this new alliance has in fact been quite effective in containing radical theory and keeping it out of the mainstream of academic practices where the majority of students are educated. As a result of the new coalitionism, theory has been relegated in the majority of literature programs to specialized courses or graduate seminars while the undergraduate courses (in which the future writers and editors who will determine which texts will be written and which will reach the reading public are trained) remain beyond the reach of radical theory. The future reader/writer/voter, the new coalition makes sure, will continue to read "realistically" and apolitically. Even when theory is made a part of the undergraduate program, it is treated as a separate discourse: one learns theory in order to "better" read what actually matters— poems, fictions, etc. In other words, theory is treated as a "methodology," something to be "applied." The success of the student in dealing with theory is always measured in terms of how well she applies it and not in terms of how rigorously she conceptualizes and theorizes. Thus, the "reading" of the political situation in South Africa is effectively separated from the reading of Jane Austen. The student is not allowed to see (by theoretical inquiry) how the reading of one in fact affects the reading of the other and how both are inseparable from the way children are raised, taxes collected, and power relations in culture organized. In his essay, "Theory in the Undergraduate Curriculum: Towards an Interested Pedagogy" (1989) William Spanos describes how at the State University of New York at Binghamton a proposal for teaching theory to undergraduate students was defeated by an alliance of creative writers and traditionalists. Creative writers/teachers are well aware of the subversive power of radical (post)modern critical theory because it undermines the authority of the workshop by questioning its underlying notions such as voice, style, subject, experience, vision, and its notion of writing itself. Theory, therefore, must be kept out of the creative writing program in order to ensure that the authority of the workshop is unchallenged and to avoid any inquiry into the power/knowledge relations prevailing in the workshop. The creative writing student who knows theory and who has read Marx, Lacan, Foucault, Lenin, Kristeva, Derrida, Gramsci, Heidegger, Cixous, Deleuze, Althusser, Luxemburg, and Adorno will not approach the workshop with the same naiveté or accept its orthodoxies, as will the student who has read the traditional syllabus of the literature department, which is composed mostly of poems, novels, and stories. The student who has read the texts of the writers above knows, for example, that the project of realism in the creative writing workshop has been problematized by theory. She who has read Marx, he who has read Cixous and Fanon, will question realism and the politics of representation of class, gender, and race that constitute realism's perspective. Such a student will realize that realism is an ideological project and that the dominant fiction workshop is an ally of the ruling class and a supporter of the status quo.

Radical critical theory is represented in the fiction workshop as an abstract apparatus of mastery: a monolithic, oppressive, inhumane discourse of power-seeking intellectuals who are alienated from "heart and head" and who are bent on depriving people/

students of their "originality" and their most authentic intuitions. Theory is said to be a new orthodoxy, and fighting it is perceived as the imaginative mission of the uniquely talented creative writer who defends originality, vision, and intuition through her irreplaceable "voice." This representation of (post)modern theory as the site of today's orthodoxy is a device used to obscure the fact that the most oppressive of contemporary textual orthodoxies is realism, especially in its most recent manifestations: minimalist fiction and what is called "experimental realism," the newest modes of what Joe David Bellamy calls "literary republicanism" (Bellamy 1985, 31). In the dominant fiction workshop, the sameness of realism and all it stands for is protected from the uncontrollable difference that theoretical discourses locate in that logocentric sameness by patching up the fissures in the texts of realism.

Radical critical theory, however, has not been totally without effect on the fiction workshop. Because of radical theory's pressures on the politics of the fiction workshop and its dominant practice of realism, both humanists and creative writers have attempted to defend their position by proposing realism itself as a means of "moral" activity in society. According to this new defense of realism, which seems to go beyond mere aesthetic considerations, (post)modern radical theory is represented as a "high theory" that is morally irresponsible in that, by undermining mimesis and by disturbing the existing processes of signification, it also undermines the viability of moral acts in the mainstream of culture. In this moral reading of realism, some traditionalist critics have looked for support in the writings of contemporary "critical realists" in philosophy and the philosophy of science. Humanist moralists, such as Terry Eagleton (1990), have found in the writings of Roy Bhaskar a place for recapturing what they call "reality." The project of "critical realism" is, in the end, a conservative one. In the name of finding an objective basis for emancipatory truth, it in fact resurrects a fundamentally nonproductive formalism. (For a discussion of the philosophical issues around the question of realism, see Wal Suchthing, "Reflections upon Roy Bhaskar's 'Critical Realism' " 1992.) For Eagleton "reality" is more or less synonymous with the experiential. Taking reality back is ultimately, however, a political and not a moral, literary, or cognitive process: Bhaskar himself (1989) states that reality is historical, that is, our understanding of it is not pregiven. If reality has to be taken back, that very act indicates that reality and realism are the objects of contestation, not self-evident entities given in advance. No object of history is mimetically pregiven, it is always materially constructed and as such is part of the political economy of knowing—it is an object of class struggle. By treating "reality" as a pregiven object of the senses, Eagleton's moral realism denies the historicity of the real and the fact that the real (what is meaningful in a culture) is produced not by the senses and the unproblematic actuality of the world nor by the playfulness (decenteredness) of signs and differential textuality, but through class struggle. This erasure of class is the main object of writings of such literary critics as Penny Boumelha (1990, 1–37), Christopher Norris (1990), and others who have attempted to stage a comeback for mimetic fiction in the wake of (post)structuralism. Their projects are, like the poetics of the fiction workshop itself, a project in bourgeois nostalgia. Fictionists and humanist critics have, for example, said that such realist writers as Nadine Gordimer are fulfilling a historical function at the present time in South Africa and that, by dismissing realism, (post)modern theory undermines moral projects such as hers that oppose ethically reprehensible acts of racism.[4]

Gordimer's bestsellers (writings) are in fact among the most interesting instances of the ideological operations of realism. Her texts, such as *A World of Strangers, Burger's Daughter,* and *July's People,* work to legitimate a reformist program by offering a local critique of apartheid and thus help to forestall a revolutionary reorganization of social arrangements in South Africa. In this respect, she is undertaking the same ideological program being undertaken by many white South African investment bankers and other capitalists, and supported, after some initial resistance, by the present South African government. Under intense pressure from the business community that wants to move into a full-blown capitalist economy as soon as possible, the government has responded by reforming some of the feudal legislation that, in a way no longer profitable in modern capitalism, denies the access of business to a vast labor force. The question in South Africa, as in other parts of the world, is not "apartheid" as such, but what is legitimated through apartheid, that is, labor relations that are founded upon the extraction of surplus labor and the laws of profit. Gordimer's fiction has moralized "race" as the primary difference among South Africans and thus has obscured existing class relations and what legitimates them – the exploitative relations of production in South Africa. Gordimer and other progressive whites are attempting to modify social relations of capital in order to save the structure of domination in the current regime. That is to say, both Gordimer and others who attempt to avert class struggle are situated in the ideological space of the slogan, "Let's be realistic!" They – and countless others who find themselves in boundary situations – have responded to this exhortation and accordingly have tried to modify and update practices that have been rendered obsolete by history. Certainly the award of the Nobel Prize to Gordimer confirms her role in cultural crisis management in South Africa and places her in the pantheon of bourgeois ideologues, along with Aleksandr Solzhenitsyn, Boris Pasternak, Albert Camus, and Saul Bellow.

Gordimer's discourses of realism are indeed collaborationist discourses. The discourse of realism has always been a mode of internal critique and localistic reform, and it is a part of the historicity of this mode of writing that its emergence is closely tied to the emergence of unresolvable contradictions in capitalism. These contradictions are systemic, but realism ignores this systemicity and instead offers, through regional critique, programs of modifications and superstructural adjustments within the system. By doing this, it legitimates the system and discourages systemic transformation – radical acts that dismantle the system itself. What cannot be solved in the contradictory relations of production and class organization is "solved" in "ideology" through the mechanisms of realism's local critique. In other words, realism has operated as a discursive technique for crisis management in capitalism and its supporting patriarchy. This does not mean that realism is monolithic, that it cannot ever, to use commonsensical humanist language, "surprise" us in its artistic richness. But, as Catherine

Belsey has put it, "of course it can do so through unexpected juxtapositions and complexities. But it assembles these juxtapositions and complexities out of what we already know, and it is for this reason that we experience it as realistic. To this extent it is a predominantly conservative form. The experience of reading a realist text is ultimately reassuring, however harrowing the events of the story, because the world evoked in the fiction, its patterns of cause and effect, of social relationships and moral values, largely confirm the patterns of the world we seem to know" (*Critical Practice* 1980, 51) It is through such "confirmation" that the regime of realistic signification, through its nostalgia for a transparent, transitive, panhistorical communicative language, seeks reference and identity in order to reproduce the "real thing." In its reproduction of the "foreknown answer," rather than the production of a question (as another critic has argued), realism reinforces the existing symbolic order and thus is inscribed in patriarchy.[5]

Radical critical theory reads Gordimer's texts as a writing regime, the ideological function of which is to propose a reformist program and thus render unnecessary a radical reorganization of social reality, and, furthermore, sees her realism as a part of that mode of the economy of signification, the purpose of which is to perpetuate the patriarchy and its self-reinforcing symbolism, such as "the name of the father" through the "illusory security of a specularly structured act of recognition" (Felman 1975, 10). Gordimer's writings raise in fact a further political problem, given the fact that she writes as a woman: egalitarian feminism is, in the last instance, supportive of the dominant order of the symbolic—it merely "reforms" the place of woman within the dominant order of signification.

In its practices, the contemporary fiction workshop has become a collaborator with the ruling regime of truth and of the class relations that legitimate that truth and thus has become an apparatus of oppression in the academy. It is only through a sustained theoretical interrogation of its practices that the workshop can be reconstituted as a site for radical reading/writing practices and, through such transgressive activities, intervene in the dominant relations of production and the existing exploitative social arrangements of contemporary U.S. society. The "voice" of the free-standing individual writer, trained in the fiction workshop, is the "voice" of the entrepreneur, and as such it is a device employed to perpetuate political and economic oppression in the guise of "freedom." Instead of "resisting" theory in the name of the free subject, the fiction workshop should be the pedagogical space in which the processes of signification in texts of culture are examined and the construction of what is represented as "reality" is made intelligible. By undertaking such an inquiry and political critique, rather than adopting the traditional stance of the humanist ideologies and "resisting" theory, the radical fiction workshop will propose theory as resistance to all semiotic constructs of culture that are offered as "natural," "eternal," "given," and "unchangeable," and will discover under their seeming eternality the historical interests of the dominant social class and its texts.

CHAPTER 5

Have You Been
to the MLA Lately?

AUTHOR

of postmodern fiction is either dead (Roland Barthes, "The Death of the Author") or deauthorized (Michel Foucault, "What Is an Author?"). As of late, however, there has been a communal effort to locate "Authors in Texts: Implied or Otherwise" in such public places as MLA Conventions.

Have you been to the MLA lately?

My aunt April (more about her in other entries) also has been after AUTHORS and has compiled files and files on them with lists, indexes, everything:

blanchot

BECKETT

MARX   NIETZSCHE

SOLLERS

JOYCE

FREUD

LACAN

HEGEL

SARTRE   PROUST

DERRIDA

HEIDEGGER

SAUSSURE

Calvino, Italo
Reed, Ishmael
Barth, John
Gass, William
Hawkes, John
Lem, Stanislaw
Bellow, Saul
Paz, Octavio
Katz, Steve
Delillo, Don
Pinget, Robert
Sukenick, Ronald
Herr, Michael
Fuentes, Carlos
Gordimer, Nadine
Johnson, B.S.
Roche, Maurice
Coover, Robert
Howe, Fanny
Lodge, David
Federman, Raymond
Beattie, Ann
Gaddis, William
Angelo, Ivan

AMERICA

America is, at best a strange place for an artist to work in. On the one hand there is the illusion of artistic freedom, constitutionally protected; on the other, there is the operative dogma of the marketplace: will it sell? In America, art—like everything else (knowledge, condoms, religion, etc.)—is a product. The discovery of this is the capstone to the

artist's alienation
He knows there is
what is good and
between what he's
used by the market
often made rich by
gets anything for
Critics may eventually
work, but then it is
it, not he. Most
others—hacks,
get rich while he is
patronized: "This is
interesting manuscript
composition, etc.),
in the present
conditions...". No
trust the general
marketplace.

Critics Have Problems, Too

process in America.
no relation between
what sells, nor
made and how it's
managers. He is
his worst work, if he
his work at all.
discover his best
they who get rich off
often he sees
imitators, faddists—
entirely ignored or
a very original and
(play, painting,
but I'm afraid that
economic
need for censorship:
banality of the

THE
   C
   R   *A dossier on (P*
   I   *O*
                        S
   T   *T)*   *MODERN fictions*
   I
   C AS archivist

WRITER

After the death of the AUTHOR (q.v.), writers were born. Writers, unlike authors, do not wield power; they just set the language in motion. Authors create BOOKS (q.v.), writers produce texts.

TEXT

there is nothing outside the text

We

since reality is only a text there is no possibility of exerting ourselves politically to change things nor is there an extratextual standpoint from which a critique of established reality could be formulated.

THERE IS NOTHING OUTSIDE THE TEXT

since social reality is not substantial nor natural but textual, it is readily susceptible to radical alteration.

found
there was no bottom.

She has been having problems though over how to list her
lists and index her indexes. She believes that postmodern
fictions are written by *younger* writers, and she has witnesses:

> *with such* YOUNGER *writers as*
> *Federman, John Irving, Steve*
> *Katz, Ishmael Reed, Gilbert*
> *Sorrentino, and Ronald Sukenick,*
> *American literature entered*
> *the laboratory of the novel with*
> *fervor and typewriter.*

She thinks that this is a good
combination

FERVOR + TYPEWRITER

But the line-ing of her authors
along *YOUNGER*/OLDER is
giving her daily agony. Some are
too old to be *younger* and some
too young to be *younger*–they
are youngest. So young in fact
that the question is constantly
asked:

Aren't You Rather Young To Be Writing Your Memoirs?

"Did you know," my cousin asked her one day, *"that William
Gaddis was born in 1922? What kind of* younger *is that?"*

My Uncle Philip has a different method for testing her
scholarly patience. He leaves Hallmark birthday cards for
absent younger authors all around the house and confuses her
abour the modern, the postmodern and the nonmodern.

```
 ┌──────────────┐   ┌──────────────┐
 │ A (   )modern │   │ a (   )MODERN │
 │   birthyear   │   │   birthyear   │
 │     party     │   │     party     │
 │          1932          │
 │ Ronald Sukenick │   │  John Updike  │
 └──────────────┘   └──────────────┘
```

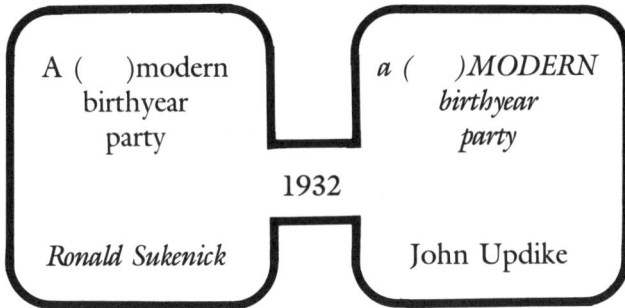

My cousin said: *"This is not, repeat, not a Hallmark card."* He thought for a while and remembered that it was very much like a picture he had seen in his physics textbook. Only there it was called *A SIMPLIFIED DIAGRAM OF MAXWELL'S DEMON.*

Fictitious Nonfiction:
Fiktionalisierungs- und Erzählstrategien
in der zeitgenössischen amerikanischen
Dokumentarprosa

WALTER ABISH

Is the author of *HOW GERMAN IS IT?*

Old or Young (pre/post) modern, however AUTHORS (q.v.) generally run into trouble with

AUTHORITY

哲學家赴捷論人權
當局逮捕控以吸毒

CHINA DAILY NEWS
January 2, 1982

Prague 31st, French News Agency.

Czeckoslovakian authorities confirmed today that 51-year old French philosopher Jacques Derrida has been arrested under the charge of taking drugs.

Paris officials expressed surprise at the charge, which they thought highly improbable.

Derrida arrived in Prague Saturday and was found missing after participating in Monday's unofficial philosophy conference which took place in the house of . . . the former spokesman for the Human Rights Constitution Movement of '77. The French Embassy in Prague said that Derrida didn't attend the second meeting of the Conference although he said that he would.

A clerk of the Central Hotel where Derrida was put up in Prague told the reporter from the French News Agency that the philosopher had removed all his luggage on Wednesday and hinted that Czechoslovakian police were accompanying him. Czechoslovakian official sources said he was under the charge of taking drugs and is facing a two-year term imprisonment or fine.

DOSSIER

A collection of papers or documents pertaining to a particular person or subject. Bundle of papers having a label on the back.

THE NEW

There are many new things around:

> NEW shoes
> NEW shaving cream
> NEW dinner napkins
> NEW poems
> NEW chef salads
> NEW authors
> NEW curricula
> NEW year
> NEW pencils
> NEW Chairwomen

"The pursuit of the new" said my uncle Philip, "is the oldest game in town." Then we all went to the New School to hear a lecture on the new architecture of the new city into which we had newly moved. My aunt demanded that I not put "new" in front of every word I used. It is crazy she said and quoted from a book on postmodern fiction saying "Crazy is ugly. And God don't like ugly." She said the book was called FOUR POSTWAR AMERICAN NOVELISTS. She reads a lot of scholarly books which is too bad because aunts in stories are not supposed to read a lot of scholarly books and with her around my story ends up being unrealistic which is ugly and of course God etc. etc. She is amazingly familiar with new things. She is in fact my new aunt because my old aunt died recently—new death in an old family; new members of a new family. What is even less realistic in realistic fiction (see REALISM) than having a scholar for an aunt is having a philosopher—cousin who after hearing the discourse of the new developing between my aunt and me asked "How do you know something is new when you see something that is new?" Somebody in the lecture hall suggested that the best way would be to directly ask the object/subject of curiosity. "Go to the new lamp shade" she said "and ask 'Are you a new lamp shade?' " The same presumably can be done with new stories.

–"Are you a new story?"

It is of course more likely that one may get an answer from a story than from a lamp shade (this the suggester suggested is the second law of vraisemblance). Stories are usually not always more willing to talk. But this too is relative (see RELATIVE & RELATIVISM); there are many stories that do not talk back and refuse to answer questions from their readers. "Ah haaa . . . " said my uncle mischievously and with a wry smile and then continued "this is why reader response criticism was invented." I am embarrassed by all these outbursts of knowledge about literature from members of my family–I have a very unrealistic set of characters in my family. "If stories do not answer your questions" my uncle Philip went on " the reader makes them do so . . . " My cousin: "But then the reader has merely answered his own questions only he has put them in the stories first." My aunt thought this whole discussion was infantile and irrelevant and there was no need to take cheap shots a reader response criticism since the real question she believed was that the stories don't answer your questions because they are:

a) either too old and are written to be read only–no talking back
b) or they are too new and don't believe that questions can be answered.

UNCLE PHILIP: But can't they just answer you and say that there are not answers?

AUNT APRIL: This is silly . . . silly and old because as soon as you have answered and said that there are no answers you have uttered an answer . . . this is saying new things in an old way which makes old people happy because it makes new things look old but it also makes the new age and when the new ages it is not new anymore which makes old people doubly happy . . . if it is new it cannot be said in an old way.

My uncle Philip as you have gathered by now is really not so much a character with a stable ego as a device who says various things according to the demands of the discourse. He has no essence so to speak and makes everything not only unrealistic but also heavy-handed and awkward. He turns to my aunt April and says:

"What is all this talk about the new?"
and proceeds to give my aunt a

QUIZ

19. Who pitched a perfect game in the 1956 World Series?

20. Who was the host of the television series "Omnibus?"

21. Syracuse was the home of what National Basketball Association team?

22. What long-running daily television series was inaugurated by Bob Keeshan?

23. Who was George Michen?

24. Who was the ill-fated star of "Giant" and "Rebel Without a Cause?"

25. Who sang "How Much Is That Doggie in the Window?"

26. What popular children's program starred, among others, Annette Funicello?

27. Name a leading American composer of symphonic music during the decade?

28. Who was the host of NBC's Today show?

29. Who was the host of NBC's Tonight show?

30. Name the star of "Marty."

31. What singer became known as an actor in "From Here To Eternity?"

32. Name three baseball heroes of the decade whose last names began with the letter "M."

33. On whose television show did Julius LaRosa, Carmel Quinn and the Maguire Sisters gain fame?

34. Who starred in "The Sands of Iwo Jima?"

35. Name the television comedy which starred Art Carney and Jackie Gleason.

36. Who was Buffalo Bob?

37. What musician played a crazy looking trumpet?

38. What National League team beat the Cleveland Indians in four straight games to win the World Series of 1954?

39. Who wrote the music for "Peter Gunn" and "77 Sunset Strip," two popular detective series on TV?

40. What cartoonist penned "We have met the enemy and he is us" in the strip "Pogo?"

41. Hair on high school and college boys ranged from the "flat top" to the pompadour to the duck tail. What greasy kid stuff did they use to keep every hair in place?

42. What playwright won the Pulitzer Prize for drama in 1955 for "Cat on a Hot Tin Roof?"

43. What member of Eisenhower's cabinet had a brother who headed the Central Intelligence Agency?

44. What did the "Flying Red Horse" signify?

45. Who wrote "The Caine Mutiny?"

(Uncle Philip speaking) "And I give you the answers too—none of this 'there is no answer rubbish'—I even give answers to questions I did NOT ask you!"

ANSWERS

1. Princess Caroline.
2. Grace Kelly and the Prince of Monaco.
3. Sherman Adams
4. Nash Rambler
5. Rich Little
6. "The Crucible"
7. "Old Man and the Sea."
8. Elvis Presley
9. Dave Beck
10. James Hoffa
11. Gian-Carlo Menotti's "Amahl and the Night Visitors"
12. Willie Mays of the New York Giants National League baseball team.
13. King of Egypt who was exiled by Gen. Abdul Nasser.
14. J. D. Salinger
15. Marilyn Monroe
16. Sal Maglie, a pitcher with the Brooklyn Dodgers
17. Leonard Bernstein
18. Matinee Theater
19. Don Larsen
20. Alistar Cooke
21. The Syracuse Nats
22. Captain Kangaroo
23. Star of the Minneapolis Lakers basketball team
24. James Dean
25. Patti Page
26. Mickey Mouse Club
27. Aaron Copeland
28. Dave Garroway
29. Steve Allen
30. Ernest Borgnine
31. Frank Sinatra
32. Mickey Mantle and Roger Maris of the NY Yankees and Willie Mays of the Giants
33. Arthur Godfrey
34. John Wayne
35. "The Honeymooners"
36. Character on the Howdy Doody Show
37. Dizzy Gillespie
38. New York Giants
39. Henry Mancini
40. Walt Kelly
41. Bryle Cream—"a little dab'll do you."
42. Tennessee Williams
43. John Foster Dulles, secretary of state. Allen Dulles headed the CIA.
44. A Mobil gas station.
45. Herman Wouk

COUSIN RALPH: What are the questions for answers one through eighteen?

UNCLE PHILIP: Do you want answers or what?

AUNT APRIL: If there are answers the questions are missing; if there are questions the answers are nowhere in sight . . .

QUOTE(ABILITY) SUBJECT(IVITY) COPY(RIGHT)

Defining the conventional academic book as *an outdated mediation between two different filing systems*, Benjamin wanted to write a book made up entirely of quotations in order to purge all subjectivity and allow the self to be a vehicle for the expression of *OBJECTIVE CULTURAL TENDENCIES*. See also Barthe's project in *A LOVER'S DISCOURSE: FRAGMENTS*.

ORDINARY TRUTHS

American Fiction: Forgetting the Ordinary Truths

THE NEW (PART TWO)

MY UNCLE PHILIP is now shifting character to fit the demands of the discourse: What is all this talk about the new this privileging of the new . . . haven't you heard that binarism is dead; that there is no NEW/OLD anymore; that all OLD things have the NEW inscribed in them and the new is always already OLD? Where have you been all these years? Structuralism is dead. Even poststructuralism is dying.

AUNT APRIL: Ahhhaaa . . . so old is new, new is old . . . no change . . . no history . . . aestheticize the whole god damn universe . . . whatever happened to history . . .

Boy Meets Boy — Or　　*Where the Girls Aren't*

LES ÉTATS-UNIS

The diversity of ethnic and social groups makes it, according to Kristeva, less subject to the totalitarian homogenization of society characteristic of other late and 'post' capitalist societies. If there is any hope for the

the land of polyvalence

Seduction

West, it can only exist in a society that at least marginally escapes the stifling influence of tradition, which accounts for the moribund state of Western Europe.

BUT

in Kristeva the

F A I L S

to emphasize the fact that the pronounced divisions in

supermarket AMERICAN

SOCIETY

are at best a mixed blessing: in fact, the latter serve more to *prevent* the attainment of a unified consensus powerful enough to challenge the system in its entirety. They represent a *token otherness* that merely enhances the system's pluralistic self-image. It lumbers on monolithically, unswerved as the potentially radical demands of each separate interest group founder in fractional strife.

REALISM (I)

'Reality' = 'Status Quo'

See also REALISM (II) and REALISM (III). They are more realistic.

ITERABILITY

There is such a thing as an original Hemingway style only if it can be cited, imitated, and parodied. For there to be such a style there must be recognizable features that characterize it and produce its distinctive effects *it was not fear or dread. it was nothing that he knew too well. it was all a nothing and a man was nothing too.* For features to be recognizable one must be able to isolate them as elements that could be repeated, and thus the iterability manifested in the inauthentic, the derivative, the imitative, the parodic, is what makes possible the original and the authentic. *hail nothing full of nothing, nothing is with thee.*

SPEEDBOAT

Is a novel by Renata Adler. In fact Best First Novel of the Year. Ernest Hemingway Award. Is that a postmodern novel? My Uncle said there were not very many postmodern women writers. My Aunt said it was because they had more important things to do than write a postmodern novel– whatever that is.

TEXT-O-GRAPHY

Village Voice

T. Todorov, *New L iterary History*

Aunt April

R. Krauss, *October*

A. Jefferson, *TLS*

J. Derrida, *Spurs*

R. Means, *Mother J ones*

G. Graff, *Partisan R eview*

R. Coover, *Stateme nts 2*

Uncle Philip

G. Ulmer, *Anti-Aes thestics*

China Daily News

J. Culler, *On Decons truction*

B. G. Harrison, *Ha rper's*

J. Gardner, *On Mor al Fiction*

Esquire

Aunt April

My Aunt April was very upset with my father's practice (that "awful practice" of quoting peo ple's words without giving their names ("What are your sources ?" she would ask him, "It's so confusing, it's not clear who is saying what . . . and by the way, what about the copyright ?") When she looked at my fat her's ("so-called" *essay* which he had titled

**THE
CRITIC
AS
ARCHIVIST
A
DOSSIER
ON
(POST)
MODERN
FICTIONS**

she declined to go to a party my father was giving for the public ation of Raymond Federman's *TWO FOLD VIBRATION.* Aft er my Uncle Philip's pleading and mediation, my father even tually consented to ("submit") a list of authors and sources that he had used in his text (he called it *"Text-o-graphy"* and kept pronouncing it, *"text-ooohhh- graphy."* Still protesting he denounced my aunt's obsession, "Copyright is just private prop erty. Copywrite is the right way to copy!"

New York Times

R. Young, *Oxford Li terary Review*

Althusser, *Reading C apital*

Cousin Ralph

Herald-American

J. Tytell, *Partisan Re view*

Telos

W. Everman, *Ameri can Book Review*

The New Republic

T. Eagleton, *Literary Theory*

New Yorker

My father

J. Harari, *Textual St rategies*

USA Today

Fiction International

M. Couturier et al. *Donald Barthelme*

DONALD BARTHELME

often, as in **Paraguay,** simply steps out of reality to play with the literary conventions which once helped us learn about the real. His form is elegant, but it suggests no beauty beyond literary shape, as if workmanship were now enough, there being no real value for that workmanship to struggle toward. Barthelme goes not for the profound but the clever.

These acts of linguistic vandalism are, of course, not as innocent as they may seem. They contribute to changing our representation of reality in drastic ways. Consider, for example, the following utterance; THE WORLD IS SAGGING, SNAGGING, SCALING, SPALLING, PILLING, PINGING, PITTING, WARPING, CHECKING, FADING, CHIPPING, CRACKING, YELLOWING, LEAKING, STALING, SHRINKING, AND IN DYNAMIC UNBALANCE. *This is not only a "constative statement" as John Austin would have phrased it. Barthelme does not simply portray a changing world; he also helps to change it in his own way by assaulting it with multiple words and unheard-of phrases. He gives the impression that reality has lost its power to force words upon him and his characters, that language is at last free from it and constitutes a private world where everything is possible at any moment.*

The Perils of Innovative Fiction

My Aunt April said that the newness of Barthelme has many sides; it is a complex kind of newness. But my Cousin did not let her finish her thought. He took a sheet from his pocket and started waving it in front of my aunt's eyes dancing and singing:

Barthelme is so complex his of-the-month club selec so clever . . . he's so

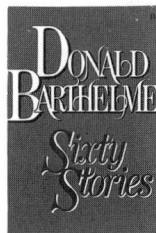

is a book-tion . . . clever . . .

BOOK

There may be nothing outside the text my Uncle laughed but there is a great deal inside the book. Publishers make money from bestseller books and supermarkets put aside shelf space for the better bestsellers. Books have covers, texts (q.v.) don't—which is one way to distinguish between the two.

A call to the American Writers Congress

WRITERS IN AMERICA FACE A CRISIS.

Rapidly advancing concentration in the communications industry threatens as never before to exclude and silence serious writers who are out of political or literary fashion. Government support for the arts is being slashed. Attacks on writers — libel suits, book-bannings, censorship — are increasing across the country. If you agree that these threats demand an active response, join us at THE AMERICAN WRITERS CONGRESS — ROOSEVELT HOTEL, NEW YORK — OCTOBER 9-12, 1981.

WHAT WILL THE CONGRESS BE?

A massive gathering of writers of all descriptions: poets, playwrights, novelists, journalists, scholars, critics, and the associations, guilds, and unions that represent them.

WHAT IS THE GOAL OF THE CONGRESS?

To help American writers deal individually and collectively with bread-and-butter problems, as well as the long-range political and economic trends that threaten the vitality of our written culture.

WHY A "CONGRESS," NOT MERELY A "CONFERENCE?"

Because at a conference people talk; at a congress, people act.

WHAT WILL HAPPEN AT THE CONGRESS?

Panels — Workshops — Caucuses — Hearings — Festivities — A plenary session to consider formal resolutions and ways to continue the work of the Congress

WHAT ISSUES WILL THE CONGRESS ADDRESS?

Government funding cutbacks — Assaults on First Amendment rights — Interests of writers and publishers: where they converge, where they conflict — Cooperative publishing and distribution methods — Who gets published/produced, who doesn't — More, more, more.

WHO WILL COME?

More than 2,000 writers from across the United States. Publishers, editors, other industry representatives, and foreign writers will also be invited.

THE INVITING COMMITTEE
(still expanding)

E. L. Doctorow • Doug Ireland • Frances FitzGerald • Kurt Vonnegut • James Merrill • Ed Bullins • Nat Hentoff • John Hersey • Alice Walker • J. Anthony Lukas • John A. Williams • Ishmael Reed • Ring Lardner • Barbara Grizzuti Harrison • Fred Cook • Morris Dickstein • Blair Clark • Studs Terkel • Calvin Trillin • Roger Wilkins • Nancy Milford • Lois Gould • Ellen Willis • Jessica Mitford • Jane Kramer • Evan Connell • Mary Lee Settle • Staige Blackford • Michael Arlen • Donald Barthelme • Penny Lernoux • Alastair Reid • Norman Mailer • Alden Whitman • N. Scott Momaday • Barbara Garson • David Halberstam • Ron Radosh • Alan Wolfe • Alta • Paul Cowan • Katha Pollitt • Lore Dickstein • Jack Newfield • Albert Innaurato • Nora Sayre • Lucinda Franks • Cynthia Arnson • A. W. Singham • Steve Schlesinger

PANEM ET CIRCENSES

Dear Mr. Zavarzadah:

> *Thank you for sending us your essay. I am afraid, however, that we will not be able to accept it for publication.*
>
> *We are afraid that your essay is advanced as a game-playing device, something that may have been offered out of "bad faith," with its own self-destruct button and charge built in.*

Sincerely,

The Editor

(POST)MODERNISM

The postmodern world in not meaningless at all; rather, it is *only* meaning,

a surfeit of meaning,

a network of sign systems

The Rosenbergs: New Evidence

which define and redefine the real and man's place

IT

within

Old Passions

THE NEW (PART THREE
WITH THE ADDITION OF NEW CHARACTERS)

"The new" my father said "is the effect of the old." My whole family is so . . . so . . . au courant . . . all of them talk like intellectual jerks; no juice (I am actually quoting from a letter evaluating my family). "There is nothing inherently new" he added "new is new only because there is something called old; difference is what does it."

MY BROTHER NORMAN: Why is it you always say there is nothing new unless there is something old? What about the old which is not old unless there is something new? How come your history is one-directional?
AUNT APRIL: No new? No old? No history? Nihilism . . . semiology is nihilism . . .
NORMAN: Who said this is semiology? [see SEMIOLOGY]

Bored by Trendy? Dare to Be Dull!

PARALITERARY

space is the space of debate, quotation, partisanship, betrayal, reconciliation, but it is not the space of unity, coherence, or resolution that we think of as constituting the work of literature.

> *drama* without the Play
> *voices* without the Author
> *criticism* without the Argument

(LITERARY) THEORY

For all the radical power it once had, theory has become a part of the intelligibility of our time, and can therefore no longer be effectively used to reveal it.

NIETZSCHE'S
u
m
b
r
e
ll
a

I have forgotten my umbrella is not caught up in any circular trajectory. It knows of no proper itinerary which would lead from its beginning to its end and back again, nor does its movement admit of any center. Because it is structurally liberated from any living meaning, it is always possible that it means nothing at all or that it has no decidable meaning.

To whatever lengths one might carry a conscientious interpretation, the hypothesis that the totality of Nietzsche's text, in some monstrous way, might well be of the type *I have forgotten my umbrella* cannot be denied. Which is tantamount to saying that there is no *totality to Nietzsche's text* not even a fragmentary or aphoristic one.

Tuesday

Monday

Language and Literature
10:00
Colin MacCabe
Realism: Balzac and Barthes
Darko Suvin
Can People be Represented in Literature?
respondent
Peter Garret

Aesthetics and Discourse
2:00
Michele Barrett
The Place of Aesthetics in Marxist Criticism
Michel Pêcheux
Discourse: Structure or Event?
respondent
Peter Haidu

MARXISM

Europeans may see
this as
revolutionar
Y
but American Indians
see it simply as still more
of the same old European
conflict between

being

&

gaining

The intellectual roots
of a new Marxist form
of European Imperialism is
in Marx's links to the

tradition

of

NEWTON

HEGEL

et al.

Afternoon

Marxism and Pedagogy
2:00
Susan Wells
Jurgen Habermas and the Theory of Communicative Competence
John Brenkman
For a New Aesthetic Education
Christopher Norris
Marxism and Deconstruction

Popular Culture and the Avant-Garde
10:00
Simon Frith
Art Ideology and Pop Practice
Iain Chambers
Popular Culture and the Avant-Garde
respondent
Lawrence Grossberg

Marxism and Postmodernism
1:30
Franco Moretti
The Spell of Indecision
Paul Patton
Rhizomatic Versus Reterritorializing Social Theory
Dick Hebdige
Pop Taste, Popular Taste
respondent
Cary Nelson

Modernity and Revolution
7:00
Perry Anderson
Modernity and Revolution
Gajo Petrović
Modernity and Revolution Reconsidered
respondent
Richard Schacht

Closing addresses, Smith Music Hall
7:00
Henri Lefebvre
Toward a Leftist Culture Politics: Everdayness and Marxism
Fredric Jameson
Toward a Political Aesthetic for Postmodernism: Cognitive Mapping and the World System

WRITING

is dangerous from the moment that representation there
claims to be presence and the sign of the thing itself. And
there is a fatal necessity, inscribed in the very functioning of
the sign, that the substitute make one forget the vicariousness
of its own function and make itself pass for the plenitude of a
speech whose deficiency and infirmity it nevertheless only
supplements. For the concept of the supplement harbors within
itself two significations whose cohabitation is as strange as it is
necessary. The supplement adds itself, it is a surplus, a
plenitude enriching another plenitude, the *fullest measure* of
presence. It cumulates and accumulates presence. It is thus
that art, *technè*, image representation, convention, etc. come
as supplements to nature and are rich with this entire
cumulating function. This kind of supplementarity determines
in a certain way all the conceptual oppositions within which
Rousseau inscribes the notion of Nature to the extent that it
should be self-sufficient. But the supplement supplements. It
adds only to replace. It intervenes or insinuates itself *in-the-
place-of;* if it fills, it is as if one fills a void. If it represents and
makes an image, it is by the anterior default of a presence.
Compensatory and vicarious, the supplement is an adjunct, a
subaltern instance which *takes-(the)-place*. As substitute, it is
not simply added to the positivity of a presence, it produces
no relief, its place is assigned in the structure by the mark of
an emptiness. Somewhere, something can be filled up *of itself,*
can accomplish itself, only by allowing itself to be filled
through sign and proxy.

THE SIGN IS ALWAYS THE SUPPLEMENT
OF THE THING *itself*

Trade

and

Defense

ALLEGORY

Grammatology has emerged on the far side of the formalist crisis and developed a discourse which is fully referential, but referential in the manner of *narrative allegory* rather than of *allegories*. *Allegories,* the mode of commentary long practiced by traditional critics, **suspends** the surface of the text, applying a terminology of **verticalness, levels, hidden meaning, the hieratic difficulty of interpretation,** whereas *narrative allegory* explores the literal—**letteral**—level of the language itself, in a horizontal investigation of the polysemous meanings simultaneously available in the words themselves—in etymologies and puns—and in the things the words name. The allegorical narrative unfolds as a dramatization or enactment (personification) of the **literal truth inherent in the words themselves.** In short, narrative allegory favors the material of the signifier over the meanings of the signifieds.

Trade Winds in the Book Biz

THE NEW (PART IV)

My aunt April shouted: "Bring me the **Sewanee Review.**" I brought her the **Sewanee Review.** She said have you read this

> there has been nothing new in the short-story form at least
> since the Middle Ages and that therefore the extensive
> contemporary emphasis upon the positive value of
> innovation is at best misguided, based on misinformation
> and misapprehension, and at worst merely another form of
> deception to be added to the luxuriant growth of large and
> small deceptions which not so much thrive in our age as
> identify it.

THE NEW REPUBLIC

My Uncle Philip summarizes all the editorials in the
NEW REPUBLIC and mimeographs the summaries for
his friends. He has such nice penmanship:

> . . . *MARCH TO NOWHERE*
> *The 1983 March on Washington reflected the malaise*
> *of America's black leadership. Understandably, even*
> *rightly, the march targeted Ronald Reagan. But*
> *what really keeps so many black people in poverty are*
> *teenage pregnancies and single-parent families.*

THE ELEMENTARY CATASTROPHES

A catastrophe, in the very broad sense Thom gives to
the word, is any discontinuous transition that occurs
when a system can have more than one stable state,
or can follow more than one stable pathway of
change. The catastrophe is the "jump" from one state
or pathway of change. The catastrophe is the "jump"
from one state or pathway to another. In the
landscape imagined by Waddington, it could be
represented as a passage of an object from one basin
to another, or as a flow of water from one channel
into another. The transition here is discontinuous
not because there are no intervening states or
pathways, but because none of them is stable: the
passage from the initial state or pathway to the final
one is likely to be brief in comparison to the time
spent in stable states.

Know Your New
Military-Intellectual Complex

OVERDETERMINATION

Freud used the term to describe the representation of dream-thoughts in images privileged by their condensation of a **Please** number of thoughts in a single image, or by the transference of psychic energy from a particularly potent thought to apparently trivial images. *Althusser uses the same term to describe the effects of the contradictions in each practice constituting the social formation on the social formation as a whole, and hence back on each* **Note** *practice and contradiction, defining the pattern of dominance and subordination, antagonism and non-antagonism of the contradictions in the structure in dominance at any given historical moment. More precisely, the overdetermination of a contradiction is the reflection in it of its conditions of existence within the complex whole, that is, of the other contradictions in the complex whole.*

Correction

(LITERARY)THEORY(PART II)

As I write, it is estimated that the world contains over 60,000 nuclear warheads, many with a capacity a thousand times greater than the bomb which destroyed Hiroshima. The possibility that these weapoms will be used in our life is steadily growing. The approximate cost of these weapons is 500 billion dollars a year, or 1.3 billion dollars a day. Five per cent of this sum – 25 billion dollars – could drastically, fundamentally alleviate the problems of the poverty-stricken Third World. Anyone who believed literary theory was more important than such matters would no doubt be considered somewhat eccentric, but perhaps only a little less eccentric than those who consider that the two topics might be somehow related. What has international politics to do with literary theory? Why this perverse insistence on dragging politics into the argument?

"pourquoi les états-unis?" *My cousin is practicing his French* with an African accent *in the other room.*

History as Farce

CHAPTER 6

A Very "Good Idea" Indeed: The (Post)modern Labor Force and Curricular Reform [1]

1 Throughout this book we have engaged the diverse arguments and discourses of cultural and critical theorists. For the most part, we have therefore addressed questions of *cultural* politics. In our arguments over cultural politics and cultural change, we have (because of the concerns of our audience) addressed the outcomes and effects of cultural change and of the contestations over these changes, without expanding on the material and historical basis of these changes. However, since no discussion of cultural change can take place without a global theory of social change, in the first chapter, we did briefly discuss our theory of social change as based on the conflicts between the forces of production and class relations. Within these conflicts and contradictions, we argued, certain historically determined questions (such as what shape the curriculum should take) arise, and, in response to these questions, particular "answers" are developed, which as an ensemble are regarded to be "knowledge" but are actually class-specific resolutions of social contradictions which are in turn the effect of exploitative class relations under capitalism. In this chapter, we would like to elaborate on the frame established in the first chapter and situate critical theory and the curriculum within this larger theory of social change.

As we have already indicated in Chapter 1, social change does not come about by voluntaristic undertakings by "free" individuals: it is, in other words, *not* the effect of personal "thinking." Nor are particular social forms of knowledge autonomous entities that can happen at any time in history. The seeming freedom of the subject to act in any way he or she "desires" and the forms of knowledge available to the subject are part of the larger material and historical frames that, in *The Eighteenth Brumaire of Louis Bonapart,* Marx calls the "circumstances" over which the subject, as conceived in bourgeois philosophy – the supposedly sovereign individual – has no control (Marx 1990, 15). (Post)modern critical theory itself consists of historically constituted forms of knowledge which have arisen out of certain social conflicts and frictions between the forces of production and property relations. The discourses that are available at any historical moment are part of the ongoing contestations concerning the hegemony of one or another form of social relations of production. Critical theory, therefore, is one site produced historically in which battles over political and social priorities are fought out.

2   Taking its cue from the conservative students, faculty, and administrators of the Syracuse University English Department, the campus student newspaper, *The Daily Orange,* recently published a feature article on the newly instituted curriculum in "English and Textual Studies" (commonly known as "ETS"). The article, "ETS Delivers Non-Traditional Approach" (see Appendix 6.1 below), hailed the new curriculum as – in the words of John W. Crowley, then the English Department chair – a "more complete transformation" (see p. 165 below) than similar "new" curricula developed in other universities. What Crowley calls a "*trans*formation" is in reality merely a "*re*formation" of the traditional English curriculum. We would like to state at the outset that such a reformation has been made necessary by radical historical shifts in the U.S. labor force. This makes the new curriculum (which provides the new necessary consciousness skills of this labor force) complicit in (post)modern capitalist practices, and not, as its proponents would like us to believe, an oppositional program of knowledge developed by progressive pedagogues through "enlightened" critique. The curricula of knowledge are changed, not by "conversation" ("enlightened" or otherwise) among faculty, administrators, and students (that is, a superstructural discursive process), but by changes in material relations and forces of production. "Conversation" is always an aftereffect—a legitimating practice.

The reformist character of the new program at Syracuse is nowhere more clear than in the way it has so easily and perfectly fit into the existing structure of the academy and its supporting knowledge industry. One might expect that a program advertised as an oppositional "transformation"—and thus as contrary to the dominant practices—would run into some transformative resistance from the dominant power/knowledge practices. However, the ETS program has not only been quickly approved by New York State educational authorities, but has also been commodified, with great success, and sold to high schools in the Northeastern United States (Syracuse University's "Project Advance") as the "latest" educational innovation.

Like all "new" transforming curricula in U.S. universities, it is a "transformation" that which does not transform anything: it simply meets the educational needs of the changing (post)modern labor force of late capitalism. This is a labor force that needs a more comprehensive grasp of the "abstract" concepts that provide the matrix of the digital logic of today's high-tech industry. In this chapter, we would like to address some aspects of the "success" of Syracuse University's new curriculum, indicate its imbrication in the capitalist economy, and, through this specific instance of curricular reform, discuss the politics of curricular reform and reformist practices in the academy in general.

The reform of the humanities curriculum in the last two decades or so has been a response to forces emerging in the postwar processes of production and to corresponding changes in the labor force. (Post)modern capitalism needs a new kind of labor force; one which, unlike its predecessor, is more capable of "abstract thinking," that is, the ability to perform conceptual operations that have become fundamental to the high-tech culture of computers and allied technologies and new modes of management. It was because of the difficulties encountered in recruiting for this new labor force that the main weaknesses of the curricula of U.S. educational systems became most clear. (The curriculum, at all levels and in all its various forms, is always an ensemble of instructions geared to producing the consciousness skills, as well as technical skills, that are required for the reproduction of the dominant relations of production.) In the late 1960s and early 1970s, when U.S. industries began to lose their hegemony in the world, the conceptual naiveté of the available U.S. labor force began to take its toll on the national economy and showed itself in the much discussed loss of "excellence" and the much publicized inability of U.S. industry to match "foreign competition."

During this period, it became evident that the students who were trained in the traditional humanities were simply unable to deal with the consequences of the growing complexity of the new forms in which capital was being deployed throughout the world. The literacies they had been taught were empirical and concrete literacies more appropriate for "low-tech" industrial societies, that justified themselves by the appeal to such traditional (humanist) notions as individuality, certainty, rationality, progress, family, heterosexuality, and a firm belief in the superiority of European intellectual and technical practices. These literacies were, on the whole, linear; they were based on the notion of time as it was formalized in Cartesian philosophy and translated into the high industrial assembly line of early twentieth-century Taylorism (developed in the management theories of F. W. Taylor).

The Taylorization of the labor force broke down work tasks into their absolute minimum units and thus produced a laborer who, with the minimum level of (pseudo)skill, could perform the job. Taylorism, needless to say, was a fetishization of empiricism and a reification of the concrete and the tangible. All the "linear" laborer had to do was to manipulate objects. Even the managers Taylor introduced into the factory in order to safeguard the "coherence" of the assembly line system were merely managers of the already "managed"–the linearized. These linear, concrete literacies were more appropriate for a labor force whose work skills and managerial expertise gradually became useless as the industrial base shifted from "low-tech" to "high-tech" and "late capitalist" forces of production emerged. It was the contradiction between the flexible and agile "high-tech" labor force that was needed and the "low-tech" labor force actually being produced by the traditional humanities program that created what has come to be called the "crisis in the curriculum." This crisis is a "crisis of knowledge" only in the sense that knowledge is produced by those forces and relations of production that are historically dominant. "Mankind," Marx wrote in his explanation of the historicity of knowledge, "inevitably sets itself only such tasks as it is able to solve, since closer examination will always show that the problem itself arises only when the material conditions for its solution are already present or at least in the course of formation" (1981, 21).

The new curriculum–the current cognitive mapping of (post)modern capitalist labor relations–is thus not the effect of the innovative ideas of individuals; it is the ideological "solution" to historical contradictions in the forces and relations of production. These contradictions have unleashed new forms of intra- and interclass war. For example, the contestation between the National Association of Scholars, on the one hand, and Teachers for a Democratic Culture (a group composed of such establishment academics as Henry Louis Gates, Jr., Stanley Fish, Jonathan Culler, Gerald Graff, Jane Gallop, and Nancy Fraser), on the other, is not a conflict over the "canon," "literature," "tradition," "artistic value," "common culture," or "multiculturalism" (as the inaugural document of the TDC suggests). These groups are, rather, struggling over those class privileges traditionally reserved for providers of the knowledge most useful to the present system, that is, knowledge necessary for the smooth reproduction of the ruling economic regime. Each group is trying to "prove" the usefulness of its own particular brand of knowledge and the necessity of the consciousness skills its members can produce. By doing so, each group hopes to assure the entitlement of its members to the class privileges that capitalism puts aside for its knowledge workers. The opposition of the right-wing academics in the NAS to the new curriculum is therefore part of the larger process of the class struggle over new forms of labor and property relations that is now taking place: it marks the struggle against the new ruling elite that is replacing the older, established one. For its part, the TDC is attempting to "normalize" the crisis in emerging class relations by supporting those modes of the new curriculum that are not "extremist" (Graff 1989, 1). The aim of members of the TDC is to save the system by incorporating moderate reform into it only so as to resecure the class position of mainstream (non-"extremist") academics, who are the current producers of abstract knowledge necessary for today's high-tech culture of late capitalism. (For further discussion of these contests, see Chapter 7.)

The change of the curriculum is, in short, a response to the change of the labor force, which is itself an outcome of the technological renovation of the means of production. The rising labor force requires skills that go beyond the linear and empirical and produce in workers an understanding, no matter how elementary, of systems operations in general. The term we use for the historically complex processes of mediating the shifts in the base into the superstructural remodeling of education is "digitalism."

"Digitalism," in our analysis, we should emphasize, is not used as the "cause" of changes (it is not a new "mode of information" that displaces the "mode of production") in contemporary capitalism and the labor force. It is deployed here, rather, as a mediating concept that points to the shift in the superstructural discourses and practices that, in response to material changes, are involved in constructing (post)modern subjectivities and the "consciousness skills" needed for the rising labor force of late capitalism. The primary reasons for the shift in the labor force, as we have already suggested, are changes in the productive forces of (post)modern society.

The class character of the changes in the curriculum we are describing here become partially clear if we bear in mind that these changes are taking place not in all U.S. universities and colleges but only in the "elite" ones, that is, in those universities and colleges that, for the most part, produce the managers for the advanced high-tech labor force. The traditional curriculum remains in effect in the universities and colleges that, in the social and academic division of labor, continue to supply the workers for that part of the U.S. labor force still deployed in more traditional (and, in terms of labor skills, "backward") industries. The graduates of these latter institutions constitute what, adapting Travis Charbeneau's term, might be called "the information underclass" (1991, 24) – the homegrown third world labor force in the United States. As the new mode of production and exchange becomes the dominant mode, the curriculum of these colleges will also change. At present, however, we are witnessing an "uneven" development.

The academy has always played an essential role in the production of the labor force: not only by teaching "practical" skills (engineering, medicine, pharmacy, law, writing) but also by producing the appropriate subjectivities for the labor force. In the social division of labor in capitalism, it is the "job" of academic intellectuals to serve capital by providing the practical and theoretical skills it needs to reproduce and justify itself. However, the focus of our attention here is not so much on the (class) role of intellectuals in producing and disseminating "theory" as on the historical necessity and class politics of theory itself for the training of the rising (post)modern labor force.

On the most basic level, the abstract knowledge the rising labor force needs is taught (to the workers who are not college graduates) through such skills as computing. There is a fundamental difference between the high school students who were taught "typing" (the trope of the linearity of the "low-tech" Fordist industrial regime) and those who are now taught "computing." "Computing" is radically different from "typing": although he knows far less than a programmer, even the computer keyboard operator needs to know not only the concrete skill of how to press the keys, but also to some degree the abstract pattern of software systems. The difference between the old industrial (typing) worker and the new (computing) worker is caused by the shift that, in response to shifts in the regime of production, is taking place in the training of the new labor force. This is a training that, in Charles R. Walker's words, emphasizes the "skills of the *head* rather than of the *hand,* of the *logician* rather than of the *craftsman*" (1957, 195, emphasis added).

Although our focus here is on the education of the "managers" of the new labor force, it should be noted in passing that abstract thinking is also needed in the (nominal) integration of laborers with managers, which is another aspect of (post)modern capitalist practices. This integration (as the more advanced Japanese model shows) has become necessary for coping with the crisis of the "alienation" of labor in the high-tech labor force. One way to integrate the workers has been to include them in the general process of problem solving in the workplace. The disalienation of the worker–through her seeming inclusion in decision making–requires that she should have at least a rudimentary "abstract" knowledge of the new industrial regime. "Digitalism" (the acquiring of abstract knowledge by workers for, in this case, their "inclusion" in problem-solving processes usually set aside for managers), it must be noted, in no way changes the antagonism of labor and capital–it does not change class conflicts. What it shows, however, is that changes in the production relations require changes in consciousness skills. Workers are not emancipated by "digitalism": they remain exploited as long as the means of production are owned by one class while labor is performed by another. Our focus here, however, is not so much on the level of the labor force produced in high schools, but on the level that is produced in universities. Managers are an important part of (post)modern capitalism: they foreground (because they do not erase) the polarization between capital and labor. In other words, contrary to the claims of liberal theorists, the increasing importance of managers does not change the character of capitalism (the extraction of surplus labor) but only articulates its particular historical shape.

In universities the students, who will move into higher echelons of the labor force (the managerial level), are introduced to abstract knowledge through the discourses of "theory." It is helpful here to bear in mind that the function of the humanities, both in high schools and universities, is to develop the *affective* makeup of the labor force, to produce in the labor force the kind of (ideological) consciousness that situates the subject of labor in a manner necessary for the reproduction and maintenance of existing social relations.

In other words, the humanities curriculum, at any given historical moment, structures the consciousness of the labor force; it teaches the labor force at all levels how to respond to the world in the "right" way. It legitimates the "feelings" one should have, the "emotions" one should "experience," the "vision" one should cultivate – in short, it teaches how to interpret the world in the "correct" way. What is proposed as "correct," of course, is ultimately the interpretation needed to reproduce the dominant relations of production. It is the humanities curriculum that teaches the subject of labor what to take "seriously" and what to "laugh at," what to accept as a "joke" and what to "ridicule." In other words, the humanities curriculum formalizes and institutionalizes (in terms of interpretive practices) the appropriate ideological responses and inscribes the subject of labor in the "immutable" values promoted as the basis of a "meaningful" life.

The new discourses of theory generated since the mid-1960s have helped to produce the consciousness skills necessary for the (post)modern labor force: they have put in question the traditional empiricism and positivism that provided the justification for the existing curriculum and argued for a more conceptually self-reflexive and interdisciplinary mode of inquiry redefined ("retheorized") as "reading" – the "skill" upon which the entire humanities curriculum was founded.[2]

It must not be forgotten that the humanities curriculum does not simply produce liberal arts majors and provide graduate training in the humanities. What makes the humanities curriculum so important to the constitution of the labor force is, we repeat, the *consciousness skills* it teaches to all students, who are – through various schemes (such as "core curricula" and "course requirements") – asked to participate in them. At every historical moment, consciousness skills are taught that are "appropriate" to the prevailing mode of production and to existing class relations.

Not surprisingly, then, the first object of inquiry of the newly emerging "theory" was "reading"—the operation through which the subject of labor is taught how to produce the "experiences" necessary for the "natural" continuation of the dominant labor relations. In the new theoretical discourses, "reading" was no longer regarded as a mimetic (linear and with a one-to-one relation of signifier to signified) activity aimed at recovering the "meaning" placed in the text by the "author," but as a nonrepresentational operation whose main purpose was to analyze the very processes of representation and the production of meaning itself. Reading as an empirical practice, in other words, was replaced by reading as a philosophical and speculative (abstract) inquiry into the conditions of signification and meaningfulness. At the core of the new practices of reading were no longer the ideas of beauty, coherence, and harmony, but the differential movement of the sign that fractured the text and marked its difference not simply from other texts (the goal of "low-tech" reading practices founded upon the notion of "identity") but rather from itself. Reading lost its "concreteness" and became a highly "abstract" and "conceptual" activity—even as it argued against conceptuality itself (for further clarification, see our discussion of textual studies in Section 5 of this chapter). Thus in this moment of the introduction of theory, reading was shifted from the level of discourse to the level of metadiscourse.

Unlike "traditional" interpretation (a practice that allowed for the full range of the reader's self-expressiveness and therefore legitimated the text as an empirical object, the reader as a "free" individual, and the imagination as supreme), reading was now understood as an operation that went beyond the mere connection of the network of reader to text to imagination. With the advent of (post)modern "reading," the reader's "individuality" was problematized into a very elaborate notion of the "de-centered subject," and the text was rearticulated as a highly subtle and complex movement of what Derrida calls "*différance*." The text was no longer a representation of the world or a "message," but an allegory of reading, an articulation of the impossibility of any reliable knowledge that can extend beyond the differential movement of the sign. In short, the mimetic knowledge ("realism") that had long served market capitalism and low-tech industry could not cope with the increasing complexities (abstraction, nonlinearity, digitalism, cyberneticity) of "late capitalist," high-tech culture. Thus in the wake of the new theory, there emerged what might be very broadly described as an antimimetic, antirepresentational humanities.

Suppressing the connection between the curriculum and economics, U.S. universities have celebrated changes in the curriculum as a sign that the academy is an "enlightened" institution that constantly "examines" itself and produces "new" and "better" understanding of knowledge. "Change," in other words, is understood as the result of a disinterested search independent from the realm of economics: It is a search for truth that is a superstructural process, merely discursive practices that produce, in their autonomy, other discursive practices. By relying on this narrative, in short, U.S. universities have suppressed the recognition of the material base of political forces that have made the "reform" in the humanities curriculum historically necessary so as to reproduce capitalist relations of production. Theory had become the discourse that produced, in a more rigorous manner, the abstract thinking needed by the new work force of the age of simulation. A new mode of intelligibility was taught to students that made sense of the world by substituting "undecidability," "supplementarity," "discourse," the "anagrammatic," and the "differend" for "harmony," "ambiguity," and "beauty." Likewise, "semiotics," "psychoanalysis," "tropology," "deconstruction" took the place of "literary history" and "biography." And of course the "texts" of Hegel, Derrida, Heidegger, Freud, Lacan displaced the "work" of novelists, poets, and playwrights. The simulacra of Jean Baudrillard were found to be more relevant to the required consciousness skills in the age of consumption and exchange value than the humanist pieties of Jane Austen, Charles Dickens, George Eliot, and Saul Bellow. The ready manner in which these shifts came to be understood locally is clear when *The Daily Orange* article quotes a faculty member as saying: "When the [ETS] program was first conceived, it was assumed that theories such as feminism and deconstruction would be intrinsic parts of the curriculum" (see Appendix 6.1).

Under the new regime, the "classics" were "read" "differentially" and the contemporary fictions that became part of the theoretical canon were either deeply influenced by theory (Kathy Acker) or, in their technomanic textuality, foregrounded high-tech thematics (Thomas Pynchon and William Gibson). Writers such as Acker and Pynchon were not only "theoretical" in their discourses but also had the additional virtue of providing newer examples of what de Man had defined as the "literary," the space of rhetorical slippage and epistemological negation. Not only did they teach theory, but they also "resisted" it. They not only offered exemplary sites for the rebirth of the subject that thinks abstractly, but also defended the nomadic self of the "feeling" and "tasting" ludic subject. The old (Cartesian) "self," which was killed in early structuralist thinking, was now reborn in the more advanced texts of (post)structuralism. And this version of self was much more responsive to the ideological needs of multinational capitalism.

3 In the Syracuse University English Department, as elsewhere, the recognition of the economic impetus of the crisis for curricular change was suppressed. Taking into account the shifts in (post)modern capitalism, we ourselves attempted in the 1980s to produce a humanities curriculum at Syracuse that did not simply produce employees for the new labor force, but also new subjects of knowledge—"criti(que)al" subjects aware of the historicity and situatedness of their knowledge, consciousness skills, and their own relation to economic forces. Such "criti(que)al" subjects of knowledge are aware of their place in the relations of production and know the close connection between types of knowledge and various social forces, especially class. In its general articulation, such a curriculum, as we argued in the Syracuse English Department's exchanges, would evolve around, among other things, a mode of critique of materialist ideology that would only succeed in reinserting the process of production (the extraction of surplus labor as the basis of capitalist exploitation) into the naturally commoditized world of the bourgeois university and its underlying knowledge industry. In other words, what was needed was not literary studies as "explication" (as both the New Critics and [post]structuralists had argued) but critical cultural studies as "implication"—a study that implicates knowledge and subjects in the political economy of knowing and working. Needless to say, our proposals were defeated.[3]

Instead of offering such a materialist pedagogy, what the new curriculum actually offered was mystified as a sign of the department's intellectual flexibility, agility, and up-to-dateness. However, if one looks at the maneuvers that the Syracuse English Department has made from the early 1980s to the present, to cope with this curricular crisis, it becomes clear that what is represented as progress is in fact a mode of containment. What is advertised as a transforming curriculum is a calculated reform designed to contain and manage the crisis (by mystifying the connections of theory to economics) and rob it of its socially progressive potential (that might allow students to see that connection and intervene in production practices, working for a new economic social order free from the division of labor).

The Syracuse Program in English and Textual Studies is the outcome of contestations, between traditionalists and theorists on the one hand, and, most importantly, among the theorists themselves on the other. In contestations among the theorists, the political economy of the curriculum became foregrounded in a fashion that was not at all clear as long as the battle was seen to be taking place only between the theorists and the traditionalists.[4] We would say that the battle between the theorists and traditionalists was over before it began. The humanists (not only at Syracuse but at other universities) failed to offer any sustained resistance to theory, that is, their countertheories were not rigorous. Their arguments retreated into nostalgic (and theological) views of the humanities and of individuality (see, for instance, Steiner 1989), into views that—like the recent Republican theories of "family values"—were no longer credible, even in the culture at large. The emerging labor force had no use at all for the values the traditionalists advocated.

However, even though the labor force did not need the notions of the free individual or the idea of interpretation or the theory of a free-standing text, the emerging labor force nevertheless still did need the *ideological effects* of these concepts, effects that, in their totality, continued to reify the bourgeois world as the "natural" world. In other words, for the new labor force to remain "cooperative," it still had to be produced in such a way that, for instance, it still believed in its own natural "autonomy." This says that the ideological effects of humanism that posit a familiar world have to be reproduced in the creation of the emerging labor force, even though the founding principles of humanism themselves ought to have been abandoned because they had become historically unuseful.

Although the emerging labor force did not need a "free" individual in the sense of a coherent, unitary, sovereign individual, it nevertheless still did need a subject that would recognize and acknowledge itself as *not* coherent, *not* unitary, *not* sovereign, a subject that was newly adept in abstraction and could arrive at its subjectivity not directly (through "identity"), but through the detour of "otherness." In other words, the new labor force needed an "individual" in a new sense, one that could think of itself as a "split subject" because (post)modern capitalism was itself a dispersed regime of capital in need of a dispersed subject of labor who would not insist on "coherence."[5] What the emerging labor force did need was a new subject that no longer thought of itself as an organic whole: what had to be saved was the notion of the subject itself (a viable self in some way separable from the social collectivity). But the way the subject was made intelligible had to be changed. This new knowledge, nevertheless, still permitted the new, split, fragmented, dispersed subject to think of itself as "free." In fact, some (post)structuralist philosophers found a new basis for this freedom that was just as "organic" and as "natural" as that promoted in the organicism of the traditional curriculum: Michel Foucault, for example, anchored the new, split, postindividual subject in the body. If the new "subject" did not have a "free" consciousness, at least it still had a "free" body and furthermore, had a new form of self-reflexivity that – in Jane Gallop's words – could "think through the body" (1988).

This new subject was no longer anchored in the idea of the indivisibility of consciousness (not in the principle, "I *think*, therefore I am"), but in the undeniability of the body (the principle, "I *feel*, therefore I am"). Hence, the crucial battle in the Syracuse English Department was not over the difference between the traditional individual and the new subject, but rather over how the new subject was to be articulated. The contestation was, in other words, over the difference of "difference." Was "difference" simply the effect of the Lacanian "symbolic order" – the post-Oedipal triangulation articulated in cultural prohibitions; the Derridean idea of "*différance*" – the disappearance of the securing "transcendental signified" and thus the everlasting slippage of representation and the unavoidable condition of "undecidability"; the Lyotardian order of the "sublime" – the apprehension of the "real" as an endless series of incommensurate "language games"; or was it to be articulated as the difference of the division of "labor" – the "difference" of private property as the effect of surplus labor? Is difference the difference of a body "free" in its libidinal playfulness or is it a body at work – that is, a body as the producer of surplus labor?

It was in this space that those at Syracuse who argued for a materialist (rather than an idealist, "pleasure-alist") understanding of the subject were excluded from the debate. The new curriculum was finally formulated by the consensus formed between some of the theorists and some of the traditionalists to reconstitute a new departmental power center. The new curriculum, "English and Textual Studies," was the outcome of this coalition between traditionalists, (post)structuralists, rhetoricians, New Historicists, and liberal feminists. What happened at Syracuse was paradigmatic of the widespread maneuver one might call "conservation through renewal." Because we believe that this reconfiguration of the departmental power center teaches a lesson in institutional politics, we shall dwell on it a little longer.

4 Bourgeois institutions are highly flexible and have immense powers of endurance. They obtain their flexibility, complexity, and staying power by constantly absorbing the elements of culture that oppose them, that is, by reducing critiques to various types of reform. Universities, as bourgeois institutions, maintain the ideological practices needed to preserve the hegemony of the ruling classes by constantly adapting to, and adopting, whatever opposes them. Among the most important strategies for absorbing the opposition and maintaining the system is the strategy of pluralistic inclusion: the institution assimilates the discourses of its adversaries. As a result, reforms take place that manage to defuse the pressure for revolutionary change. This was the strategy that was deployed to ward off radical change in the Syracuse English Department. Those radical faculty members and students who insisted on producing discourses that resisted assimilation, and thereby transgressed the boundaries of the "reasonable," were excluded. They were excluded because their "extremist" views of knowledge were characterized as "nonknowledge," "propaganda," "dogmatic," "doctrinaire," "homogenizing," "nondifferential," in short, "illiberal."[6]

Of course, these tactics for exclusion of the radical must be explained more fully because, in the university as in all other liberal bourgeois institutions, nobody should be *formally* excluded. These institutions acquire their legitimacy by claiming total inclusivity (the "liberal" claims a pluralism that ought never to exclude any point of view). But what happened in the Syracuse English Department happens all the time: the radical thinker is situated on an axis of alternatives such that she has the "free choice" either of working from within the system or being marked as an "extremist" who can therefore be "legitimately" excluded because she can be regarded as "self-excluding." In other words, the options come down to either being "persuaded" of the legitimacy of working within the system and thus accepting the existing structures, or finding that there is no space for radical change. "Persuasion" (the model of democratic conversation) is, in other words, an alibi for a pernicious system of surveillance and punishment built on the principle: "Be persuaded, or else. . . "

The maneuvers we have just described in the Syracuse English Department have not gone unnoticed on the national scene. Writing in *The Chronicle of Higher Education,* Scott Heller, referring to the "Marxist professors" (that is, us) at Syracuse University who were resisting the reformist project, wrote: they "ultimately refused to work on a committee that drew up a statement of purpose about the new curriculum [that is, 'Not a Good Idea']" (Heller 1988, A17). Our concern here is to point out how the refusal to serve on committees is construed, in bourgeois institutions, as a mark of "unreasonableness," "irresponsibility," "extremism," and even as a form of "terrorism." If professors decline to serve on committees and thereby refuse to go along with reformism and "pragmatic" solutions, such refusals are interpreted as a sign of their "absence," as a "failure" of "collegiality" and "citizenship," rather than as a protest against the existing terms of "collegiality" and "citizenship." In other words, the only way that a dissenting faculty member can prove his "collegiality" and "responsibleness" is to attend committee meetings, be soundly defeated by the "majority," and accept that defeat as a mark of "democratic" governance. Any protest against the way this "machinery" of democracy is set up is interpreted as an act of "extremism" and "nondemocratic" behavior.

We want to argue that in order to produce any radical change of the system, one has to maintain the notion of an "outside" to the existing system's "inside." This notion is necessary if critiques are to avoid being reduced, and then openly "absorbed" by the status quo, and simply disarticulated and "added onto" (tolerantly included side by side with) the existing structured practices. One way to mark the outside is to invoke the notion of "disparticipation." But of course, existing institutions have no place for political disparticipation—a concept that marks the illegitimacy of the existing system by a refusal to "play the game" according to its oppressive and exploitative rules. To disparticipate is to refuse to accept what actually *is* as the "real" and insist on what *ought to be;* it is to point to the *possible* which is suppressed in the pragmatic *is.*

According to the dominant regime of power/knowledge, change can only be brought about from "within" the system by playing by the rules of the games the system engenders, that is, "games," because they in no way threaten the existing system. Of course, at the core of these games (participation in committees, etc.) is the game of voting – the assertion of "free choice." But what is mystified here is the politics of voting as a device of system maintenance. When one votes, whether one votes for or against, one has, above all, accepted the legitimacy of the system of voting: one has "voted for voting" as a legitimate, democratic mode of conducting public life. In other words, one is regarded as "reasonable" only if one accepts the fundamental frame of participation from within. The rejection of the idea of disparticipation in the dominant games is nothing but a repetition of Roger Kimball's notion that the "tenured radical" is an unacceptable member of the academic community. Kimball's position gains its force, of course, from its commonsensical appeal to the notion of "participation" as well as "pragmatism." In the discourse of bourgeois institutions there is no room for nonpragmatic thinking because it questions the legitimacy of the actually existing and argues for other possibilities. "Pragmatism" pervades all practices of bourgeois institutions and in a "reasonable" and commonsensical manner institutes a regime of anti-intellectualism that in effect subjects all knowledge to this test: Does it work? The question, however, should be: Does it work where, and when, and to do what? It might "work" in the present situation and under the existing circumstances, but such "working" does not in any way indicate the legitimacy of these practices. For instance, during the 1991–1992 academic year, when the Syracuse English Department was discussing – through diverse contesting discourses – its priorities for hiring new faculty, we argued, against the main departmental current, that new faculty should be invited to join the department to help it bring up the level of its intellectual discourses and not simply continue business as usual. The response of John W. Crowley, the chair, was to mark such arguments as unacceptable by stating that: "the arguments that will have weight with the Dean are not apocalyptic narratives about programs in decline but hard facts on the critical mass for meeting instructional needs" (Syracuse University Department of English Executive Committee Minutes, March 25, 1992). In his discourses, then, the "pragmatic" becomes once again an ideological alibi for perpetuating the status quo by adding to the already existing discourses and thus reinforcing the monolithic and totalitarian knowledge that dominates the department.

5 So far in this chapter we have indicated (among other things) (1) how the crisis in the curriculum is not an internal crisis of the academy but the effect of a shift in the forces and relations of production in advanced industrial democracies, and (2) how the changes in the curriculum of contemporary U.S. universities are not radical changes but in fact reformist changes within the existing system so as to make it more responsive to the need for a labor force appropriate for late capitalism.

We would like to conclude this chapter with a brief discussion of "Not a Good Idea" (Cohan et al. 1988), the statement of purpose for the ETS program, which has become the semiofficial account of the new Syracuse curriculum written by those who supported it. (It is available from the Syracuse University English Department.) This statement has been widely distributed throughout the U.S. academy as offering a model of "change" that might be adopted elsewhere, and it is frequently quoted in professional articles about the new curriculum. We wish to show how the "new" Syracuse curriculum is simply a rearticulation of familiar, reformist strategies.

In order to do this, we must first elaborate more fully than before the broad shift in humanistic inquiry that has been under way in the U.S. academy in recent years. The shift away from humanist traditionalism has moved, on the one hand, in the direction of the new "textual studies" promoted by those under the strong influence of (post)structuralism, and, on the other hand, in the direction of the new "cultural studies" promoted by those who oppose pantextualism – the limiting of cultural analytics to questions of signification and representation, and the consequent erasure of the political economy of knowledge. Unlike (post)structuralists who deny that any difference is "decisive," we believe that there are decisive differences between the two forms of study. While both were produced under the pressure of (post)modern thought, the two approaches have quite distinct preoccupations and political implications.

Textual studies is a superstructuralist mode of analysis in which "writing" – as the trope of intelligibility – is taken to be an autonomous practice: it is nonrepresentational and differential, and it works not according to a social logic but in terms of its own immanent logic. Although textual studies rejects the notion of an intentional consciousness and the associated philosophical vocabularies, it is in the end an argument for the independence of human consciousness. It is, in Bakhtin's words, an analytics that posits that "the word [consciousness] gives birth to the thing [the world]" (Morson 1988, 182). Thus textual studies is an attempt to occlude the social production of ideas and feelings in order to produce the (post)modern subject as autonomous, that is, free from class and class struggle. Cultural studies, on the other hand, attempts to write the social back into consciousness and relate its products to the material base and not simply to the materiality of language. Cultural studies is, therefore, an attempt to demonstrate that "it is not the consciousness of men that determines their existence, but their social existence that determines their consciousness" (Marx 1981, 21). Ultimately, what is involved in the academy in the contestation over the cultural logic of intelligibilities between textual studies and cultural studies is the role of mode of production and class relations in capitalism.

To expand the distinctions: textual studies is concerned with the mechanics of signification (the relation of signifier to signified, thus the emphasis on Saussurean linguistics in the new Syracuse curriculum), whereas cultural studies is concerned with the production and maintenance of subjectivities, that is to say, with language as a social praxis and not merely a formal system of differences – with language, in Marx's words, "as practical consciousness" (Marx

1988, 51). Textual studies puts in question the validity of cultural studies by proposing a theory of textual *différance*. Because of the effects of *différance,* culture is not available in any reliable way, according to textualists; through language as representation, culture is itself subject to the laws of *différance*. But the results of these textualist moves–because they operate on a political agenda–must also be elaborated. Textual studies defines "politics" as those reading activities that "delay" the connection of the signifier to the signified: deconstructive politics, in other words, is the interruption of the easy trafficking of meaning in culture (the disruption of *con-cept*uality by *text*uality). This move, far from being a trivial "philosophical game" (as traditional humanists seem to think), is aimed ultimately at rendering knowledge itself as unreliable. Although it takes the materiality of signification into account, cultural studies, by contrast, in its focus on the politics of the production of subjectivities rather than on textual operations, understands "politics" as access to the material base of power, knowledge, and resources.

The story of recent developments does not end here, however; for under the impact of current academic/intellectual politics, cultural studies diverges strongly into different modes of understanding. On the one hand, there is what might be called "Experiential Cultural Studies" (the work of Raymond Williams, E. P. Thompson, Janice Radway, Teresa de Lauretis, and Naomi Schor–if indeed the practices of the latter two are anything more than a kind of "deviant textualism"). On the other hand, there is what might be called "Critical Cultural Studies" (the work of Fredric Jameson, for instance, which is informed by the notion of "totality"). By "cultural studies" the academy now means, for the most part, "experiential cultural studies" or at the very most the writings of authors like Stuart Hall, who, by giving a liberal reading to Gramsci's notion of hegemony (in the wake of Laclau and Mouffe's readings), manage to subvert the relation between subject and class and who, in this way, try to occupy a place between experiential and critical cultural studies.

These modes of knowledge–that is, textual studies, experiential cultural studies, and critical cultural studies–promote (as we have suggested) distinct and competing understandings of the political, the historical, and the material, although today's renovated U.S. academy (under the dominance of the first two closely collaborating modes) is making a strenuous effort to occlude the differences, specifically the difference of the latter. "Not a Good Idea" is an exemplary instance of this occlusion through curriculum reform.

In light of the distinctions just drawn, "Not a Good Idea" can be read as an emblem of academic schizophrenia and careerist anxiety about saving the subject, because it expresses the wish to reconstitute the English department as a department of "textual studies," There is also a desire to hold on to "cultural studies" out of fear of not being "politically up to date." The deeper logic of this apparent indecisiveness becomes clearer when we examine the several discursive strands with which "Not a Good Idea" is constructed. First, there is its subject-serving narrative of institutional history; second, its reliance on a politics of coalitionism (that is to say, on an evasive political eclecticism and pluralism that avoid facing their own ideological complicity in perpetuating the regime of exploitation by reifying the subject as "volunteer"); third, its striking abandonment of (post)modern theory in a desperate rush to relegitimate thematics; and finally, its curricular effects, as suggested by the supposedly "new" course offerings announced by the department for the first two years of the "new" program.

The "history" to which the document points as the enabling condition of curricular change at Syracuse is an occlusionist history. At the level of culture at large, it cites the climate of unrest of the 1960s and 1970s (it mentions, for instance, "the feminist movement," "the Vietnam War," "the Civil and Gay Rights movements"—all of which it sums up as "recent American social *experience*" [see Cohan et al. 1988]) and the impact of (post)structuralist theory. In other words, its general narrative articulates events so as to foreground the categories of "experience" and "textuality," the two structures of understanding that unobtrusively reinstall the subject in the discourses of dominant knowledges. The document's uneasy, but necessary, hold on these categories requires explanation.

Following the ludic (postmodernist) common sense of the academy, "Not a Good Idea" assumes that everything is textual, cultural, made, and constructed, and that the subject of pedagogy is thus irretrievably distanced from "origin" and "the original."

In spite of this "knowledge," however, there persists in the academy an unrelinquishable yearning for "origin" and the unconstructed, the "natural." The articulation of "experience" with "textuality" in "Not a Good Idea" reproduces the ideological effect so necessary for the working of the bourgeois knowledge industry. In the midst of the "constructed" (theorized in differential "textuality" by [post]structuralism), "experience" provides an oasis of "nature"—the nonconstructed, spontaneous, and originary (subject). This is a double move that reproduces, by appeal to the subject of experience, the "natural" amidst the "cultural," and is the founding gesture of experiential cultural studies. Suppressing the logic of domination that underlies the vast political eruptions of the 1960s in the seemingly local and heterogeneous, experiential cultural studies fetishizes the nomadic, the cellular, and the local experience. By the deployment of "experience," experiential cultural studies has been successful in reducing "exploitation" (as a global strategy) to the "experience" of exploitation, and thus has substituted for the political economy of knowledge, courses in the experience of the gay, the feminine, the ethnic. The popularity of "social movements" in the ludic academy, which is taken to be a sign of "political" engagement, is, in other words, a strategy of avoidance—a repression of the global logic of domination by privileging the local site of the experience of the dominated.

At the level of institutional history, the document's narrative grants several preconditions for the department's "change," but pivots climatically around the hiring of Steven Mailloux as the new chair (the subject), whose arrival is seen to coincide with the arrival of "theory" itself, and whose first year in office is described as a time of "nearly constant flow of memoranda and position papers" (Cohan et al. 1988, 2). Change, in other words, is tied to the subject as the origin of action and transformation. The theory of history implied here is an extension of history as experience that we have already mentioned. What is occluded by this narrative is the history of change and change as history: the fact that the flow of memoranda and position papers (*discourses,* as distinguished from the subject) had a complex history, which to a very large extent determined the arrival not only of Mailloux but also of quite a few of the others who signed the document. That is to say, the discourses of change were historical and transsubjective. They determined the space of the arrival of Mailloux, not the other way around. What's more, although the writers of the document take great satisfaction in stressing the "openness," "freedom," and "publicness" of the exchanges on the curriculum (they describe it proudly as "the product of the *agora,* the public meeting place" [1988, 2]), they nowhere mention the fact that they had blocked the publication in book form of the memoranda and position papers, which would have made the historicity and materiality of the contestations inscribed in them truly public. They cited as "reason" their unwillingness—as one professor put it, in the best tradition of common sense—"to launder dirty linen in public." A close reading of these texts shows that there was no dirty linen in the discourses, unless of course what they mean is those strong critiques that do not find their way into the consensus documant they have written. "Not a Good Idea" thus suppresses the transsubjective work that initiated the department's curricular debate and suppresses any record of those historical moments of departmental contestation. Rejecting critique when it doesn't serve their interests, they persist in trivializing it as a merely personal "venting of spleen." This was the phrase used to describe our critiques of Carnegie-Mellon's supposedly "revolutionary" practices. (See our text, "War of the Words: The Battle of [and for] English" [*In These Times,* October 28, 1987] and the letter to the editor by David Shumway and Paul Smith in the November 18 issue of *In These Times.*) The response that critique is a venting of spleen is by no means exceptional, but an instance of a coalitionist discourse that circulates widely in the academy to contain critique. For instance, when our critique of the "new" Syracuse curriculum was articulated in a paper given at the MLA Convention in December, 1989, in Washington, D.C. (at a session titled "The Cultural Wars and The Classroom," see Morton 1987), in his response Gerald Graff—

adopting other language used by Shumway and Smith–called our critique a demand for "re-education camps" (see Graff, "Response to Papers" 1989). The phrase, "re-education camps," is of course part of the "Cold War" heritage of the established academy and it is used as the "final argument." By using it, Graff–relying on the coalitionist common sense of the audience–was sure that our critique had been completely discredited. Graff believes that by naming our discourse as the discourse of the "re-education camp," he has uttered the final judgment from the perspective of a unique vision of "freedom." However, the triviality of his observation is further marked by the commonality of his position. For example, in an essay titled "Syracuse University and the Kool-Acid Curriculum," Nino Langiulli writes, "For those with an ear for analogy, these courses are curiously reminiscent of those given as 're-education' in such places as Kampuchea, Ethiopia and, until its deliberate demise, Jonestown, Guyana" (1990, 6).

Graff and other high priests of the dominant ideology blindly follow this "Cold War" legacy in their own practices; they believe that such a phrase is self-evidently negatively coded. We believe–to go on with Graff's Cold War rhetoric–that the MLA Annual Convention (like countless conferences, symposia, and colloquia sponsored by the dominant academy) is indeed nothing but a "re-education camp" where academics, who in their day-to-day lives encounter social contradictions and class fissures, are "re-trained" back into common sense through the ideologies of such ritual academic occasions. The articulation of our critique at the MLA was indeed a demand for "re-education": it aimed–like all our work–to open a space in culture not where the contradictions of late capitalism can be reconciled in the spirit of reform, but where they can be brought to a crisis, in the spirit of revolution. Indeed all acts of pedagogy are demands for "re-education": the question is, What do those acts educate people for?

To return to our narrative: far from heralding the advent of theory at Syracuse, the arrival of Steven Mailloux signaled the end of theorizing. Since the vigorous and ongoing theoretical inquiries seemed to be "getting out of hand," attention had to be shifted from theoretical questions to the pragmatic business of putting together a (consensus) curriculum. The policing role of the new administrative regime and its control of theory can be seen in the department's understanding of "knowledge" and "subjectivity" as reflected in advertisements placed in the "MLA Job Information List" before and after the arrival of the "new chair." In 1985 (the year before Mailloux's arrival), the department was seeking those "who wish to undertake teaching and research in reading and writing texts" (1985) and with an interest in the politics of pedagogy, reading, writing, and was thus stressing the materiality of reading/writing practices. In 1989, after the new chair was in office for a full term, the department sought candidates "with a focus before 1900" (1989) and thus had violently reverted to a historicist periodization. The politics and economics of these job announcements take us back to the point that contestations over the curriculum are finally and always contestations over subjectivities, over, that is, the construction of students and teachers as subjects. "Jobs" are the material ways through which the required subjectivities are legitimated and recognized. The new curriculum that "needs" teachers with "period" expertise is, in short, an ideological apparatus for recognizing that "knowledge" is knowing the subject of a chronologized, experiential history. We have already pointed out how the consequences of the pragmatic and antitheoretical practices promoted under Steven Mailloux's chairship were institutionalized by his successor, John W. Crowley. Under Crowley any discourses about the direction of (post)modern knowledge and its relation to the structures of the department (curriculum, personnel, funding) were regarded, as we have already indicated in our discussion of the debate over hiring, as nonpragmatic, unworkable, and thus as abstract and theoretical. Under Crowley's regime as chair, theoretical discourses were treated— again as he put it in the already mentioned departmental executive committee meeting as useless "apocalyptic narratives." What he regarded as useful were "hard facts on the critical mass for meeting instructional needs" (March 25, 1992).

Working by a process of amalgamation, the department's shift to a businesslike pragmatism finds its key political method in "coalitionism." "Not a Good Idea" produces the department, not as a collective whose general interests are to be theorized, but as a set of factions—sets of individuated subjects that must be united by "consensus" (taking competing "interests" as inherently and equally legitimate). This, then, is how the limits of theory are set: Pragmatism suspends the pressures that theory can put on the various "positions" in the name of "getting things done." Theorizing stops and the work of the "real world" begins. What is meant here by "real world" is the existing world as reified in the pragmatism of such apologists of the subject as Rorty, Fish, Walter Benn Michaels—which is to say, the world "as it is." In other words, the consensus curriculum aims, at best, to reform the world but not to change it. It may be necessary to add here that by "theory" we mean a grasping of the world historically for the sake of transforming it in a collective fashion. By postulating departmental politics (and intellectual exchange) as basically factional and single-issue politics, "Not a Good Idea" works specifically to block any effort to articulate the curriculum in terms of the kind of global theory promoted by critical cultural studies and finally localizes issues to the extent that the new curriculum itself becomes, in our view, just a set of local topics: history, theory, politics.

The privileging of pragmatism leads to a local politics and to localizing the curriculum. This localization is sanctioned by moves made in the name of Foucauldian micropolitics and the Lyotardian war on totality. "Not a Good Idea" implies that the new Syracuse curriculum is conceived to be a (post)modern curriculum informed by *différance* and *self-reflexivity*. Yet what "Not a Good Idea" proposes is finally just a set of expanded thematic tabulations and localized issues: to the traditional issues of genre, period, and figure are added the new (post)modern issues of subject, text, and representation. (Post)modern thought thus becomes merely an expanded scheme of terminologies, typologies, and conventional classifications. We are returned again to the traditional curriculum-as-encyclopedia-of-topics-and-themes, to a curriculum in which each course becomes an ethical project for the instructor as the subject-of-self-fashioning, thereby avoiding the transformation of the course into a historical site of sustained inquiry into the structures of the political economy of knowledge. We are, in other words, returned to the very set of academic practices that *différance* and self-reflexivity were supposed to displace. (Regarding the possible power of *différance* and self-reflexivity to produce modal change, we must note that we are engaged here in an immanent critique of "Not a Good Idea" and are not endorsing the effectivity of textual *différance* and self-reflexivity.)

That the new Syracuse curriculum is just a set of thematic tabulations is evident from the course offerings proposed for the first two years of its operation, 1990–1992; for instance, "Psyche and Symbol in Medieval Romance"; "The Enlightenment"; "Modernism"; "Gender in Brontë, Tennyson, Hardy"; "Renaissance Poetry"; "History and Psychoanalysis"; "Faulkner"; "Epistolarity and the Novel"; and "The American 1890's." These courses–and almost all the others–could have easily been offered under the old curriculum. The new curriculum is merely the standard curriculum-of-the-subject turned inside out through the sleeve of the "special topics" designation. Some may suggest that it is a signal curricular change that students at Syracuse can now take Dickens without Dickens being a "required course"; but is this what the much-discussed politics of canon busting has come down to in the end? Has the curriculum that can merely celebrate its non-bindingness actually come to grips–as "Not a Good Idea" claims to have done–with the materiality of the contestations over reading/writing the texts of culture (that is, with materiality understood as the overdeterminedness and effectivity of cultural phenomena)? Or has it silently underwritten traditional liberalism with the updated vocabulary of deconstructive "undecidability"?

In a more recent example (from course offerings for the 1993/94 academic year), the ideological character of the "new" program in English and textual studies becomes still clearer. After several years of work in theory that has supposedly "problematized" the humanist notion of the subject, Syracuse students are now invited to participate in a seemingly new, fresh, and exciting form of knowledge by taking a course called "Living Writers and Dead Pals," described as "a reader's/writer's dream come true!" in which "students read works by living poets and prose writers" and "meet those writers for question-and-answer sessions" (English Department, Syracuse University, *The English Newsletter*, March 1993, p. 3). Not in any sense "new," the course reverts to the familiar notion that "knowing" means "knowing through the senses," that the most reliable knowledge is knowledge that is "naturally" derived by the student from his or her unmediated contact with the world, with literature, with writing, with authors, and so forth. Such a course reinstitutes the bourgeois understanding of the autonomous subject needed by the labor force of capitalism: it reinstitutes the ideology of individualism by presenting subjectivity in the form of the writer–subject whose vibrating, sensual voice becomes the medium of instruction, and simultaneously in the form of the student–subject whose experience of that voice becomes the very means of knowledge. (This course description is available from the Department of English, Syracuse University.)

While the document tries to pass itself off as the result of a compromise made between departmental "factions," it actually represents the coalition that has recently formed in the dominant academy between traditionalists and (post)structuralists – in other words, between "experientialists" and "textualists," – the political aim of which is ultimately to occlude the politically directed agenda of a (materialist) critical cultural studies. At several points the document stresses that "no one is satisfied" (3, 5) with the new curriculum, as if this were a result of all the compromises made in order to arrive at a consensus. Actually the text, in a repetition of a Lacanian gesture of desire, celebrates (quite cannily) the uncertainties of "satisfaction" and underwrites the department's pragmatism with characteristic deconstructive moves. If the new curriculum is "Not a Good Idea," we need not worry since – as (post)structuralism teaches – there are no "good" (in the sense of "autonomous") ideas, for ideas are inseparable from their discursive production. By putting the issues into quotations marks (by problematizing them), the contestation is assumed to have been "settled." As for the three basic categories used as the "template" of the new curriculum (History, Theory, Politics), "Not a Good Idea" has this to say: "Each may claim dominance, but their necessary intersection can only undermine such claims" (3). In other words, the categories behave in approved (post)structuralist fashion: they are reversible and emblemize the unending "play of signification." If the curriculum is uncertain and "does not know" what it is teaching, it then fits quite nicely with that notion of pedagogy as "teaching ignorance" which Barbara Johnson, among countless others, has so effectively promoted (see Chapter 1). Rather than offering global theory and politics, the new curriculum offers the "pleasures" of ignorance—with ignorance standing (in the humanistic tradition) for the "richness" of the "experience" of the subject for which no theory/politics of knowledge can possibly account. Ignorance, in other words, is a new knowledge of excess. As throughout the dominant academy, the moves made in "Not a Good Idea" are aimed finally at fracturing and containing the public space of concept formation by returning everything to the private sphere. The point of its coalitionism is to refer everything, after all, to "what individual faculty and students want." The subject is again violently reinstalled.

We have ended this chapter with a critique of "Not a Good Idea," the document which several years ago (1988) announced the inauguration of the new ETS curriculum, but we wish to return finally to the recent article in the *Daily Orange* (1992, Appendix 6.1) because we see its appearance as one mark of the bringing to completion of the process of institutionalization of the ETS curriculum as an intellectually "up-to-date" and "transformative" curriculum of which Syracuse University can be "proud." A materialist reading of the *Daily Orange* text once again reveals, on the contrary, the reformist (not transformist) character of the new curriculum—and the theoretically and politically regressive character of current local discussions of it: in the *Daily Orange* text the new curriculum's "radicalness" is equated with nothing more than its "avoidance" of the "conventional canon" and with a desire for an unspecified and undirected "constant change" (p. 165 below). Furthermore, the new ETS curriculum's allegiance to *re*formation rather than *trans*formation is clearly captured in the historically and politically freighted slogan, summarizing the effects of the program, with which article begins: "Literature is dead! Long live literature!" (p. 164 below). Even more politically telling is the following statement: "The ETS curriculum . . . teaches you to critique responsibly" (p. 166 below). In the light of what we have said here, it should be clear that "responsibly" is finally a code word for "reform." The lesson that such a proposition teaches—and the basic lesson of any reformist curriculum—is ultimately that the only legitimate and acceptable kind of critique is the "safe" and unthreatening critique that comes from "within" (plays the games of) existing institutional structures.

APPENDIX 6.1

ETS Delivers Non-traditional Approach: New Method for Studying English Aims to Avoid Conventional Canon

SCOTT McINTOSH

Literature is dead! Long live literature!

Syracuse University's new program of English and textual studies (ETS) breaks from a traditional approach to teaching English.

The program does not believe that "coverage of a canon is the goal of an education in English," according to a proposal titled "Not a Good Idea: A New Curriculum at Syracuse."

The "canon" often refers to a set of "great books" predominant in traditional English curriculums.

The proposal also says the program seeks to produce not "the traditional 'well-read' student, but a student capable of critique—of actively pressuring, resisting and questioning cultural texts."

The curriculum evolved, according to associate professor Steven Cohan, co-author of the proposal, when professors began offering special topics courses, showing "there was a need in the curriculum" for a different kind of study.

A New Leader

In the mid-1980's, a new department chair, Steven Mailloux, was hired for the express purpose of developing a new curriculum, Cohan said.

From *The Daily Orange,* February 3, 1992. Copyright 1992 by *The Daily Orange.* Reprinted by permission.

The ETS program was then developed and finally installed as a major program in 1990. Mailloux continued as a professor, but the department is now chaired by professor John Crowley.

The curriculum is divided into lower- and upper-division levels. The lower division consists of two introductory courses, ETS 141 and 241.

In the upper division, there are three groups of study—history, political and theory. This changes the curriculum from one "organized by chronological period . . . to a curriculum organized by modes of inquiry," according to a 1990 issue of *The English Newsletter*.

ETS majors are required to take courses in all groups.

Crowley said the ETS program is a "more complete transformation than others."

"We're labelling the approach that we're taking."

"Once you change the categories, you change the way in which knowledge is perceived. Knowledge itself is constructed. It is not natural.

"Every discipline goes through an evolution. Even the most traditional departments have changed."

Constant Change

Kenneth Rosen, a visiting professor from the University of Southern Maine, agreed with Crowley. "All departments are in flux," Rosen said. "Few are willing to be museum custodians.

"Statues stand in the park and collect bird droppings. The change is a good thing."

Associate professor Patricia Moody expressed the same idea. "Language is not artifactual," she said. "You don't just study the written word.

"Reading is an ongoing transaction. It can never be finished. The artifactual page and the student's mind are both culturally produced."

Moody said the ETS program brings to the forefront the fact that "there are other countries, other genders, other races. It's more aware of difference. It creates a greater consciousness."

According to Cohan, when the program was first conceived, it was assumed that theories such as feminism and deconstructionism would be intrinsic parts of the curriculum.

Rosen, who considers himself a relatively traditional professor, nonetheless approves of courses in these theories.

"I like ideas," he said. "I'm stimulated by ideas. I'm enriched and rewarded by colleagues who make ideas their business."

Rosen said students who take courses in theory "bring new insights to the texts I teach in my class."

Against the Canon

Critics of programs like ETS claim there is too much theory and not enough stress placed on the literary canon.

But Moody questions this criticism, claiming the canon is explored sufficiently by her students.

"It's possible that a student could go through the ETS program and not read some major works, but I believe that my students don't read just in the classroom," Moody said. "I expect that they read on their own.

"The ETS curriculum is empowering," she said. "It teaches you to critique responsibly. The ETS student is going to understand more about less, and that's a fair trade-off."

Joann Blaszczak and Deborah Hepburn teach the introductory ETS class to seniors at Clinton Senior High School in Clinton, N.Y., as part of SU's Project Advance.

They had to "relearn" English to accommodate the ETS program. They originally learned English according to a chronological order of great works and authorial intent, they said.

"I want an integration of both traditional and theory," Blaszczak said. "To ask a student to read a work from a different point of view is great."

Gretchen Murphy, a junior ETS major, agrees. "Literary theory is more important politically than teaching traditional literary canon," she said. "The program should have literature survey classes built into the system.

"We should read books from the literary canon, but we should read them from a different perspective."

Hepburn feels the ETS curriculum is an imposition of beliefs that she would not normally teach in her class.

Moody agrees that "there's a danger of being just as oppressive and blind as the old which it seeks to replace," she said.

Hepburn said the ETS program tends to create an elitist class where "if you learn the discourse, you can join the club."

However, Blaszczak said even though they don't teach major works implicitly, the application of theories to these works is important to the teaching of English.

CHAPTER 7

Signs of Knowledge in the Contemporary Academy

1 A curriculum is a space in which the signs of culture are articulated with meaning and disseminated to produce desire and subjectivity. The signs of culture, however, are always the sites of class struggle over meaning–over the real–and it is therefore not surprising to see that at times of crisis, such as the one we are presently going through, the curriculum itself becomes a space of crisis and also a place where the crisis has to be "managed" and "mastered."

Today bourgeois literary and cultural studies are in a state of crisis–hardly a day goes by without one's hearing of curricular debates. On the one side of the debates are the curricular "innovations" proposed by liberals who are attempting to reconstitute the center of the academy by updating their practices in (post)modern language and thus, through superstructural changes, trying to conserve the old structures of knowledge in the academy and to preserve the class interests that bourgeois higher education has always served. The approach of these liberal academics is "pragmatic": they use whatever "works," without much worry about "principles." In fact they put worrying about "principles" in question as the mark of a dogmatic modernist concern with the origin and epistemological grounding of practices; in their view, such worry has no place in the (post)modern curriculum. The changes at Duke, Stanford, Carnegie-Mellon and all other elite universities are innovations of this "pragmatic" kind: they attempt to save the capitalist knowledge industry by using the capitalist method – that is, by constantly renovating the curriculum as the means of production of knowledge. "Opposed" to the liberals are the neoconservatives, who continue to assert the necessity of "principles" and thus see the efforts of their "enemies," the (post)modern "pragmatists," to be a compromise with the "other" – that is, the "other"-as-Marxism. The differences, however, between the "modernist" neoconservatives such as Roger Kimball, Dinesh D'Souza, Hilton Kramer, . . . , on the one hand, and the (post)modern pragmatists such as Stanley Fish, Gerald Graff, Frank Lentricchia, . . . , on the other, are ultimately differences over strategies, not over goals. In the end, both groups are working to preserve the interests of the ruling class: the fact that there are contradictions within the bourgeoisie and quarrels and contestations among its various factions by no means indicates that the ruling class does not have a common class objective. The fact is that the growing complexity of class structure in late capitalism amplifies antagonisms among the ruling class's various factions. These antagonisms are articulated in the theoretical works of the academics who, by profession, rely on and support the interests of the ruling class in the knowledge industry. In general these competing bourgeois groups are fighting over knowledge (the limits of the real) in the form of various "theories" in the academy on behalf of the ruling class as a whole. They are simultaneously fighting more locally in support of one of the ruling class's particular (elite) strata. These intraclass conflicts among ruling class factions are, in short, "mediated" in terms of different abstract "ideas" promoted by the bourgeois knowledge industry. In a way, then, the seeming differences are only differences over which group is the "legitimate" defender of the "truth" (of the ruling ideas and the class that makes those ideas to be the ruling ideas – the "obvious" truths). The difference, in other words, is not – and has never been – over *whether* the ruling truths should be defended, but only over *how* they should be defended.

The triviality of these "differences" (which function as an ideological smoke screen to divert attention from the political economy of knowledge) and their absolute similarity at a higher political level can be clearly seen in the fact that these "differences" are now packaged and marketed as forms of entertainment for academic audiences. For a fee of $10,000 Stanley Fish and Dinesh D'Souza (a former Reagan policy advisor and one time editor of *The Dartmouth Review*) appear before "packed houses on college campuses to engage in orchestrated verbal fistfights" (Begley, "Souped-Up Scholar" 1992, 50). Going one step further in "orchestrating" the fistfights, Gerald Graff has institutionalized the "difference" between the two factions of bourgeois professionals of ideology competing with each other in serving the ruling class by establishing an organization he calls "Teachers for a Democratic Culture." The debates between "Teachers for a Democratic Culture" and their seeming adversaries gathered in "The National Association of Scholars" are as contrived and trivial as the fistfights between Fish and D'Souza. "Are Fish and Graff running another Rumanian revolution?" asks Curtis White, who effectively points out (in "The War Against Theory" 1992, 4) the underlying similarities between these two strata of the ruling class by reminding us that it was not all that long ago that Graff published a book called *Literature Against Itself,* which in many ways articulated the very ideas that today his "enemies," D'Souza, Kimball, and other conservatives, embrace. For instance, it is difficult to see any "difference," except in local terms, between Graff's attack on radical and revolutionary thinkers and writers and the attacks on the same group that Hilton Kramer publishes month after month in his editorials in *The New Criterion*.

What we are witnessing is the fact that in the bourgeois academy curricular innovations and opposition to them has become a boom business on which many careers in the humanities are being made. John Ellis, author of *Against Deconstruction,* is now one of the editors of the right-wing publication *Heterodoxy,* which is devoted almost entirely to curriculum bashing, to discrediting curricular innovations. On the other side, various humanities departments "in crisis," rather than hiring a Hawthorne "man" or a Jane Austen "man" as they used to do, are now routinely hiring a curriculum "man" (or occasionally, "woman"). A curriculum man usually knows the language of contemporary theory and is familiar with that politically harmless mixing of texts which has become known as "interdisciplinarity," but his main expertise is academic troubleshooting: he delivers "change" without conflict or bloodshed and thus supplies the academy with defused bombs. In short, he is a systems manager whose speciality is to resecure the existing system of reform and renovation and to contain any radical transformations in the construction of the social "real."

2 The present crisis in culture at large as well as in academic and educational policy-making circles involves a powerful struggle over how certain controversial signs of culture (for instance, "woman," "property," "African-American," "scholarship," "lesbian," "objectivity," "terrorism," "poverty," "polemic") are to be understood and over the role played by the teaching of the humanities in articulating this understanding. Typically the question gets staged as a "debate" over the content of the curriculum for literary and cultural studies between two supposedly bitterly divided camps, camps which, as we have already suggested, are in fact two (different) strata of the (same) ruling class. On the one hand, there are the traditional humanists (Allan Bloom, M. H. Abrams, E. D. Hirsch, Wayne Booth, Saul Bellow), who argue for a curriculum nearly exclusively comprising the "great books" of the Western tradition with their supposedly "eternal" truths. On the other hand, there are the (post)structuralist theorists (such as J. Hillis Miller, Barbara Johnson, Shoshana Felman, Gregory Ulmer), who support the "opening up" of the canon on the grounds that since "truth" is ultimately the effect of textual difference and thus undecidable and therefore plural, the curriculum itself should also be plural. "Truth," Derrida declares, "is plural" (*Spurs* 1979, 103). The arguments of such other renovators of the canon as mainstream liberal feminists and radical democrats and experientialists such as Paul Lauter and Henry Giroux are ultimately founded upon a version of traditional liberal pluralism that has its theoretical justification in (post)structuralist proposals, even though these pragmatic pluralists may in fact oppose some aspects of (post)structuralism. In Giroux's more recent texts—such as *Postmodernism, Feminism, and Cultural Politics* (see pp. 1–59), *Postmodern Education,* and, especially, "Post-Colonial Ruptures and Democratic Possibilities: Multiculturalism as Anti-Racist Pedagogy" in which he has absorbed (post)structuralism, liberal feminism, and (post)modernism into his theories—are interesting indications of this common genealogy. (Post)modernism, in other words, has allowed Giroux to articulate the underlying liberalism and experientialism of his theories in a more appealing manner in the ludic academy. His growing interest in the writings of Ernesto Laclau and Chantal Mouffe simply foregrounds what has been the unsaid of his texts. The question here is not, of course, about Henry Giroux the person, but about how his ideas represent the tendencies of the (post)modern academy and the way in which the center of this academy is being reconstituted by mixing traditional liberal discourses with those of (post)structuralism.

This staging of the issues in the contemporary academy is an ideological strategy calculated to obscure the collaboration of these seemingly opposed theories of knowledge which aims at relegitimating the curriculum of the dominant forms of knowledge by ensuring that certain kinds of questions about literary and cultural studies are never raised in the public debates over education, much less addressed.

It is interesting to note that in the current struggle, the more the mainstream position—that is, humanism and (post)structuralism and its variants—is revealed to be inadequate for dealing with the economic and political issues involved in education, the more its proponents retreat into either the pursuit of "pleasure" (as the mark of the autonomy of the human imagination) or the search for "moral priorities" (as an indication of the timelessness of human values). To defenders of the educational, institutional, and political status quo, pleasure and ethics/morality have come to represent the final grounds of the meaning of the signs of culture and the basis for (new) subjectivities–the definition of "reality." This is clear not only in the many published and broadcast commentaries,[1] but also–and more alarmingly–in the way these values are being institutionalized in literary and cultural studies curriculums in various U.S. universities today. One way to sort out the proliferating ad hoc comments on the question of how students should make sense of reality–and for what reasons–is to look more carefully at the underlying presuppositions that inform not just the current "debates" but also the existing institutional structures, and to investigate more closely the economic and political issues which are at stake.

Today the U.S. university curriculum in literary and cultural studies evolves around three basic theories. The first, the oldest and most familiar, is what might be called the "transcendental curriculum." This curricular mode assumes that the aim of liberal education is to instill in the student moral values beyond the reach of history, politics, and economics, values which are said to be true "forever." As Gertrude Himmelfarb recently put it, in this curriculum "ideas transcend race, gender, and class" because beyond them lies the everlasting domain of "truth, reason, morality, and artistic excellence" (Himmelfarb 1988, A31). In terms of semiotics, this moral curriculum is also the curriculum of "correspondence": the regime of meaning legitimated by it is grounded on the theory of the sign in which the signifier, in a more or less transparent fashion, settles on the signified. In a sense the signifier is a mere repetition and reproduction of the signified, which, as an instance of the plenitude of meaningfulness, precedes it. The "interpretation" of the texts of culture in this curriculum is grounded in the self-evidence of free-standing and transdiscursive meaning (the experiential "signified").

The second major curricular theory also has a long history in Western pedagogy, but is not as familiar to the common reader as the first one, which he "naturally" equates with education itself. This curriculum, which might be called the "textualist curriculum," goes back to the preoccupation of Alexandrian scholars with the reading of texts, but it became especially influential only in the current century, with the rise of the "Russian formalists," and with their influence on the Prague structuralists, the U.S. New Critics, and the French (post)structuralists. In this program, the "text" is understood to be not so much a site of signs or the locus of signifying activities, but the very logic of those activities: in the language initially made popular by the OPOYAZ (the acronym for an organization that was part of the Russian Formalist Movement of the early twentieth century), this logic is called *literaturnost,* a term that was later turned into a deconstructive theoretical category, the "literary," by Paul de Man and others. In the textualist curriculum, the "textual"/the "literary" is, for the educated person, the exemplary means of resistance to bourgeois pragmatism and utilitarianism. The class bias of such an understanding of pedagogy as the articulation of the textual/the literary is clear in the conservative writings of Shklovsky, Eichenbaum, Tomasjevsky, Tynyanov and other members of the OPOYAZ and their mediator to the West–Roman Jakobson; the class politics of "literariness" becomes even more pronounced in the texts of Derrida, de Man, Barbara Johnson, Lacan, Gregory Ulmer, Judith Butler, and David Halperin. The literary is the name of that Kantian structure of understanding that resists the connection of the signifier to the signified, the normative and the theoretical, in a rebellion against the social and the public (as they are defined in opposition to the "private"). This resistance to the social and the public (made intelligible as the boring, dull, and work-a-day life of the bourgeois) takes the form of a rebellion against the signified itself. The more the facing of the signified is delayed, the greater the space in which the imagination of the educated can roam, and invent what Barthes calls "fantasy" (*A Barthes Reader* 1982, 477) and Lacan calls "desire" (Lacan, *Ecrits* 1977, 292–325).

The "pleasure" of this resistance is eventually reified in the textualist curriculum by its "radical" proposal that there is no such thing as the "signified," only floating signifiers (Derrida, *Of Grammatology* 1976, 6–93). The space between the signifier and the signified, in other words, is unbridgable and the two are in an eternal fissure and rift. This, as we shall see, becomes the basis of what the textualist curriculum posits as "the political," that is to say, an intervention in the easy trafficking of meaning in culture. De

Man, the most power-*full* pedagogue of this textualist curriculum and its most conservative theorist of the idea of politics as rhetoric, in fact deconstructs all the marks of materialist politics in his essay, "Resistance to Theory" (1986). There he proposes the "literary" as the mark of the impossibility of the connection between language and the social and then goes on to state: "What we call ideology is precisely the confusion of linguistic with natural reality, of reference with phenomenalism. It follows that, more than any other mode of inquiry, including *economics,* the linguistics of literariness is a powerful and indispensable tool in the unmasking of ideological *aberrations,* as well as a *determining factor* in accounting for their occurrence" (de Man 1986, 11, emphasis added).

The theory of the sign that underwrites the textualist curriculum is then in ostensible opposition to the curriculum of transcendence. Here the signifier not only does not "correspond" to the signified, but, in its constant permutations, denies that there is such a thing as the signified. The signified in this regime of meaning is merely a temporary illusion produced by the signifier in its ongoing transfiguration from one signifier to another.

In the textualist curriculum, reading is taught not so much to instill overtly moral values as to make the student sensitive to what Roland Barthes has called "the pleasure of the text." Although this now famous phrase has the ring of novelty that makes reading for pleasure seem like a recent invention of (post)structuralism, the notion actually has a very long history in pedagogy, going all the way back to the transcendentalist moralism of Horace, who insisted that reading should *delight* and instruct. With Horace as their shared archetext, it is therefore not surprising that both the traditional humanists and the new deconstructionists are in total agreement when they talk about the necessity of the pleasure of the text in the curriculum. Thus when Arthur Gold defends the traditionalist view of reading as an act of pleasure (Gold 1988, A19) or Noel Perrin advocates the expansion of the pleasureable in the canon (Perrin 1988, A44), they do little more than agree with the defense of "the joy of reading" put forth by one of the United States's leading deconstructionists, J. Hillis Miller, in his book *Theory Now and Then* (1991).

For Miller the joy of reading is the possibility of transcending the political – transcending the discussions of class, race, gender, sexuality, which Himmelfarb regards to be obstacles to grasping "artistic excellence." In the discourses of such critics as these, the term "artistic" is to be understood as the unique space for the "excentric" experience of the individual – a space that is "private" and thus free from the social. Miller, in a voice undistinguishable from those of such humanists as Gold, Abrams, and others, writes: "For me the joy of reading . . . is something like Wordsworth's sudden joy: surprising, unpredictable both in nature and in its possible effects, a break in time, in that sense anarchic, a dissolution of preexisting orders, the opening of a sense of freedom that is like a new earth and a new heaven, an influx of power" (*Theory Now and Then* 1991, 296). The influx of power that Miller experiences as a result of "reading" is exactly the ideological effect that bourgeois cultural studies and the humanities aim at producing in the subject of (post)modern labor. The alienation (powerlessness) that is produced in the practices of capitalism – through the extraction of surplus labor – are covered up by the power-fullness that the subject experiences in the "privacy" of self-contemplation and anarchic freedom. The oppressive "order" of the workplace is compensated for by the "anarchy" (the surprise-full orderlessness) of "reading." "Reading" as the experience of the joy of powerfulness is, of course, in late capitalism itself an (upper) middle class pleasure power. For the working class, popular culture (especially popular music) does what "reading" does for the (upper) middle classes. This incidentally is one reason why "rock" music has become such a central subject in contemporary cultural studies and why such publications as *South Atlantic Quarterly* publish special issues on the topic. "Rock" is the site in which the process of the imaginary disalienation of the subject of (post)modern labor takes place. Bourgeois apologists in cultural studies such as Constance Penley, John Fiske, and Lawrence Grossberg "defend" rock and the popular in general because they believe that, through the unfettered pleasures it offers, the popular mounts a "resistance" to capitalism. This "resistance," however, is already allowed for in the capital and wage-labor regime, it is, like other modes of bourgeois resistance such as "realism," a form of immanent critique of capitalism and is therefore a reformist but quietistic collaboration. The program of "reading" (or "listening" as "textuality") proposed by Miller and other pleasuralists, of course, bypasses socioeconomics; in contemporary literary and cultural studies socioeconomics is treated as a mere inconvenience of life that one puts up with so that one can, whenever possible, get to the *real* freedom and joy of reading/listening. The purpose of radical pedagogy is, of course, not to allow "reading" ("listening" to music, "seeing" films) to become such a recuperative practice. (It is of course significant that the mainstream pedagogy of pleasure no longer allows for "listening" or "seeing," but absorbs these into the archeproject of "reading"–see Morton, "Renarrating the (Post)Modern.") Radical pedagogy works to deploy reading as a device for developing class consciousness. The goal of radical pedagogy in the project of reading (or more precisely the goal of the project of "critique") is to enable the subject of pedagogy to realize–in a total fashion through a global theory–the connections between labor and leisure, the powerlessness in the workplace and the powerfulness in the private zones of bourgeois life, and to further ask herself how free this private freedom is and how and at what cost it is achieved. In short, the goal is to understand the relationship between the order of the capitalist production system and the anarchy of bourgeois freedom.

Yet the pleasures of reading, which both the humanist and the textualist curriculums propound, are neither as private nor as purely aesthetic and ethical as we are asked to believe. Behind these pedagogies lie unstated assumptions that need to be investigated. The dominant pedagogy is the pedagogy of pleasure, the pleasure of surprise, "surprise" being the most clear evidence of the impossibility of "determination" and "necessity"–a mark, in other words, of uncontainable contingency. It offers the pleasure of shattering the solemnities of bourgeois life by indicating that what appears to be that life's solid and stabilizing foundation is in fact shaky– only the effect of textuality. (We want to point out that as used in [post]structuralist and [post]modernist discourses, the term "bourgeois" is a purely cultural category and has nothing to do with the position of the producer in the regime of wage labor and capital. It is, in other words, a space in cultural politics and not a relation of classes under capitalism.) Since textuality itself is understood as a moment of "excess"—the slippage of language (*différance*)—(post)structuralism sees all ideas as unfun moments of conceptualization (solemnities). Truth, therefore, in this regime of knowing is nothing more than the illusions and mirages of interpretation. This pedagogy represents its subversion of bourgeois solemnities as a form of pleasure, the pleasure of resistance to predetermined "meaning" through the displacement of the sign and the discovery of the drift of meaning. In predictable bourgeois fashion, (post)structuralism justifies (gives a "utilitarian" teleology to) the pursuit of pleasure as ethical, that is to say, as the indication of "individual freedom" as the pleasure the spirit takes in its own unboundedness. This theory of pleasure as freedom, however, is itself determined by the historical circumstances under which it developed: it arose from the efforts of those French right-wing intellectuals of the 1970s known as the New Philosophers (people like André Glucksmann and Bernard-Henri Lévi) for whom "pleasure" was at the heart of an agenda of human rights and ethical priorities.[2]

In order to show their political right mindedness, (post)structuralists have worked hard to associate the solemnities of truth with masculinity, and in fact such (post)structuralist pedagogues as Barthes, Lacan, Felman, Derrida, Cixous, and Jardine have equated pleasure not only with freedom, but also with femininity. However, (post)structuralism's proffered pleasure is finally a very masculinist pleasure of mastery: what is represented as the pleasure of unmastering (the feminine subversion of received truth) is in fact the deep pleasure of mastering a new form of truth, truth as laughter and the truth of positing culture as farce. This easy "dispensing with" of the truth in the textualist curriculum of pleasure guides students away from a confrontation with the boring, unfun realities of exploitation, repression, and oppression in late capitalism and instead offers them a permanent feast of *différance*. (Post)structuralist teaching in fact reinforces existing social arrangements and regards the very idea of commitment to social change as not merely untenable, but ridiculous. Like New Criticism, (post)structuralism places the student in the position of being a consumer of intellectual subtleties, of the "joys" of reversibility, in short, of novelty.[3]

In urging the subjects of reading to celebrate the pleasure of the text, humanist and (post)structuralist pedagogues are actually instructing them to celebrate the virtues of individualism: the "pleasure" of the text, in other words, is that unequalled experience through which the reader reaches new heights of (private) "reality" and thus achieves irreplaceable identity, unique personhood—in short, individuality. In the textualist curriculum, as we have already argued, pleasure is employed as a means for affirming the uniqueness and inviolability of the individual. "Pleasure," the effect of the literary, is resistance to the pieties of the bourgeoisie and its regime of closural reading (which is nonenjoyable, since in it the distance between the signifier and the signified is unexpandable). The privileging of "pleasure" in the traditional/deconstructive literary curriculum is finally a "political" move: by setting the pleasure of the text as the main activity of reading, as both humanist Gold and deconstructionist Miller advocate, this curriculum instructs the subject to regard pleasure as a testimony to his freedom (from the foreordained meanings of the bourgeois) and by virtue of that "freedom" to understand himself as a unique and free individual. The pedagogy of pleasure as a curriculum of freedom is not only reified in the text of high culture but is also extensively circulated by the culture industry, as one of its latest texts, the film *Dead Poets Society* (with Robin Williams) indicates.

Contemporary capitalist society is founded on the idea of the *free* individual who can *freely* participate in the activities of a *free* market. Here is where the underlying "moral" thrust of supposedly amoral deconstructionist pedagogy merges with the more overtly moral instruction of the transcendental curriculum. Deconstruction, in Horace's words, also textually "delights" the student in order to "instruct" her into "freely" complying with the dominant economic laws and rules of the existing world. Neither the old traditionalist nor the new (post)structuralist version of the dominant curriculum is interested in changing the world (see our discussion of Graff's essay, "Teach the Conflicts" in Chapter 1) because both are pedagogies of the dominant class and as such have a vested interest in keeping the world as it is: rather than changing the world, both curriculums "instruct" (by delighting) the student to join the status quo.

Changing the world, however, is the main agenda of the third and least familiar—indeed the suppressed—curriculum in literary and cultural studies, which is distinctly "modern" in the sense that its main theoretical and political assumptions came to be articulated after the French Revolution: this is what might be called the curriculum of the "political economy of knowledge." Here reading is not grounded in "pleasure" or in arriving at eternal moral truths, but is approached as the articulation of the ongoing social struggles over the signs of culture and over the definition of (social) "reality"—over what it is posited that various texts mean at any given historical moment and over what kind of values get legitimated through those meanings. The ultimate outcome of these struggles over meaning—although mediated by the aesthetic—is, of course, not aesthetic as such, but ideological and economic: texts, by means of the meanings attributed to them, make—on the cultural and superstructural level—"natural" and thus "stable," class relations, which are in fact historical products of economic forces and the relations of production. Through such "naturalizations" they legitimate the existing distribution of wealth in society. It is this overtly economic and political reading of literature that offends mainstream practitioners of literary and cultural studies and makes the editors of *Heterodoxy* and commentators like Jonathan Yardley complain that "literary standards" have fallen victim to political "relevance" (Yardley 1988, B12).

In the transcendental curriculum, the signifier of knowledge settles upon a coherent and intelligible knowledge, producing an instant of self-presence and cognitive plenitude. In the textualist program, knowledge is never fully available ("ignorance" in these discourses is the mark of the knowledge of this impossibility) since the signifier of knowledge, in its everlasting drift, cannot be grounded so as to faithfully "represent" knowledge and its object. All that is available by way of knowledge in this mode of literary and cultural studies is a "reading," that is to say, a "fallen" knowledge that is deprived of any unproblematic access to a founding signified. In the curriculum of the political economy of knowledge, in contrast to the two other modes of knowing, the signified is proposed as "corresponding" neither to an already existing and determined signified nor to a transhistorical playfulness of the indeterminable signifier itself. In other words, the political economy of the sign refuses to accept both "reference" (in the transcendental curriculum) and *différance* as reversal and substitution (in the textualist curriculum) as the site of meaning. The meanings of the signs of culture are produced, in this curriculum, through social struggles along the lines of class, gender, race and the state's power to subjugate. Signs are neither eternally predetermined nor panhistorically undecidable: they are rather "decided" or rendered as "undecidable" in the moment of a social conflict. The project of *différance* that shapes the textualist and the transcendental curriculum–as the movement of textuality and the effect of literariness, in the former, and as the outcome of the activities of the self-evident and unique (and thus different) subject, in the latter–is itself retheorized in the political curriculum as the outcome of such social practices as (alienated) labor and its congealment in private property.

We turn now to an exemplary instance of management of the crisis in contemporary knowledge in the U.S. academy. We want to emphasize that our discussion, in the following pages, of Duke University's curricular changes is not a "conventional" one; namely, it is not an immanent critique of the Duke program, nor a reading of the program "in its own terms" aimed at demonstrating how the program is in contradiction with its own assumptions. Such an approach–the only mode of inquiry which is legitimated as substantive and rigorous in the dominant academy–has severe political limitations (thus its privileged status in the academy). Immanent critique is basically an ahistorical and formalist mode of understanding that accepts that which already exists. Instead of raising the questions, "WHY does this practice exist?" and "WHY are these the terms of its operation?," immanent critique focuses instead on analyzing their mechanics and their rhetoric (HOW they exist).

This form of critique thus cuts off the relations of the system's "own terms" from the economic and historical series that have produced those terms. Thus immanent critique makes it impossible to ask questions about the consequences of these terms. Questions about the historicity of the system's "own terms" or their political and economic consequences are rejected as extraneous, in other words, as the effects of a totalizing–and thus "totalitarian"–"outside." This "outside" is exactly where our inquiries into Duke's program lie–as well as into all other curricula of knowledge in the moment of the (post)modern. In short we are not interested in an epistemological inquiry into Duke's curriculum, in taking its "arguments" apart by offering "counterarguments." This form of investigation will eventually reify "logic" and abandon "history" (Zavarzadeh, " 'Argument' and the Politics of Laughter" 1992a, 120–124). We grant arguments their "truth," and then ask: "If this is true, then what? What kind of world will be produced if these truths become the lived realities of the daily lives of student–citizens? What makes the 'truth' of these assumptions historically necessary?"

3 Duke University's massive renovation of its English department is a monumental effort in (post)modern discursive crisis management. In Duke's (new) regime of knowledge the theory of the sign that grounds its proposal for a new way of reading texts of culture (in spite of some local differences) adheres to the notion of "reference"; but, as befits a crisis management strategy, it redefines "reference"–broadly following classic formalist (post)structuralist theories of signification–so that it becomes more an effect of the processes of signification than of a signified pre-existing them. This strategy is reproduced, for example, in Stanley Fish's notion that there is no "fact" (that is, "referent," what Derrida calls "the proper") as such; instead facts are the effects of the processes of intelligibility used by the "reader." But this erasure of "reference" does not, in the end, open a space up for political contestation. Rather a new closure is imposed – this time through textuality and desire. "Reference," is reproduced not as a global entity (the mark of commonality), but as a local effect (the sign of heterogeneity). The reader (student) is thus first given the "insight" (by means of the "subversion" of the outdated) that the older notions about meaning production are no longer valid in the (post)modern moment. But then, immediately, the ideological effects of reference – the securing of the hegemonic real – is reproduced by a revised, (post)modern notion that posits reference not in an "outside" (a social space) but in the immanent laws of signification itself and in the symbolic order of desire. It is a "reference" that "refers" to itself: a new moment of plenitude and securing is thus (again) achieved.

The effects of such semiotic maneuvers is that social commonality (part of the theoretical legacy of the Enlightenment) is erased: the commonality of the social (following the ludic post-Marxism of Laclau, Hirst, Mouffe, Aronowitz) is broken up into a series of incommensurate special interests such as the environment, the feminist, the queer.

In other words, citizenship as collectivity is turned into citizenship as an eclectic (Mouffe and Laclauian) "hegemony" – the social as the regime of heterogeneity. As Zavarzadeh has argued (in *Pun[k]deconstruction and the [Post]Modern Political Imaginary* 1993), what is contested in the theory of reference (or any other theory, for that matter) is not a purely cognitive matter to be resolved through finding the epistemologically "true" solution. Theory is in fact, as Althusser has stated, the site of class struggle in philosophy. The theory of language that underlies Duke's (renovated) curriculum in literary studies is a conservative political theory that aims at fracturing the social collectivity in the name of the contingent, the ex-centric, and the nonrepresentable. It is to the actual daily political effects of such linguistic and logical maneuvers by Fish, Smith, and others that Terry Eagleton refers when he says: "we begin with a proper dismissal of disinterestedness, a suspicion of objectivity and an apparently hard-nosed insistence on the realities of incessant conflict, and we end up playing obediently into the hands of Henry Kissinger" (quoted in Begley 1992, 52).

The Duke program's ahistorical relativism is "strongly" theorized and legitimated in the theory of "value" propounded in Barbara Herrnstein Smith's *Contingencies of Value: Alternative Perspectives for Critical Theory* (1988), in which a modified form of relativism is employed in order to (1) jettison the now historically irrelevant theories of value of the transcendental curriculum and (2) at the same time prevent values from being understood as the effects of social classes. In other words, Smith provides a "theory" of the norm that is appropriate for advanced capitalist democracies in which the illusion of the freedom and the sovereignty of the self is a founding principle. Smith's maneuver is to deconstruct the traditional, modernist idea of "value" as an absolute ground, but at the same time to reproduce a (post)modern notion of norm that does not allow norms to be seen in terms other than ethical. The politics of norms – the fact that norms are superstructural legitimations of labor relations under capitalism – is thus obscured. What we get from Smith is therefore a ludic normativity.

On the level of daily practices, it is politically significant that Smith, who seems to think of her book as "radical" (as a text that fractures the dominant academy's practices), is herself a steadfast defender of the values of the dominant academy. After David Brooks's article, "From Western Lit to Western as Lit," appeared in the *Wall Street Journal* (1988), Smith took it upon herself to clarify the misconceptions about Duke. Another value crafter, Frank Kermode described her reply, "She explained . . . that . . . her colleagues were not 'trashing' the classics. They were teaching people to read literature . . . thus enabling them to grow familiar with American culture and Western thought and even, she went so far as to add, with 'eternal truths' " (Kermode 1989, 38). In her clarification, which is anything but "radical," Smith suggested that "there had been no real changes in purpose, only in means" in the Duke program (Kermode 1989, 39).

Jane Tompkins's contribution to "relativism" at Duke is of a more practical nature. She renovates the canon, replacing Melville with Louis L'Amour (*West of Everything: The Inner Life of Westerns*). Here the idea of the canon – the universal "law and order" in the curriculum – is preserved but in a form that is open, democratic, participatory, pluralistic (relative), and expandable. In other words, the canon is rearticulated so as to produce the illusion that it is nonexclusionary, a form of canon more appropriate for large capitalist democracies that have almost completely substituted consensus for coercion, hegemony for force, and which have installed institutions that produce the same outcome as force and coercion by pluralistic "consensus," that is, as an effect of *invisible* violence. When Tompkins announces that instead of reading Melville, she now reads Louis L'Amour's novels (in Heller 1987, 13), one would like to draw attention to the fact that in this celebration of the popular, the assumption seems to be that the mere replacement of Melville with Louis L'Amour involves a revolutionary breaking up of the canon. That the popular, by its promise of unbounded "pleasure," is in fact the most effective strategy for the interpellation of the subject compatible with capitalism does not seem to bother the proponents of the new canon. Melville, in other words, is no longer "pleasurable," that is, does not reward the compliant subject. Louis L'Amour, by contrast, does. Yet what we are witnessing is not the displacement of the canon, but only the formation of a new one, which, like the old, has its own rules and regulations and dominant hierarchies. These new hierarchies may seem "upside down" to traditonally trained "scholars" turned "theorists,"—that is, to those persons *The New York Times Magazine* refers to as that "heretical brigade of academics who [are] fed up with hierarchies of literary value" (Atlas 1988, 26)— but they are hierarchies nonetheless. In this new regime, the discourses of Deleuze, Guattari, and Foucault are marshaled to focus attention on the merely local aspects of the upside down canon (making it appear nonhierarchical), distracting attention from its persistent global hierarchical logic. Responding to the desires of consumers of texts, Annabel Patterson insists that she is engaged in the production of the "new" for the new program by proposing that her reading of Shakespeare's *King Lear* as "an economic critique of seventeenth-century England" is "heretical" (quoted in Heller 1987, 13)—that is to say, dangerously transgressive and thus worthy of the attention of novelty-seeking readers/consumers. Not at all clear, however, are the political, pedagogical, and theoretical *consequences* of such a reading or why it should have any serious claim on our attention. By presenting her views as "heretical," Patterson has in mind responses from people, like Frank Kermode, who "criticize" the Duke program from a right-wing point of view and find her reading of Shakespeare "ideological." However, by such a (mis)addressing of her practices, Patterson tries to postpone the recognition that her work conforms quite conventionally to the (post)modern codes of reading Shakespeare, codes which are developed at various levels in such books as Susan Wells's *The Dialectics of Representation,* Malcolm Evans's *Signifying Nothing: Truth Contents in Shakespeare's Texts,* Terence Hawkes's *That Shakespearean Rag,* and many, many more.

The Duke program's attempt at conservation by renewal, aimed at producing radicalness without radicality, norms without normativity, reference without referentiality, an ethics of ambiguity and heterogeneous vacillation – in other words, this systematic erasure of systematicity – is nowhere more clear than in Frank Lentricchia's illuminating statement: "I am too American to be a Marxist" (quoted in Atlas 1988, 27), the two categories being, according to him, mutually exclusive. Of course, the "American" in Lentricchia's phrase is the allegory of the heterogeneous – the nonsystematic permutation of the self and the joyful surprise that it produces. Marxism, by contrast, is for him the totalitarian totalization that places an end to these playful and joyous permutations of nonrepresentable surprises. With this phrase, Lentricchia tries to block the critique of his pleasuralist pedagogy. What he does instead, of course, is – at one blow – erase the history of Marxism in the United States and obscure the plight of the country's oppressed groups by effectively equating "American" with "bourgeois" and by insisting that liberal politics – and liberal politics is underwritten, as we have argued, by the "new" (post)structuralist *différance* – is the only kind that is viable in the late twentieth-century United States: all more radical forms of politics are "beyond the pale." In the struggle over representations in the (post)modern moment, the effect of Lentricchia's remark (which though ostensibly a remark about "himself," is actually aimed at setting discursive/representational/political limits in culture) is to deny the viability in the contemporary United States of powerful Marxist concepts such as "history," "totality," "class," and "the material."

The themes of surprise, joy, and detotalizing "vision" that underlie Lentricchia's statement here are opened up and developed in a set of his more recent essays, "En Route to Retreat: Making It to Mepkin Abbey" (1992a), and "My Kinsman, T. S. Eliot" (1992b). These texts, each with a somewhat different emphasis, reveal the same notable turn towards mysticism – this time in an "American" intellectual – that we have already observed in European intellectuals (such as Derrida, Kristeva, and the *Tel Quel* group) faced with similar political dilemmas (see Chapter 2). While they appear at first glance to be straightforwardly "traditionalist," an unmistakably ludic aura pervades these texts: "the point of Mepkin Abbey," Lentricchia remarks, "is that there is no story adequate to what occurred during those three days in late April of 1991" (1992a, 70). Mepkin Abbey, then, is posited as a good ("ludic") space in which stories are de-story-fied and narratives de-narrative-ized, but (we contend) narrative nevertheless persists there. The visit to the abbey turns out to be a political allegory of the path by which the one-time "Marxist" has entered (like some other intellectuals in the Reagan–Bush years) the space of "post-Marxism" by confirming – in the merely commonsensical belles-tristic mode of a late (in fact, too late) twentieth-century man of letters – the post-Marxist high priest Laclau's notion of the impossibility of society. "Retreat" is ostensibly an apolitical and purely "aesthetic" story (punctuated by Wordsworthian "spots of time" updated with ludic assumptions and references to contemporary popular culture icons such as Robert de Niro and given a conventional "spiritual" relevance through the intertexts of Robert Merton's parallel journey) by "an ex-Catholic" and "half-assed ascetic" (1992a, 68) who is ineluctably and mysteriously "drawn" to visit a monastery. In fact the text is an inquiry into and rejection of – following Lyotardian ludic injunctions – the "master narrative" of "two worlds" (what exists and what ought to be). While couched predominantly in religious terms, the two-world theory is given a political twist. In Lentricchia's dominant religio-aesthetic framework, the story traces the movement between two modes of society: the "ordinary" active society of everyday life and the "extraordinary" contemplative society of the monastic order. There is, however, a submerged political story (a version of Lentricchia's narrative of the incompatibility of "American" and "Marxist") inscribed in the seemingly "minor" details of the history of Mepkin Abbey: its founding through the patronage of those "true" ("major") "Americans" Henry and Clare Booth Luce (the one "a major force in the Republican Party," the other "a major American convert to Catholicism," 1992a, 71) and Henry's death-bed declaration that "a Trappist monastery" is "the only place in the world . . . where communism works" (1992a, 71). Here the secular–religious binary is transmuted into the choice between capitalism and communism. Represented mainly as a "test" of Lentricchia's "religious vocation" (a vocation he in the end declines), "retreat" is finally an exercise in nostalgia, an allegory of the death of ("retreat" from) social (though not philosophical) idealism ("I cannot imagine what the secular world would have to become . . . ," 1992a, 78). Lentricchia's story, in a completely commonsensical manner, posits social idealism (Marxism) as requiring an "asceticism" too rigorous for a full-blooded "American," expecially one caught up (never mind Wordsworth!) in the rapturous enjoyments of the sensuously performative space of ludic (post)modernity. These pleasures Lentricchia pursues in the second text, set in part in New York's Little Italy, where Lentricchia hoped he'd "meet again what I thought I had found at Mepkin Abbey" (1992b, 5).

In "My Kinsman, T. S. Eliot," Lentricchia continues the search for transcendence by recasting the two-world narrative of "Retreat" (transcending the world as it exists by moving to an alternative one) as a "two-self" narrative, involving a more frankly secular "individual" with a second spiritual "self" rather than a "society"-centered narrative in which the social individual transcends society (citing Eliot's remark in "Tradition and the Individual Talent": "What happens is a continual surrender of himself as he is at the moment to something which is more valuable," 1992b, 5). Solicited to write a "brief intellectual autobiography" (1992b, 1), Lentricchia aspires instead to produce a ludic "self-reflection with the desire not to have a self to reflect upon" (1992b, 1). Here the (post)-

modern cliché of the "death of the subject," a notion which might have enabled a shift from the individual to the collective, is articulated as mystical "self-transcendence" (a shift from the "self" to a ludic ineffable, indefinable, and unconceptualizable "not-self"). New York City (a "foreign" site to which Duke University apparently sends its students, the way other universities send students "abroad," and to which Lentricchia has gone for the fall semester of 1991 as faculty "sponsor") becomes in this story the exemplary scene of "othering" or "splitting" the self. The "splitting" of the self, understood not politically as a historically produced marker of exploitative/privileging structures against which opposition might be mobilized, proceeds in predictable pleasuralist ludic fashion: The particular "scene" which is momentarily taken as the "focus" of experience (Angelo's restaurant, for instance) is first "textualized" so that it can be "read"; then the Barthesian mode of reading for the "pleasure of the text" is inaugurated. This results in the "splitting" of the subject in the sense that the supposedly "unified" and "coherent" self "experiences" the irruption of previously unacknowledged (unconscious) libido-charged elements of its own imaginary. These elements arise in a supposedly "spontaneous" "response" to the unexpected and unanticipatable "meanings" suddenly encountered. The result is a text that, by combining the "high traditionalism" of T. S. Eliot and the "high theoreticism" of Jacques Derrida with the "popular" appeal of "Ripley's Believe-It-Or-Not" and "Star Trek," titillates bourgeois sensibilities with representations of "surprising" encounters with "other others"—for instance, with such ethnic and gender "impossibilities" as a "Chinese Calabrian" and a "man" with a "major [male] body" (1992b 8) who is transmuted (via the alchemy of "imagination") into a "woman" (1992b, 7). The fact that under Lentricchia's voyeuristic gaze (so keenly attuned to the dominant—to a "major" Republican, to a "major" Catholic convert, to a "major" male body, . . .) there hangs about the "other others" a hint of the side show freak indicates that the "liberation" he purportedly experiences is still only a liberation for "self" number one.

The strongest mark of the "success" of the curricular trouble shooting undertaken at Duke is another remark by Lentricchia that further clarifies his political position: in answer to anxious inquiries from those who suspect that in any radical upheaval there will be a great deal of "bloodshed," Lentricchia proudly announces that in the hallways of his department, where presumably a revolution in English studies is taking place, there "ain't any [bloodshed]" (quoted in Heller 1987, 12). This painless revolution requires some explanation, because, we believe, there are no bloodless revolutions, only bloodless *coups d'état*.

If there is no bloodshed at Duke University, it is because–in spite of its claims to the contrary–what the new team hired to "change" things at Duke is trying to do, as Smith's "clarifications" demonstrate, is not at all different from what the old team has been doing all along. What is presented as a bloodless revolution is in fact a bloodless *coup d'état* conducted by the administration of a bourgeois university that has realized that its capital invest-ments in the humanities (as a set of socially stabilizing practices) will just go down the drain unless a heavy reinvestment in "blue chip stocks" is immediately made: thus the hiring of luminaries in the profession. Duke is only one of the many private universi-ties in the United States that at this moment, in a mode of aca-demic panic, are attempting to appropriate recent literary theories in order to update their practices without radically questioning them. The old practices, as we have already suggested in Chapter 6, are no longer productive for the reinscription and recruitment of the subject of labor needed by late capitalism. Because the sole purpose of the bourgeois academy is the interpellation of such sub-jects, its failure in this undertaking would mean quite simply the loss of its usefulness and the loss of jobs for its administrators and faculty. The updating of practices now going on is part of routine procedures performed by technocrats and professionals of ideolo-gy who must constantly stay on top of current technologies–or, as Lee Patterson of Duke puts it, "new methodologies" (Heller 1987, 13)–in order to satisfy their social mission, the production of subjects compatible with the ruling relations of production. What the faculty and administrators at Duke are doing is what all good capitalists do: they constantly renovate the means of production.

At such (expensive) private universities as Carnegie-Mellon, Stanford, and Duke, where the prestige and reputation of the school is based on its professional programs (in computer sciences, medicine, law, . . .), there is an urgent need to keep these programs closely associated with the humanities so that they can be represented as being more than mere "career" training. Stanley Fish is, of course, quite aware of the role of cultural studies and contemporary theory in the constitution of the (post)modern labor force. He is also concerned that English departments may no longer be able to do a good job at this hailing of the subject of labor. In fact it is believed that Fish himself "would like to switch horses, to have his tenure at the Law School [at Duke] and his secondary affiliation with the English Department" (Begley 1992, 52). This pedagogical desire is, of course, politically quite significant and points to the shifts in the pedagogical center of gravity in the knowledge industries of late capitalism. It is the sciences and professions that now provide the crucial (post)modern subjectivities of the labor force, not the "literature" departments (which used to do the job in the earlier, simpler days of capitalism). The attention paid to literary theory and the new curricular patterns at these universities (and to a growing degree in their professional programs) is, in other words, in the last analysis a means of providing (post)modern subjects with the appropriate affective make up. By this we mean (as we indicated in Chapter 6) that cultural studies at Duke and other universities is an ideological apparatus through which the subject of labor is taught what to take seriously and what to ridicule, what to regard as intelligible and what to dismiss as nonsense, that is, how to conduct oneself in the world in a manner appropriate to one's "class." We wish to repeat here that class is never taken as an economic category in these pedagogies (not as the place of the subject in productive relations) but as a marker of "taste" and an indicator of "life style." This obscuring of "class" in the categories of "taste" and "lifestyle," and the confusion of class with "profession" is one of the ways in which the dominant cultural studies hails the subject in advanced industrial democracies. Places like Duke University—in late capitalist economy they have the social and cultural role of providing the emerging bourgeoisie with a sense of class cohesion through the strategic use of the humanities—have realized that the social cohesion needed to maintain existing class relations is no longer achievable within the available traditional humanistic concepts. The teachings of Arnold, Leavis, and Trilling are no longer capable of reading the complex texts of (post)modern culture or of making "complex" sense of the classic text that can produce the desirable ideological effects usable in constructing the (post)modern subject. In other words, liberal ideology has failed the pedagogues of late capitalism: a reading of the texts of culture based on their theories can no longer endow the bourgeoisie with the consciousness skills necessary to produce the coherence of social classes. Thus, the recuperation of the views of Derrida, Cixous, Foucault, Lacan, Deleuze, and "Marx" in organizing subjectivities in the ludic (post)modern moment.

Derridean *différance,* for example, which in terms of various interpretations is articulated as the difference of ethnicity, gender, queerness, Westernness, . . . is the informing principle of "identity" of the new curricular practices at Duke ("Intellectually, the department emerging at Duke defines itself more in terms of what it isn't than in terms of what it is," Heller 1987, 13), is now deployed to update and "make new"—and thus respectable—the most oppressive form of bourgeois liberal pluralism which was at the core of the Arnoldian tradition. (Pluralism is the political strategy of bourgeois democracy through which the operation of relations of exploitation are concealed by positing power as equally locatable in plural regional sites and by positing these diverse sites as merely "different" from one another rather than as in conflict—organized equally–horizontally, rather than hierarchically–vertically.) In its deployment of *différance* as variousness (the "variousness" that Lentricchia celebrates in his "Retreat" as the experience of the unexplainable intrusions of the transcendental into the routine of bourgeois life), the new curriculum produces an ex-centric self for the bourgeois subject and thereby produces and maintains the unique subjectivities required by the dominant relations of production. In "My Kinsman, T. S. Eliot," Lentricchia narrates the mysterious morphologies of this subject, morphologies that can only be hinted at and at best *described* immanently but never *explained*. According to him, the closest that one ever gets to *explaining* the morphologies of the ludic subject is in experiences of the whispers and elusive gestures in the dim corners of a restaurant in Little Italy, where the imposed codes of gender, ethnicity, and class evaporate and in their wake produce a transsocial zone of intimacy and disalienation, a zone in which the "authentic" self emerges. Such nontotalizable and transsocial subjectivities, which are "centered" in the idea of the free and initiating individual (who, like the new Duke program, is *not* what others *are*) and which are so essential to the practices of the professional programs at these universities, are then further strengthened by concepts derived from the "New Historicism" in the new humanities so privileged at Duke (Heller 1987, 13). This new historicism has its ideological roots in a rereading of Foucault's molecular politics and the theory of power as decentered and dispersed in all sites of the social, a politics and a theory that, by emphasizing "the particular," manages effectively to undermine a global analytics of the logic of the underlying relations of exploitation in capitalism. Furthermore, the "New Historicism," by substituting for the concept of exploitation the Foucauldian concept of "power" as a dispersed and nonrepressive (in fact enabling) element, has collapsed the "difference" between the powerful and the powerless, the ruling class and the ruled. In a Foucauldian social analytics – the kind underlying the practices at Duke and celebrated in Lentricchia's *After the New Criticism* (1980) – the powerful are indistinguishable from the powerless since "power" in fact produces "resistance" in the powerless and makes them as powerful as anyone else.

The political effect of such a view of power is then to blur the lines between the powerful (the exploiting ruling class) and the powerless (the exploited proletariat) and through the notion of "resistance" (as the agency of the singular subject) eliminate social collectivity and, consequently, defuse class conflicts and erase class struggle as the only force for social transformation. This form of experiential and nonsystematic "resistance" (which is, by the way, the kind of "resistance" that John Fiske, Lawrence Grossberg, and Constance Penley attribute to popular culture and by doing so eliminate the space of critique and radical transformative politics and practices), however, is already provided for by existing networks of power. In the Foucauldian formula, power begets counterpower (resistance) and as such it actually enables the powerless. The important point in this pedagogy is that power itself produces resistance, which means there is no way out. The "New Historicist" theory of the social announces the end of the (Enlightenment) project of emancipation and transformation. Fish explains this idea of the social in the following aphorism: "The maintenance of the status quo is always and simultaneously its alteration" (quoted in Begley 1992, 52). In the last analysis, the "new" Duke pedagogy is the pedagogy of submission: the subject of labor is taught that the only way for her to be is to accept the existence and inevitability of the existing system and attempt to work within it—locally, experientially, and by rejecting any global theory that produces the social as a totality. The educated person, in the Duke pedagogy, is one with a subtle and nuanced mind, a sophisticated person whose project in life is captured in the injunction to "only de-totalize!"

The most effective way of obscuring class struggle as the force of history and thus of occluding the economics/politics/knowledge nexus is to articulate, as at Duke, the new curriculum according to this new menu of (post)structuralist pluralism. The new pluralism is inscribed in the new curriculum through what at Duke, as elsewhere, is called interdisciplinarity (Heller 1987, 13). Almost all the members of the new Duke "team" seem to be innocently self-congratulatory about the breakthrough their interdisciplinarity has achieved in the curriculum, evidently unaware that what seems like a curricular breakthrough to them is in fact nothing more than political collaborationism. The displacement of the curriculum will not take place by means of interdisciplinarity, but only through a politically interested transdisciplinarity.

"Interdisciplinarity," as we have already indicated in Chapter 3, is a version of the "great books" teaching model that is necessary for the expansion of the intellectual horizons of students in professional programs (to produce them as "rounded individuals") and as such it is in fact a mode of "varidisciplinarity": a reinscription of political "pluralism" in the reigning curriculum. Both varidisciplinary and interdisciplinary models (like political pluralism) are modes of eclecticism – forms of acknowledgement: the accumulating of knowledge without having to confront the ideology of the production of knowledge. Transdisciplinarity, by contrast, is aware of the status of knowledge as one of the modes of the ideological construction of reality in any given discipline and thus, through its political self-reflexivity, attempts not simply to accumulate and juxtapose knowledge pluralistically but to ask what constitutes knowledge – why and how and by whose authority certain modes of understanding are certified as knowledge and others as paraknowledge or nonknowledge. Transdisciplinarity is a "*transgressive*" space in which configurations of knowledge are displayed as ultimately the relations of social exploitation. This space is not the quiet "*inter*active" realm where Marx and Freud and Nietzsche and their progeny live in peaceful coexistence. The dominant notion of interdisciplinarity is grounded in the concept of a discipline as a coherent (that is, theoretical) articulation of a subject. In other words, institutionalized interdisciplinarity presupposes a "logical" configuration of a field and then places itself at odds with it. But disciplines are not logical: the discourses of ideology merely represent them as such. Our theory of transdisciplinarity emphasizes rather the institutional arrangements of knowledge in response to labor relations: "discipline," in other words, is historico-political, not merely theoretico-logical.

At the heart of the "interdisciplinary" program at Duke lie the ideas and practices of Stanley Fish, who, as we have already indicated, tellingly links the humanities with the legal profession. Like all "curriculum men," Fish has effective troubleshooting skills: "Colleagues say that his reputation for irascibility does no justice to his administrative skills" (Heller 1987, 14). In addition to his administrative skills, however, Fish's claim to the intellectual leadership of the new Duke team derives from his own interdisciplinary undertaking, "legal and literary studies." Fish's interdisciplinary project, reading law texts in the light of recent literary theory, is itself another instance of political collaborationism. At the present moment in the United States, the pressure on legal texts and on reading them (through a combination of "new methodologies" – but primarily through Derridean deconstruction and its accompanying neopragmatic antifoundationalism) is a last-ditch effort to assign to law texts the status of textual "uncertainty" so that the very question of exploitation in existing social relations will be rendered "shaky." In such readings, "justice" is, in the last instance, nothing more than the slippage of a sign, a (mis)reading, an inherently unstable textual (mis)construct. Justice is indeed unstable, but not because of the slippage of the sign (which in Fish's theory is essentially a formal entity), but rather because it is the site of class struggles. There is no indication that the innovative curriculum at Duke is at all interested in the hiatuses of the texts of culture (not just in their aporia) that come about because of the operations of ideology that attempts to offer an imaginary social unity by concealing the real contradictions of society. Fish's "revolutionary" reading of law texts really provides hermeneutically impressive but socially oppressive ("The maintenance of the status quo is always and simultaneously its alteration," Begley 1992, 52) and reactionary support for the liberal concept of justice. This is why Fish's reading has had immense influence, particularly among law students and professors, who have more to lose if the present system is actually displaced and not merely deconstructed. It is also one of the reasons that the inquiries known as "critical legal studies" have been taken over more and more by the textualist curriculum and the politically radical reading of texts of law is once again being marginalized through the institutional influence of textual revisionists like Fish. The reading of law that Fish produces captures the contours of the subject of the (post)modern labor force that the program at Duke aims at constructing: a subject who knows that "law," like all other practices under capitalism, is an open space for the hermeneutic entrepreneur.

CHAPTER 8

Texts of Limits, the Limits of Texts, and the Containment of Politics in Contemporary Critical Theory

TRANSGRESSIONS: 1

In the 1988 presidential campaign, well-paid crisis managers continually produced limit-setting texts in order to screen from view more serious and disturbing political issues: thus, for example, the debate over Michael Dukakis's furlough program was used to deflect attention from the collapse of the inner cities of the United States. Similarly, at times of stress in the literary studies "field," the academy's professional managers, such as Stanley Fish, go to great lengths to reassure their "worried" public that, after all, "peace and prosperity" reign; there is nothing on the horizon to upset settled expectations, no "October surprise" or "Black Monday" to disrupt the profession's business as usual. The key to such calming maneuvers, directed in Fish's case to members of the MLA through his essay, "Guest Column. No Bias, No Merit: The Case Against Blind

Submission" (published in *PMLA* in 1988), is of course to set the limits of the horizon surveyed in such a way as to occlude the "troublesome," while claiming to open up issues to the full spectrum of "reasonable" views.

Fish's strategies of occlusionism begin by focussing on the nagging but ultimately trivial question of whether submissions for publication should be blind. What renders the point trivial is the philosophical and political nostalgia that produces the basic premise of Fish's text – the sovereignty of the subject as professional – on which Fish's argument, both in the nine-year-old main text and the recently added post text, proceeds: the history of the literary studies field, according to him, is the history of the succession of great and originative minds (the "consciousness[es]" [1988, 746] of Frye, Bowers, Lewis, Hartman . . .), who own as their private property various subfields of study (this is Frye's archetypal criticism, Hartman's Wordsworth . . .) – a regal lineage with its heirs in what Fish admiringly calls today's "most influential and up-to-date voices" (1988, 747). It is this "saving of the subject-of-the-profession" (1988, 747), and the reassurance that such a salvage operation provides to the MLA's largely humanist and theoretically updated neohumanist members, which is the ideological goal of Fish's cautionary text. If he derides those old-fashioned aesthetes who might be tempted to offer to the profession an article "as the report of a communion between the individual critical sensibility and a work or its author" (1988, 739), nevertheless he still insists that an acceptable article must be a communion between one subject of the profession and others, to wit, between its author and other members of the professional community. Thus, in (re)making the case against blind submission, Fish is finally no different from, though perhaps more "up-to-date" than, William Schaefer, who, according to Fish, performed exactly the same task of defending "humanistic values" for a earlier generation (1988, 739). If, however, the subject is taken to be the speaking subject, the subject of discourses, blind submission becomes a less compelling issue because the attention once directed to "individual" persons and their "achievements" is refocused on the discourses circulating in the books, journals, conferences of the professional domain and their ideological inscriptions. The profession will then no longer be conceptualized as a set of property owners, but as a field without a subject, as an ensemble of collective texts.

To be sure, Fish exploits—in the spirit of the alert and energetic professionalism he defends—the (politically) safest elements of contemporary thought; he has, as already indicated, abandoned the most overt and thus embarrassing aspects of the old theory (the recognition of the author as the guarantee of meaning for the text). Futhermore his text is, from beginning to end, a deconstructive dismantling and reinscription of a series of binaries, a recuperation of deconstructive "undecidability" (reunderstood as the inevitable changes in argumentative stances the profession goes through) in the service of liberal pluralism. But he is himself very careful not to go "too far" in the absorption of new ideas and furthermore—from the platform of the *PMLA* "Guest Column," for which his own theory is a leading justification—gives his readers a clear and authoritative definition of the limits of reasonable discourse, beyond which the dangers of extremism (they might contribute to "the possible erosion of the humanistic community" [1988, 739]) lurk. Whereas in the main text, he had set these limits in terms of the opposition between "the timeless realm of literature and the pressures and exigencies of politics" (1988, 747), in the posttext he resets those limits in terms of the opposition between the traditional "aesthetic vision" and New Historicist "Politics" (with the emphatic capital "P"). What, according to Fish, these two positions share and what therefore places them beyond the pale of the acceptable is that they are "extreme" ("pure" is his term [1988, 747]) in seeming to scorn, if for different reasons, the mere careerism that is part and parcel of the literary studies institution. Fish does not seem to see that his cardinal claim in support of the status quo, which is the very heart of liberal humanism—that "in this profession you earn the right to say something because it has not been said by anyone else" (1988, 739)—is utterly belied by the maneuver of declaring *in advance* what is beyond the pale of (acceptable) intelligibility. Such a maneuver effectively blocks any investigation into the significance of significance, that is, into the politics of signifying practices in culture.

The "slippage" in Fish's text by which the New Historicism's supposed commitment to the material (its threat to turn "politics" into "Politics") is both affirmed and denied ("As Donne might have said, small change when we are to [materialist] bodies gone" 1988, 747) reveals an "uncanny" awareness that to find a more credible "materialism" one would have to look beyond the New Historicism, which is to say, beyond the limits permitted by Fish's text itself. It hints at the fact that the "dangerous" limits his text constructs are not really dangerous at all, and that the New Historicism provides no threat (any more than does deconstruction) to the dominant liberal humanism of the contemporary academy. The discourse of professional "erosionism" in Fish's text is a version of that discourse which, on the national political scene, renders the United States as the bastion of the free world, the site of a logocentric sameness, whose only unhappy fate could be its wearing away as a result of the misguided acts of the "faithless." The theory of disciplinary conventions that Fish's work articulates is a justification for keeping the present professional game going, with gradual "evolutionary" changes over time, not an inquiry into the status of the game itself. This theory of conventions is thus as "transcendental" as either the aestheticism or the New Historicism he rejects: it is in fact a theology of games, updated (of course) by being silently underwritten by the (post)structuralist notion of "play." In Fish's view, the going game is "the only game in town," one has no choice but to play, and indeed one should be grateful that everyone can play ("everyone's Wordsworth is someone's Wordsworth," Fish generously remarks [1988, 741]).

The justification for setting "limits" to the professional game is simply that, in Fish's narrative, as in other conservative narratives, the end of the present game/regime of knowledge can only be seen as the end of history itself. In the scheme of things constructed by careerists, professionals of ideology, academic managers, team players, and power brokers, there may be a place for the fringe (those who don't play very well), but there is certainly no place for an effective oppositional margin, with a vision of how things might be based on an "other" set of premises than those of the dominant regime. This is, for the establishment, unintelligible, a contradiction in terms: as Fish makes quite clear, if "there are some of us who" can take risks (1988, 740), they are only the established people (the C. S. Lewises), those whose professional capital accumulation is great enough to make the risk "bearable"; in other words, there is no risk at all. Thus while urging the members of the MLA to reject, in the name of professional integrity, a trivial "blind submission," Fish at the same time urges on them a seriously damaging one.

Fish's effort at institutional and professional crisis management through occlusionism is no isolated instance, but rather part of a system-wide maneuver aimed, *in the present historical moment,* at containing "dangerous" thought. What Fish was called in (as a "guest") to do for the Modern Language Association, historian Robert Berkhofer, Jr., was called in (at about the same time, October 1988) to do for the American Studies Association, that was, to deliver at that group's annual convention a showcase session address on the state of the American studies "discipline" in the late 1980s. Berkhofer and Fish needed to acknowledge "new" thought but they also had to be sure to do so in a manner that would preserve the status quo.[1] Berkhofer's text, "Poetics and Politics in and of a New American Studies," is "uncertain" and "parodic," qualities that might be taken to signal its "(post)modernity." These features, however, are merely conventions of a more ordinary game, familiar elements of the significatory modality that governs all texts belonging to the knowingly naive "what are we to make of it all?" genre (this is one of Berkhofer's opening formulas; and the emphasis on "all" is underscored by 12 pages with 81 footnotes that accompany the 23-page text of the lecture). The text's uncertainty derives not from the writing subject's resituation in the discourses of (post)modernity, but from the rhetorical maneuver of the "feint," that is, momentarily "giving up control" – admitting the challenges to, if not the inadequacy of, its own ruling categories – in order ultimately to restore control once again and thus to reassure its liberal–humanist audience of the survival of the dominant academy's cherished premises.

To mobilize the discourse of abandonment-to-the-new, Berkhofer deploys both tongue-in-cheek neologisms and *faux*-(post)-

modern interrogatives that become – in his rhetoricization of them – conundrums. More important, however, are Berkhofer's text's own situatedness and the operations of its analytic strategy. It was not for reasons of relative "distance," "objectivity," and "non-implication" that a historian was asked to defend American studies from the intrusions of (post)modern thought, but because, as Berkhofer remarks, "the linguistic turn . . . appears more devastating to historians and social scientists than [to] literary and other humanistic scholars" (1988, 11). For Berkhofer, (post)modernism's "devastating" effects on history appear to be limited to the unsettling of the status of "documents": he does *not* acknowledge that if (post)modern assumptions are more "dangerous" to the discipline of history than to that of literary studies, it is so for the political reason that, as a key empirical discipline in the humanities, history is more crucial than literary studies for legitimating the reigning cultural narratives. Berkhofer's strategy is to renarrate the tale of textuality versus *con-cept-uality* as the story of textuality versus *con-text-uality* by proposing that what all the contending parties and claimants to American studies have in common is a concern for "context" (1988, 2) and that the litmus test for truth in American studies is whether "context" is understood as anything that can possibly be called "historical" at all, a distinction that will determine whether issues are being addressed "politically" or merely "poetically."

As Berkhofer sees it, three conflicting definitions of "context" are at work today in the wake of the "linguistic turn"; but in the definitional phase of his essay, its feigned rhetorical "uncertainty" turns into a conceptual muddle, for the only effective distinction he is able to draw is the traditional one that recognizes "context" (his "context 3" [1988, 3]) as "the extra-textual(ist) world" (1988, 13), that is, what he calls a "(truly) (properly) contextualist" one that reintroduces "history" in its quite familiar guise as relying on the notions of "reference" and "realism." What he identifies as "contexts 1 and 2" are products of that troublesomely "self-referential" and "solipsistic" post-Saussurean understanding of meaning. Here Berkhofer's analysis collapses upon itself when he is unable to distinguish between contexts 1 and 2 except to say that the first is restricted to the single text, while the second is intertextual. All that the resulting tautological discussion finally suggests is that contexts 1 and 2 are mere "textualities" anyway and have no right to be referred to as "contexts" in the first place, a denial that reveals the entire point of the text's various "feint" maneuvers. In the end, Berkhofer's staging of the question of "context" adds up to a revalorization of traditional views, for his account represents as patently impossible a contextualist position that would take history seriously at the same time that it takes (post)modernist textualism seriously.[2] Hence the received idea of "history" is saved—without any sustained inquiry into that notion, as are all disciplines, including American studies—that rely on that "history."

In all texts of the "what are we to make of it all?" genre, after a rather tedious rhetorical journey, readers/auditors find themselves right back at their point of departure, and so it is with Berkhofer's performance, which begins with the (predictive) observation that although "proponents of both poetics and politics seek to constitute the conceptual framework(s) of a new American Studies, . . . they basically . . . deconstruct each other" (1988, 1)—that is, they cancel each other out. He concludes with the (confirming) rhetorical question: "Must all who would mediate between the polar positions remystify as they demystify, reconstruct as they deconstruct, reify as they rematerialize, politicize as they poeticize?" (1988, 23). To carry out this return to the point of departure, Berkhofer begins and ends his discussion with a lengthy quotation from Sacvan Bercovitch that catalogs what Berkhofer sees as the "dangerous" presuppositions of the "new" reading practices (again, as for Fish, represented by the New Historicism) and that for him not only represents the "outer limits" of the political (it demands attention to race/class/ gender . . .) but also emblemizes the hopeless "incompatibilities" he sees in (post)modern discourses.[3] "Surveyor" Berkhofer might easily have read Bercovitch's text as a "survey," but instead constructs it as a dangerous political manifesto, ignoring the fact that its catalog is a rather innocuous mixture of traditionalist and (post)modernist premises (for instance, it introduces the idea that art is "material" while robbing it of its force by claiming that it also "transcends culture").

But Berkhofer's goal here is by no means to think through the contradictions he sees, but to reject any intellectual undertaking based on the (post)modern concept of the "problematic" (as opposed to the traditional concept of the "problem") as being from the start incompatible with anything like "rigor." A mere "problem," after all, can be "solved" (that is, provide the relief of closure on which traditional historical narration rests), whereas a "problematic," Berkhofer laments again and again, just leads to other "problematics." Berkhofer finally reassures his audience that the "new" thought is just a contradictory mishmash that, while answering some questions, only manages (inconveniently) to raise new ones. An audience sympathetic to Berkhofer's ideological goals will not notice how much of this presumed "confusion" is *produced* by Berkhofer's text: when, for example, he grossly distorts (post)modern discourses to suggest that they *deny* that there is such a thing as biology (1988, 7) (that is to say, they deny the existence of an "actual" as well as a culturally produced "real"), or when he charges that they transform "strata or groups into class(es)" and convert "sex into gender and peoples or races into racism" (1988, 7), as if (post)modern discourses do not know that there is "sex" as well as "gender," "peoples" or "races" as well as "racism." Such distortions are exemplary instances of the intellectual and political anxiety in the face of the radical potential of (post)modern thought that produces the "demand" for articles like Fish's and lectures like Berkhofer's. Ultimately, what Berkhofer "found" is what he was expected to find: because things are still so much "up in the air," any serious concern about the new thought can be safely deferred.

Berkhofer's lecture is symptomatic of the recent ideological and programmatic shifts in American studies: classical American studies—which was an attempt at an earlier historical moment to go beyond monodisciplinarity and produce new forms of knowledge and pedagogy—arose after World War II, as the postwar world hegemony, dominated by the United States, developed. In the wake of (post)structuralism, however, when the bankruptcy of the form of this hegemony was revealed, American studies began to attempt to suture new theoretical understandings onto the established, "classical" ones. As in Berkhofer, however, the result has been a form of confused eclecticism that one can see in the curricula of many American studies programs all across the U.S. academy. While Berkhofer struggles to provide a "logic" for this new historical conjuncture, in the end what he offers is nothing more than another justification of the old classical American studies and a clear sign of the very tenuous and uncomfortable truce that prevails today between American studies and (post)modern theory.

TRANSGRESSIONS: 2

In another region of contemporary discourses, the question of the political is being fought without the overt patriarchal heavy handedness of Fish and Berkhofer. Their maneuvers, while somewhat more polite, are not much different from those of a group of conservative "limit-setting" academics who organized themselves recently as the National Association of Scholars, and whose agenda is to combat what they call the "radicalization . . . of American universities." Because of "affirmative action" programs (clearly a threat to the patriarchal state) and the rise of political consciousness in the academy, today's curricula have—according to these academics, who follow the line of William Bennett, Allan Bloom, and E. D. Hirsch—lost their "objectivity" and created what they derisively call "oppression studies" (Berger 1988, A22).

In this discursive arena, where the traditional understanding of rhetoric as persuasion has been replaced by the (post)structuralist understanding of rhetoric as textual (self)-dismantling, questions of historical specificity and the material are also at issue: what is taking place, however, is not so much a battle over constructing "texts of limits" for the sake of holding a buffetted professional structure together (although the effect is pretty much the same), because here the premises of (post)structuralism have unsettled the self-certainty implied by such constructions, all structures—as well as the subjects of them (unlike those of Fish and Berkhofer)—

having already been de-centered. Furthermore, because the scene of this battle is marked with the designation "feminism," it has a nearly automatically "liberatory" and "otherly" valence. In this presumably more thoroughly "undecidable" domain, the question being contested is not what are the "texts of limits" but rather what are the "limits of texts": in other words, whether and at what point should readers of the texts of culture–who accept the premises of (post)structuralism–allow for, permit, or produce an "arrest" of the play of signification? Whereas the Fish/Berkhofer issue is that of saving the subject of the profession, the issue at stake here is the limits of textual play. Symptomatic of this line in current "political" conflict is Jefferson Humphries's essay, "Troping the Body: Literature and Feminism" (1988), an attack on the version of tropics elaborated in the work of Naomi Schor.

Undecidability and the play of signification are inscribed in the very self-representation constructed by Schor's various texts: unlike the "assured" self-representations of Fish and Berkhofer, hers is marked by changes in intellectual approach resulting from the vast shifts in critical theory itself in the past several decades. Fish's argument is a plea to be thought of as a "founding father" of contemporary criticism: Schor's texts testify to her own "unfounding" through an alertness to insights of theory harnessed to serve the interests of feminist politics. It is the political harnessing that, as we shall soon see, so disturbs Humphries.

Before getting to that, however, it is necessary to investigate Schor's various theoretical moves, which her self- reflexive texts both enact and (in their own way) mark.[4] Schor theorizes a mode of reading based on what she calls a "restricted thematics" and "female paranoia," interdependent practices with a "logic" that deserves investigation. While at one point she summarily defines "female paranoia" as the "privileging of odd, eccentric textual details referring to parts of the female body: eroticized wounds, bound limbs, the clitoris" (1987, 7), she nevertheless (being engaged "not so much with the *representation of woman* as with the relationship between *woman and representation*" [1985, x]) presents it not merely as a reading strategy, but more significantly as a theory of theory: that is, as "the female critic's" contestatory intervention "into patriarchal theoretical discourse" (1985, xi). Freud's observation of the connection between theory and the paranoid patient's "delusions" is the basis of Schor's argument that theory, being itself a form of paranoia, is dangerous particularly when extended (totalized, as patriarchal theory "totalizes") and intensified (in its male-associated, "extreme" forms). She reads one of Freud's cases and associated intertexts as posing the question not only of whether there is such a thing as "female paranoia" but such a thing as "female theorizing." By her own practice she answers both questions in the affirmative and distinguishes "female paranoia/theorizing" (in Freud's terms, represented as a " 'jealous paranoia' " which is " 'closer to the normal and the neurotic' ") as "decidedly less systematic and elaborate" than "male paranoia/theorizing," which is – and here she also quotes Freud – a " 'persecutory paranoia' " (indeed " 'a highly organized and masculine psychosis' ") marked by a " 'high power of sublimation' " (1985, 151–152).

Connecting then the hypersystematicity of "male theory" to the drive of structuralism for a universal mode of intelligibility, she argues not only for the liberatory effects of (post)structuralism (in its salutary, if uneasily related feminist and deconstructionist versions) but also for the reemergence of "theme" (as presumably more associated with the particularities of the surface texture of texts than with the totalizing modalities of "deep structures"), and thus for the renewed acceptability of critical "thematics" as a result of the break with the former tyranny. Furthermore, since thematics – in the hands of the wrong kind of readers – can itself be totalizing and oppressive, the new thematics must be a "restricted thematics" (which is like "female paranoia" in being a "restricted paranoia" – a concept for which she finds further support in "practical paranoia-criticismm" embodied by Salvador Dali) [1987, 101]). Although Schor posits this "restriction" in a somewhat simple-sounding formula ("new thematic criticism must not go beyond the framework of the individual novel [poem, drama]" [1985, 28]), she argues that this requirement will introduce a certain "intermittence" (diachrony) into critical practice that will always tend (with or without the sanctions of structuralism) toward a totalizing synchrony. Another way to express her reservation is that, as against "traditional thematics" which pursues across many texts the thread of a single interwoven discourse, "restricted thematics" creates pressures for (in the manner of, say, *S/Z* or *A Lover's Discourse*) a certain "sectioning" of the text in which the "sections" are inspected for their multiple cultural discourses. This is explicitly understood to be an antipatriarchal and antiacademic move by which the reading/writing subject becomes not the subject of just *langue* (merely the subject of a set of academically acceptable disciplinary codes, like linguistics, for instance) but of *langue* and *parole* together (a culturally situated subject of a multiplicity of codes, including for instance, gender).

There is of course nothing in the procedure of restricting thematics that guarantees the investigation of all available discourses of culture, for the project is not aimed at such a guarantee (indeed it finds such interests "suspicious"), because it represents itself not so much as an agenda for finding new power as an agenda for mitigating existing power: for Schor, female theory "seeks to transcend not the sticky feminine world of prosaic details, but rather the deadly asperities of male violence and destruction" (1987, 97). In other words, rather than being itself a cultural force that presses the "claims" of the "feminine," feminine theory counters dangerous male theory by dismantling its "conceptual systems" (1987, 97).

If one observes that even Schor's "feminism" does indeed hold a place in present academic institutions and intellectual structures; in other words, the meanings her theorizing constructs occupy a cultural space that is—as it is situated within (post)structuralism—dominant, if not "imperial," and can only be dominant by virtue of the displacement of another occupant. In this respect at least, it is a form of violence; she anticipates with the reply—drawing on Barthes—that the agenda of her work is to arrive at an "exemption from meaning" (1987, 88), that is, at the "scandal" of the utterly "useless," "inessential," and "meaningless" detail (1987, 85). From this perspective, "female paranoia" becomes not merely a countertheory, but ultimately an antitheory, a space outside the symbolic: whether conceived of as the space of Kristeva's "semiotic" or of Barthes's "exemption from meaning"; it is a space in which, for Schor, as for them, the body plays the obviously crucial role.

In order to extend the previous (post)structuralist argument, theorizing the subject as the speaking subject—to be understood diachronically as well as synchronically, as being in a particular historical and material situation—does not simply *in theory* "open up" to examination the whole array of culture's discourses; it also, according to Barthes, is a move that factors (so to speak) the body into the signifying chain. If the body is not exactly "exempt" from meaning (any more than is Kristeva's semiotic), it tends in the direction of such exemption, an outcome that in Barthes's view would not be bad. In dialogue, he says, "the body . . . flings toward another body . . . messages that are intellectually empty [that is, of meaning], the only function of which is in a way to *hook* the Other (even in a prostitutional sense of the term) and to keep it in its state of partnership" (1985, 5). Whatever else this says, it suggests that at least in some quarters the urgent (post)modern program of dedisciplining the body is bound up with rendering it exempt from meaning, with its theorization as a site of opacity.[5]

With this understanding of Schor's project in mind (that it is a deconstructionist–feminist project which, unable to work outside masculinist theory, is therefore aimed at mitigating its violence, that this mitigation hinges on a general strategy of "restriction"—of paranoia, or a thematics of the body), we can turn to the objections to it registered in the peculiarly anxious text of Jefferson Humphries. That anxiety (he sometimes seems not to be paying attention) appears immediately in the charge that Schor is guilty of "fetishism" (Humphries 1988, 19), an odd charge because, in the preface to the book by Schor he is reviewing, Schor had already "confessed" that fetishism is integral to her entire method (Schor 1987, x). Even more surprising is the procedure adopted by (post)structuralist Humphries (writing, by the way, in one of deconstructionism's staunchest sanctuaries) to define "fetish": he relies on a commonplace dictionary definition of it ("any material object regarded with superstitious or extravagant trust or reverence" [Humphries 1988, 19]), which he does not bother to "deconstruct" or even to problematize. He only extends the definition of "fetish" slightly, to claim that "extravagant" means "unsupported by logic or argument" (1988, 19), a charge which the foregoing discussion not only belies, but which (again odd for a [post]structuralist) depends on a commonsensically unitary notion of both "logic" and "argument." No, it is neither Schor's fetishism nor her supposed lack of argument that worries Humphries, but another part of his definition, the question of "the material" (the same question that worries Fish and Berkhofer), because, in this "exchange" between Humphries and Schor, we are witnessing the "political" trials and tribulations of deconstruction; and in this encounter Humphries plays the role—against Schor—of deconstruction's more "orthodox" defender.

What worries Humphries is that Schor's practice threatens to become "materialist" and form the basis for political intervention by equating genital organs with tropes (for instance, "synecdoche = knob = clitoris = femininity" [Humphries 1988, 19]): in other words, she dares to "arrest" the play of signification for basically political reasons. Thus her move, which "refetishizes" in the sense that it restructures the symbolic clitero-centrically (rather than phallo-centrically), implies a questioning, not of the desirability of deconstructive decentering, but of its axiomatically "political" benefit. Schor's "deliberate fetishization of sexuality," her tendency "not to treat the female body as metaphor . . . " but to "virtually conflate . . . the body as trope with the body as material reality," reproduces—according to Humphries—the "fundamental error" of "Jamesonian marxist criticism," which is "to *intentionally* conflate matter, the real, as trope with literal matter, 'reality' " (Humphries 1988, 21). This is an "error," Humphries says, because "textual 'energy' . . . does not have gender" (1988, 22). As Humphries's analysis goes on to suggest, Schor's and Jameson's "error" results basically from a misunderstanding of reading itself: they believe reading is an act of intervention, of (to use Schor's term) "desublimation." Indeed, Schor follows Barthes in insisting that reading as desublimation will in fact show how sublimation has covered over the materiality of cultural (and in particular, gender) relations (Schor 1987, 184). By contrast, Humphries insists that reading is an act of *sublimation,* in which "we all [emphatically, both men and women] submit to being 'tied up' in the representation of a desire not our own . . . for the duration of the reading" (Humphries 1988, 23). He adds that the "pleasure of reading or writing is a pleasure in sublimation, in deferral to the illusion of an alien(ated) desire which one can only participate in as a spectator" (1988, 24). For Humphries, the trouble with Schor's reading of Stendhal, say, is that the meaning ends up being Schor's, not Stendhal's (Humphries 1988, 23), a conclusion that will not surprise or alarm Schor, or her attentive readers. Furthermore, the latter— who will take seriously the commitment to reading as writing that Schor pursues (after Barthes) will see the triviality of Humphries's understanding of "the material" as "brute matter" (a hopelessly naive reduction of the "real" to the "elemental") rather than as the effectivity and overdetermination of cultural relations. Schor is actually proposing that reading must be more than a matter of what Humphries calls "pleasure" (and what J. Hillis Miller calls "joy" [see Miller, "The Joy of Reading" 1986, 2]).

Humphries's text is ultimately a desperate attempt to deny that texts have limits: in his view, the "body is fake, a trope, and within the text of which it is part, gender difference is merely another trope. Male and female are tropes which may be freely substituted, one for the other. What Schor and Freud [at his worst, according to Humphries] try to accomplish is to contain, 'enchain,' the truly liberating force of the text, its playful insistence on the interchangeability of male and female" (1988, 25). "Literature," Humphries, the orthodox deconstructionist believes, "already contains the antidote to phallocentrism" (1988, 27) and must simply be allowed to "deconstruct the 'fetishization' of gender difference" (1988, 26). Politics, therefore, can safely be left to the operations of textual self-dismantling. In fact in Humphries's hands, deconstruction (represented as theory itself) gets promoted to the status of a kind of political "magic." In another domain of cultural studies (the literature of the South), in which Humphries also works, he repeats the reductive pattern just noted. In his recent essay, "On the Inevitability of Theory in Southern Literary Study"

(1989), he defends his generation of "theoretically informed" southernists against an older generation of tradition-minded southernists by charging that the traditionalists' practices (he brings them into relation with those of the Nazis) are hopelessly "ideological" as compared with "the essentially anti-ideological force of theory" (1989, 182). The rather complacent claim that theory is "anti-ideological"–a proposition that might well be seen as "ideological" itself–certainly requires argument which Humphries doesn't provide. Thus, for Humphries, a "magical" (post)structuralism in the southernist debate will take care of the ideology of race, whereas here in the Schor debate it will supposedly take care of the ideology of gender.

In the last instance, Humphries's charge that Schor is dangerously "materialist" is a trumped up charge meant to screen from view–as do Fish's worries about the New Historicism–a more powerful political materialism; Schor's "materialism" depoliticizes as it politicizes: what Humphries anxiously represents as Schor's activist, "materialist," interventionist theory is an ideological misrecognition of what is ultimately a passive subversionism (apparently justified, like Barthes's own, as the only move possible in today's supposed "impasse of militancy" [Ungar 1983, 129]). It merely substitutes for the ruling automaticity of self-deconstructing texts the automaticity of bodily "pulsions." Ultimately, Humphries's critique of Schor represents the nonpolitical (deconstructionist tropism or rhetoric) challenging the political (clitoral theoretics), while Schor's work itself represents the deployment of the political *against* the political: for although–as Humphries perceives–Schor's texts "threaten" to perform the "awful" transgression of breaching the deconstructionist code by which "woman" and all other cultural phenomena are rhetoriciced, her texts (by isolating one inequality from others) still exempt the body of "woman" from the historical and material specificities of race, class, and so on. Ultimately her project becomes an example of the very "erosionism" that, as we have seen, establishmentarian Fish knows is no threat.

TRANSGRESSIONS: 3

Although deconstruction has done its part, nothing has contributed more to the current tendency to deploy the political *against* the political than the dominant reading of Foucault. Not all Foucauldian presuppositions work equally against the political. Political analysis has certainly been advanced by the denaturalization of cultural phenomena carried by the moves of the abandonment of representation as mimesis, the displacement of the subject, and the discursivity of meaning—to name concepts Foucault shares with others. But political analysis has also been advanced by the archive, the genealogy, the episteme, and countermemory—some concepts that are more closely associated with his name. The difficulty arises with his limiting understanding of specificity, that gets inscribed in the other concepts he deploys in theorizing the domain of culture: in the concept, for example, of "emergence" (culture is thought of as a surface on which phenomena "emerge," island-like) the job of the intellectual is to interpret the "emergence" of cultures without doing so from too "high" (too "totalizing") a level of generalization. In Foucault's view, discursive practices should not be investigated through the appeal to "higher" levels of conceptualization. For example, a decisive difference, according to him, between the initiation of a science and the initiation of a discursive practice (such as psychoanalysis) is that while "in a scientific program, the founding act is on an equal footing with its future transformations" and "is merely one among the many modifications that it makes possible," the initiation of a discursive practice "is heterogeneous to its ulterior transformations" (Foucault 1977, 133). One quite significant political consequence of this kind of distinction is that to expand any discursive practice "is not to presume a formal generality that was not claimed at the outset" but "to explore a number of possible applications" (Foucault 1977, 133). However "noble" the intention to avoid "totalizing" (and the spectre of "totalitarianism," which is thought to lie beside it) through such notions of specificity, the move has other results: it not only encourages, on the philosophical level, an eclecticism that places ideas in a colloidal dispersion and "suspends" their force, but, on the political level, also continues to underwrite a supposedly displaced liberal humanism, the pluralism of which places persons in a colloidal dispersion that "suspends" their oppositionality. It is Foucault's understanding of genealogy, governed by such principles as "emergence," that, as John Rajchman has argued, makes Foucault's a "nominalist history" one committed to "no transformational scheme at all" (Rajchman 1985, 61). Foucauldian specificity has, however, been readily recuperated to reinforce (through a change of vocabulary) the eclectic, pluralist, and applicationist close-reading practices already so firmly entrenched in the academy: it has, in other words, prompted an avalanche of easily managed "transgressions" through which the bourgeois academy can exorcize its guilt—*without cost*—by exercising its nostalgia for something called the political.

A notable instance of such nostalgia is the recent special issue of *diacritics,* "Culture and Countermemory: The American 'Connection,' "(Mohanty, 1987) in which—as a set of "political" essays—race/class/gender and reading practices themselves appear to be investigated "historically" and "materially," through Foucauldian "specifying," but end up being treated in a localized and localizing manner. In this manifestation, "specifying" appears finally to mean only opening up new cultural terrain for established reading practices, not the transformation of those practices. Here, in an issue that "responds" to Berkhofer's call for American studies to relate text and context—that is, to situate interpretive and critical reading in relation to "reality" (the *diacritics* issue gives attention to the "reality" of the Native American, the "reality" of the African-American, the "reality" of Hollywood . . .)—the limit-setting task performed by Berkhofer is performed instead by the conceptual self-limiting through which the *diacritics* issue proceeds. But the conceptualization of "reality" is as indecisive and inconsistent in the *diacritics* issue as it is in Berkhofer's text: at some moments "reality" is mediated by discourses/concepts (frames of intelligibility), while at others it is unmediated "nature." The result is a set of essays marked by a "discriminating" indiscriminateness on a number of levels.

Such indiscriminateness appears in Arnold Krupat's eagerness (in "Criticism and the Canon: Cross-Relations" 1987) to welcome the varieties of "historicism"—including those associated with (post)modern thought—while at the same time calling for "a little more anthropology" (Krupat 1987, 11). This rhetorical move is an early mark of the *diacritics* issue's theoretical inconsistency in ignoring the incompatibility between the discourses of the traditional social sciences and the discourses of the (post)modern human sciences. Krupat makes his political logic clear: he welcomes the return of "historicisms" to *balance* now dominant formalist excesses (such as those of deconstruction). Yet, through his desire for balance rather than contestation, the political dimensions of the question of the "other" (the native American in Krupat's essay) are effectively tamed. An equally basic contradiction is evident in Susan Willis's "*Fantasia*: Walt Disney's Los Angeles Suite" (1987), in which archaeology appears to be located more in the space of inquiries into "material culture" than in the space of (post)modern thought—where the traditional understanding of the value of historical study (the achievement of "critical distance") as necessary for approaching the present (too close, too immediate) is modestly "updated," and where an unexplained privileging of metaphor threatens to bring her "political" investigation quite easily under the control of contemporary rhetorical (deconstructive) studies.

Ranged against these self-contradictory essays in the *diacritic* issue are several texts of greater theoretical coherence that in fact *do* employ primarily (post)structuralist discursive strategies. The least interesting of these seem to take special delight in the possibilities of the strategy of reversal, though the technique is used so predictably and to such little effect as to give the impression of mere cleverness. Both Robert Miklitsch's essay on the canon ("The Poppies of Practical Criticism: 'Rabbi, Read the Phrases of This Difference' " 1987) and S. P. Mohanty and Jonathan Monroe's essay on the poetry of Ashbery ("John Ashbery and the Articulation of the Social" 1987) rely for their "politicality" on the silent grafting of Foucault's notion of reversal (deriving from his insistence on the multidirectionality of power) onto the "philosopheme" of reversal as elaborated by Derrida (understood as a crucial stage in the deconstructive dehierarchization of binaries). This grafting is carried out as a "self-evident" operation with an inevitable "political" benefit. Miklitsch's strategy for resituating Helen Vendler and her canon of American poetry is to give her a reverse reading: Vendler, who in a review established a Hellenic versus Hebraic paradigm for poetry criticism and thinks of herself as a "Hellenic" reader (in deconstructionist terms, a "canny," "Socratic," "Apollonian," "rational" reader), is reunderstood by Miklitsch as a "Hebraic" reader ("uncanny," "irrational," "Dionysian")–she is the "rabbi" Miklitsch addresses in his title. In their own reversal, Mohanty and Monroe systematically (and predictably) "disclose" Ashbery's (post)modernity by arguing that his texts can be read according to (post)modern assumptions about the self, textuality, and so on. Their reversal, they imply, demonstrates that Ashbery's poetry is "open" to the social and thus automatically "political." Yet because it does not take an aware reader at all long to "see" what Miklitsch identifies as Vendler's "pedagogical imperialism" and her "orthodox impulse," his essay appears to serve the function of merely holding "traditionalism" at bay on behalf of an uninterrogated deconstruction. Similarly, in their haste to reclaim Ashbery for the political "left," Mohanty and Monroe do not pause to ask how it is, if Ashbery's texts are as "oppositional" as they claim, that those same texts turn out to hold the number 2 position in "orthodox/conservative/reactionary" Vendler's canonical list of contemporary American poets (as Miklitsch's article plainly indicates). *Doesn't "oppositionality" cost something?* Furthermore, if all texts have contradictions within them and indeed deconstruct themselves, why can Miklitsch not find enough contradictions in Vendler's discourses to "save" her the way Mohanty and Monroe "save" Ashbery; after all, as another deconstructor has proclaimed, "deconstruction has shown [that] there is no text so politically determined that a clever reading cannot show how it simultaneously undermines its own strategy, thus allowing the text to be claimed for an opposing view" (Young 1988, 133). Evidently what is at stake in these texts is not getting rid of the canon, but producing a new one, not getting rid of thrones, but dethroning one academic claimant for the sake of enthroning another.

More interesting and politically ambitious are the texts by Hortense Spillers ("Mama's Baby, Papa's Maybe: An American Grammar Book" 1987) and Dean MacCannell ("Marilyn Monroe Was Not a Man" 1987). Spillers's "archaeology" is decidedly Foucauldian/discursive, though its discursive power is reduced by her tendency toward the "florid." Here, at the level of enunciation, where she fights out her own battles between the libidinal and the political, the libidinal wins and that is really the general message behind her essay, as it is the general message behind the later work of Foucault—and of Barthes, for that matter. Following Foucault, Spillers theorizes the bodies of black (particularly female) captives suspended on slave ships between their home cultures and New World cultures as "flesh," that is, as bodies that somehow fall outside ideological categories, particularly the category of gender. It is in this way that she theorizes African-American women as "ungendered." Again following Foucault's "specifying" strategy, she assumes that below a certain level of microcultural analysis ideology no longer operates. Thus Spillers, like Schor and most other American academics, privileges the local and localizing kind of investigation over investigations that connect the alterities of race/class/gender together in a politically systematic and global manner. Although aware that her project, which to some degree reaffirms biologism and the gender system, can be regarded as "reactionary" (Spillers 1987, 66), she thinks that the only alternative offered by (post)modern thought to reaffirming gender positions is an unacceptable kind of "gender 'undecidability' " (1987, 66). This is indeed *not* the only alternative, although it is the one the *diacritics* issue reinforces (whether its arguments are traditionalist or deconstructionist). What about investigating the politics of gender through materialist–feminist or Marxist–feminist analysis? Shunning these possibilities without explanation, however, Spillers turns back to a familiar form of (theoretical) transcendence: woman (specifically the African-American woman whose inheritance is her "ungenderedness") is "privileged" here as being rooted in nature. Being/having once fallen "outside" the established subject position (that of gender, as she is arguing) appears in Spillers's text both as a kind of rootedness in nature and simultaneously as a kind of "oceanic" (Freudian) floating state of being nowhere. In her essay the concept of "race" hovers at first uncertainly between a cultural and a natural definition before settling down with the natural. This contradiction does not bother Spillers, no doubt because she is so urgently trying (as her introductory paragraph indicates) to theorize a ground ("flesh"/the body) for solidarity among African-American women (but it is a solidarity that depends more on sameness and psychological supportiveness than on political awareness and mutual critique). Of course, to introduce the political (the kind I am suggesting here) would be "costly" to Spillers, not only in terms of a certain kind of internal "solidarity" among African-American women, but also therefore in terms of the perceived "representativeness" any one of them may hold in dominant institutions by working, say, to "solve" the problem of race by such reformist moves as "affirmative action." In the end, while Spillers aims to displace with her own understanding the kind of analysis of the African-American family (with a matriarchal structure that is "inconveniently" out of step with the dominant patriarchy) proposed by Daniel Moynihan, her basic theoretical maneuver repeats Moynihan's. Whereas liberals like Moynihan think that the plight of disadvantaged minorities is to be explained by a "fall" through the nets of "the system" (which only needs reform to work "right"), Spillers's explanation of the situation of African-American women is a "fall" outside the parameters of gender, and she calls not for a displacement of the gender system but for its "reform." Neither Moynihan nor Spillers sees the "plight" of the "disadvantaged" as a result of positions *assigned* to marginal groups by the machinery of the present cultural/social/economic system.

A similar localizing specificity that refuses to examine the global system of relations and the positions they assign to subjects underlies Dean MacCannell's investigation of the cultural representations of Marilyn Monroe. His is a way of inquiring into the operations of the power/knowledge relations of the gender system by tracking the trajectory of desire as it is "sited" in the discourses of recent texts about her (including those of Norman Mailer and Gloria Steinem, which—this is supposed to surprise us—cooperate in producing a similar "Monroe"). MacCannell produces Monroe as the Lacanian "Other" ("a genuine, unyielding, radical insistence, one that knew itself to be in league with other radical movements but way out ahead of them" 1987, 114) and argues that the patriarchy's need to control this "radical" energy (Monroe) led to the development of a (discursive) system of "containment strategies" that his text elaborates as being primarily "male," but in the creation of which even the "liberated" Steinem had a hand. The question that remains is the political complicity of MacCannell's own text: if it–like other texts in the *diacritics* issue– operates a series of reversals to "reveal" a certain kind of politics (he identifies it specifically as a politics of "transgression" [1987, 126]), a reversal similar to his own reversals can be performed on it. One can say that "Monroe" was not just the space of some flow of endless erotic energy (as MacCannell asserts in an unexplained complicity with the interests of pleasure), but that "Monroe" was "solicited" to occupy the position of the "uncontainable erotic" and that the machinery of and reasons for this solicitation must be examined. What MacCannell's "feminist" text, like those of Spillers and Schor, reveals is the inadequacy of theoretical sophistication alone for a political project.

Certainly the most telling feature of the *diacritics* issue is the fact that its most explicit and direct call to politics coincides with the call for a retreat from (post)modern theory. In their "(Re)watching Television: Notes Towards a Political Criticism" (1987), Best and Kellner rightly reject as politically ineffective the kind of reading practices reflected in and promoted by the work of Derrida, Foucault, Baudrillard, Lyotard, and Kroker and Cook, but they overhastily urge that (post)modernism (to them nothing but a formalism through and through) be grafted onto a Gadamerian "political hermeneutics," by which they hope to achieve several goals: (1) to recover the sense of depth lost in surface-oriented (post)modern criticism (as if either depth or surface were inherently preferable), (2) to combat the "waning of affect" registered by and produced in (post)modern thought (as if affect were the motor for effective political action), and (3) to avoid what they call (post)modernism's "elitism" (as if the particular historical situatedness of intellectuals can be either ignored or erased). While they call overtly for a theory that "passes through the (post)modern problematic so as to appropriate its insights and to overcome its limitations" (Best and Kellner 1987, 98), they are covertly calling for a return to a kind of commonsense (political) criticism focused on content and readily disseminated to an audience larger than the one Derrida, for example, might seem to be addressing. Their suggestion not of a reversal but of a "return" nostalgically ignores history: there is no "going back" except by way of the kind of theoretical/ideological forgetfulness by which their text is marked. For instance, they deploy (post)modern thought to deny a "universal meaning" for television's texts, but at the same time claim that (post)modern thought "occludes the polysemic, multivalent nature of the texts of popular culture" (1987, 106), in spite of the rather obvious fact that (post)structuralism energetically promotes what Barthes calls "the *irreducible* plurality" of the text (Barthes 1986, 59, emphasis in original). What they mean is that the *dominant* strains of (post)modernism do not promote effective political practices. Although they in fact acknowledge (post)structuralist polysemia (Best and Kellner 1987, 105) as "friendly" to their call for a "plurality of interpretations," they do not see its politically disabling effects—after all, it does dominate the collection to which they are contributing. Wanting to be "radical" readers of television, Best and Kellner fail to ask these salient questions: Do "radical" readers really endorse a "plurality of meanings"? When does the call for the production of a "plurality of meanings" turn into a mere "interpretation-ism" that only serves the interests of liberal pluralism? And most important, how does oppositionality/radicality have to be theorized to take care of both politically unproductive traditional reading methods and politically unproductive (post)modern ones? But Best and Kellner—their project suggests the inadequacy of commitment alone for a political project—do not dismiss unproductive (post)modern readings: indeed their text reproduces Spillers's (and the entire *diacritics* issue's) "traditionalism or (post)structuralism" dilemma and thus unwittingly helps to fulfill the issue's covert ideological goals—corroborated, as we have seen, in variations by Fish and Berkhofer,

Schor and Humphries. These ideological goals are the occlusion of the politically unproductive common ground shared by older and newer reading strategies, the distraction of attention away from alternative possibilities for political understandings, and the consequent deferral of efforts for radical change.

Speaking "Criti(que)ally"[6]

"[Critique addresses a] constitutive tension . . . the tension between an approach built on genesis and a construction premised on normativity . . ."

"[Marx's model of critique] does not definitively establish at the theoretical level the relation between intellectual objectification and social reality but . . . views this relation as a contradictory one. It thus allows individual analysis the necessary cognitive scope that will prevent it from becoming a mere demonstration of an already established schema."

"Critique cannot 'seek to be political,' . . . the political is not some existent thing or structure to which the critique seeks to become adequate or whose realization it wants to bring about. Critique *is* political. . . . "

"Dogmatic criticism sets its own theory against the one it criticizes and infers from the claim to truth of the former the untruth of the latter. Such criticism remains external to its object. . . . Dialectical criticism [that is, critique], by contrast, proceeds immanently."

". . . The *Critique of Political Economy,* or, if you like, the system of bourgeois economy critically presented . . . is at once a presentation and, thereby, a critique of that system."

"To take hold of the process [of historical development] in its entirety, it is necessary to go beyond the present that first makes knowledge possible. Marx takes this step not by introducing the dimension of the future but by introducing the concept of the self-criticism of the present."

"In its most general form, capitalist ideology functions . . . as 'second nature.' . . . The goal of the Marxian critique is the defetishization of this second nature . . . [and the exposure of] those contradictions–be they economic, social, or political–which suddenly cause a crisis which shows the holes in the fabric of second nature."

"Critique . . . is concerned with the *receptivity* of the historical world to the particular judgments of politics."

"Understanding history is . . . an 'exact phantasy.' History is . . . at once memory and hope, past and future shooting through an open present."

"Critique makes possible the opening to the New."

TRANSGRESSIONS: 4

It should by now be evident that the point of the critiques we have undertaken here has been to demonstrate the *systematic* character of the strategies deployed to contain the political in the contemporary American academy. What remains to be indicated is that, at its core, this containment effort is aimed at restricting or blocking the process of concept formation. Today the war on concept formation is being conducted, in broad terms, by means of two moves: one (the popular "activist") move is to disrupt the space of concept formation wherever it appears and shut it down in whatever way possible (the seemingly manifold methods through which this is accomplished involve, chiefly, calling on that widespread anti-intellectualism so easily tapped in America by referring to experience and common sense); the other move (the "philosophical") is to *theorize* the restriction of concept formation by making it merely an element in another and more encompassing process. Obviously, this second line of thought has already been extensively developed in (post)structuralist texts such as those of Derrida, de Man, Deleuze, Lacan, and more recently in texts like those of Ulmer, in which the concept-mitigating understandings of desire, the tropological and the undecidable have been elaborated[7]; it was carried further, emerging as Baudrillard's unsettling vision of the world as thoroughly "simulacral." Recently, however, there have been signs that Baudrillard's notion of an utterly "distinctionless" culture (an "unreal" real) is not being taken very seriously—Baudrillard himself having been transformed into a kind of "pop" theorist.[8] Now it is rather Lyotard's more "solid" reading of the (post)modern condition that appears to inform dominant views.

What makes Lyotard's reading of culture so appealing, currently, is that it continues and extends understandings needed by the mainstream in order to block radical social change: for one thing, Lyotard reinforces the localizing tendency—an important part of contemporary critical practice, as we have already seen—by dismissing "master narratives" and by disconnecting the various "language games" played by subjects in culture (emphatically separating, for instance, the "descriptive" from the "prescriptive"). Most importantly, Lyotard promotes the *libidinal economy model* of culture (which he associates with "freedom" and "openness") and rejects the ("outmoded Enlightenment") *conceptual economy model* (which he associates with oppressiveness). Although not finally vanquished, the conceptual model (of which he is suspicious) has—as his argument is currently received—nevertheless been subsumed by the libidinal (the only "saving" element in culture, if there is one). There are two ways the relation between the two economies may be understood. One might say, from one perspective, that desire "takes in" reason; at the same time, however, the libidinal economy stands in a relation of excess to the conceptual one. On this view, the demystification of politics is impossible because it would require a critical practice launched from a conceptually grounded and decided position. What supposedly remains to us is only the deconstruction of politics – which says positions are themselves undecidable, "in excess."[9]

Following the line developed by Derrida, de Man, Foucault, Lacan, and extended by Lyotard, the dominant American academy today posits a cultural criticism in terms of a (libidinal) economy of excess: in this criticism – it promotes its own kind of "critique" (to which we will return shortly) – concepts are understood as tropologically produced truths that are thus delusory and must be resisted in the name of a something that exceeds those truths, in other words, exceeds the public representational systems of culture, that is, in the name of a private and individual body, desire, space. . . . Thus, for all its avowed "openness," this kind of criticism privatizes cultural issues, placing them in a domain where they cannot be addressed as issues of the collectivity. The political function of this privatized excess, governed by undecidability, is to block ideology critique, which depends on the publicness of representational systems and, thus, on concepts and categories. If Lyotard finally has to admit that things do get "decided," he nevertheless insists that they are decided undecidably, so to speak. In his account, it is neither "time" nor "the concept" nor "categories" nor "history itself" that decides: otherwise "one would have to presuppose that history proceeds by concepts, dialectically. Whereas it guides us only after the fact" (Lyotard and Thebaud 1985, 14–15). Rejecting the conceptual economy model that promotes political struggles grounded in a particular understanding of the historical, the dialectical, and the conceptual, Lyotard promotes (as we saw Barthes do before and as many are doing in the United States today) a cultural politics of "unrepresentable" excess.[10]

Instances of the politics of excess in the United States are not difficult to locate, but an exemplary one is the work of Alice Jardine. To be sure, her effort to broaden interest in the (post)structuralist-inspired French feminisms in this country is already widely recognized, but the question of the political effects of such an effort also needs to be investigated. In connection with her own political concerns, Jardine opened the issue of "unrepresentability" a few years ago by announcing (paraphrasing

Derrida): "I . . . truly *do not know* if it is to a change in representation that we–as feminists–should entrust the future" (1986, 96, emphasis in original). One of her recent writings, "in the name of the modern: feminist questions *d'après gynesis:* in five acts" (1988) is in fact a performance of this politics of unrepresentability figured in "a mixture of appropriation, collage, parody, and pastiche" (1988, 157). In the introductory text read to the audience just prior to the performance, Jardine situates it within a narrative that pivots, on the one hand, around a historical moment referred to as "gynesis" when "with the demise of 'Man,' 'Woman' has become a dominant trope of otherness in the West" (1988, 157) and, on the other, around her own enunciation of this moment in her influential book, *Gynesis: Configurations of Woman and Modernity* (1985). Indeed she represents the performance piece as an extension of her earlier investigations, inasmuch as it traces and responds to "a fierce and growing reaction against, both poststructuralism [which she defines as the "feminocentric logic" theorized by persons such as Lacan, Derrida, Deleuze, Guattari, . . .] and postmodernism (most often dubbed 'Theory') and their attacks on dominant Western logic" (1988, 184). By specifically targeting "the humanist academy in the West" (1988, 186), Jardine locates her intervention in the arena where Fish and Berkhofer are working and on behalf of theory as if against their kind of traditionalism and academicism: "my overriding concern," she says, "was to upset the scene of academic respresentations in some modest way" (1988, 185). In taking this tack, however, Jardine obscures the degree to which (post)structuralism has already achieved acceptance in the American academy, signs of which–as has already been indicated–are present everywhere, even in Fish's current work. Indeed there is no better indication of the thoroughness of the absorption of (post)structuralism by the humanist establishment than Jardine's own position at Harvard, that is, her position in the center of the center of the American academy. This gives her the power and prestige to write what she wants and publish in the preferred presses and journals. She might say that her subversiveness is shown in the fact that she has written the piece, now under discussion in an "oppositional" collection of "feminist cultural criticism," published by a left-leaning press (Verso); but that doesn't explain, for instance, how *at the very same time* she is in the (political) position to receive—as she recently did—a multiyear grant from the National Endowment for the Humanities in the Reagan–Bush years to hold summer institutes in order to teach other teachers about the avant garde.

Actually Jardine's interventions take place more in the domain of the Schor–Humphries debate, where the influence of (post)structuralism is an accepted fact and where what is at stake is the question of its political effectivity. In that context, in which it is recognized that "the political" cannot be evaded (as, say, Berkhofer wants to do), the effect of Jardine's work is to shift the grounds of the debate: she neither accepts Humphries's naive notion of an all-encompassing textuality nor Schor's very restricted notion of the material, as the body of woman. In other words, her work goes far beyond the question of writing "texts of limits" or setting "the limits of texts." Furthermore, it outflanks the New Historicist perspective represented in the *diacritics* issue on "Culture and Countermemory" discussed above (Mohanty, 1987). Instead, like Lyotard, she suspends the question of the material/the historical by throwing the focus of inquiry elsewhere. Readers familiar with her work will know that Lyotard had already made a brief appearance in *Gynesis,* but as Jardine herself indicates, the terrain of the academy is shifting very rapidly, and *Gynesis* was written well before the resurgence of the political struggles we have recently witnessed.[11] Under these new circumstances, in which the contestation is no longer that between an entrenched traditionalism and a surgent (post)structuralism, but a contestation between an entrenched coalition of traditionalists and (post)structuralists against those seeking radical change, the best Jardine can do is to redirect the focus of inquiry away from materiality ("Is it a text or a body?") toward the kinds of issues Lyotard favors: the status of representation, the roles of various "language games" (especially the question of the "performative"), and related forms of inquiry and their consequences.

Like all texts, Jardine's performance piece not only offers us something to read, but also proposes a modality for "reading."

While not "totally inclusive," her reading mode is implicitly "generous": her pastiche encompasses a large series of discourses from different cultural spaces concerning "modernity," "*la modernité*, "postmodernism," the "avant-garde," "theory," "the patriarchy," "feminism," and so on, thus giving a place to a variety of "specificities." Reinforcing this sense of "openness," Jardine declares that she has avoided taking "either a geographical or gender position," preferring "once again [as in *Gynesis*] to sift these male debates through a series of feminist questions" (1988, 157). She furthermore insists (speaking of the cast, which consists of three male and three female voices, five of them recorded and thus "fixed") that ideally the role of "woman-live" ("her" role) should be left blank in the circulated text so that "others – in other contexts" (1988, 157) could fill it in with their own interventions. Yet for all its apparent "openness" and "unsettledness," Jardine's text generates a system of urgencies, intensities, and hierarchies, in other words, it has a structure and constitutes a representation. What Jardine calls her "sifting" or "questing and questioning" (1988, 183), follows a specifiable trajectory: Act I concerns "naming" and emphasizes the scholasticism and academicism of (pointedly male) definitional obsessions; in Act II, the "postmodern condition" is understood to be a "new male condition"; in Act III, "postmodern positions" are again largely male, because "feminist theorists . . . have not particularly wanted to get into the act" (1988, 184); in Act IV, "postmodern connections," the "feminocentric theorists" – Deleuze, Derrida, and especially Lyotard – are prominent; and in Act V, "feminist questions" are given over entirely to female voices, "starring" those feminists whose inquiries have been so heavily influenced by the male writers of the previous act: Kristeva, Cixous, Wittig, Irigaray. If, as it appears, the text moves in the "right" direction, it is crucial to note its discursive trajectory: the shift away from "names," "conditions," "positions" (all understood to be heavily masculine) toward "connections" (presumably more feminine). The endpoint of this discursive series, which is the category of "the other" (which though not explicitly mentioned in the title of the last act, is nevertheless clearly identified in the text).

Other features give the trajectory of Jardine's text a decided force: the first three acts are dominated by masculinist presuppositions (even when voiced by "women") that begin to take on a monotony and emptiness signalled by their fading repeatedly into the monotonous "sucking stones" discourse from Beckett. This "movement" (it enacts the "demise of 'Man' " put forward in Jardine's larger narrative) is followed by the "gynetic" (post)structuralist discourses, which are then succeeded by discourses of a presumably even "greater" feminine authenticity/identification. In case one misses the point, Jardine/"woman-live" prods the audience/reader from time to time by means of asides. In one of them, she declares Habermas a "dinosaur" because he persists, for political reasons, in holding onto something like "modernism" and the "Enlightenment" conceptual economy model (1988, 163). In a contrasting aside (whispered to the audience), "woman-live," having listened to a string of observations by "sympathetic" male theorists, Lyotard being the ultimate, she grants them a grudging admiration: "I wish I could say these guys aren't any good!" (1988, 176).

The point of the present analysis of Jardine's text is by no means to object to her concern with "the other" – nor indeed to deny that there has been a crisis in representation: for any oppositional political project it is necessary to theorize a space for the cultural/political margin in the wake of the (post)modern crisis of representation. What is important, however, is to indicate that Jardine's text not only follows the pattern (already discussed above in relation to Schor and Barthes and even Spillers) of positing for cultural studies the necessity of a space for the gap in, intermittence of, and/or exemption from meaning. But also – in line with Lyotard's recent interventions – her argument extends this space so as to situate "the other" as in fact "unrepresentable" (which is to say, beyond the conceptual). Jardine, furthermore, *performs* this unrepresentability by refusing, as already mentioned, to take a "position" and by suggesting that her "role" in the text should be thought of, ideally, as a "gap." The question is, What is the political significance of an "openness" that in fact becomes a "gap" in the system of culture?

Her text's claim to "openness" must be addressed finally in

terms of its genre or modality; one has to ask, in other words, what "sifting" means in her program of "sifting these male debates through a series of feminist questions" (1988, 157). The discursive apparatus of this sifting (of fragmentary inscriptions)–a familiar apparatus from the work of Sterne through Joyce and Beckett to Federman, Barthelme, Sukenick, Barthes, and Hassan–has always been a device for outraging the bourgeoisie, for shaking the solemnities of bourgeois life to the delight of the rebel. However, such acts of "outrage"–as we have already suggested more than once–are only "trangressive" acts that serve not to enable radical political change but rather to distract attention from it. Jardine's practice of fragmentary inscription is the kind promoted by such mainstream humanists as Ihab Hassan (*Paracriticisms: Seven Speculations of the Times* 1975) who have used the collage as "performance" (rather than as a further stimulus to concept formation) in order to (re)inscribe the subject in writing twice over. For the key to the effectiveness (unsettlingness) of such collages of fragmentary inscriptions is that they achieve the status of the "unsummarizable" and frustrate the possibility of conceptual coherence: their very modality is thus one of excess.[12] And the appreciation of this modality of excess through the transcendant reach of imagination (exercised by the two subjects, writer and reader, who decode it) becomes a mark of membership in the subversive group. The now growing academic interest in "performatics," its (post)structuralist inspiration (which, we may add here, is forcefully shown in a recent issue of the journal *Qui Parle* (Jacobs et al. 1989) devoted to "Theatricality & Literature," stressing especially the work of Cixous, and giving even Marx a performatic reading) and its (non)convergence with traditional dramatics, has lately been noted by Thomas Whitaker. Although Whitaker asks, "Is the text now becoming its own self-reflecting performance?" and sees the academy as showing "signs of capitulating to the rhetoric of theater and the impulses of performance, often without accepting or clarifying the assumptions they may entail" (Whitaker 1989, 145), he himself does not inquire into the political presuppositions or effects of this new "trend."

Of course what qualifies some male theorists for even Jardine's grudging admiration is that, like her, they theorize this kind of "gap" so as to localize and restrict, if not entirely block, the space of concept formation; they help to theorize (actually, to mystify) otherness as something excessive (it is "*not* another discourse" [Jardine 1988, 174], one says), which thus transcends the arena of public representations. By "theorizing" otherness as something excessive, Jardine and her male cohorts restrict the already limited politics of textuality more and more to a politics of enunciation; while this is carried out under the aegis of a "constructionist" rather than "essentialist" theory of the subject, it nevertheless "individualizes" (does not "collectivize") this subject, thus causing the subject to fit quite smoothly in the American pluralist political context. As the discussion above suggests, although Jardine claims to take no "geographical or gender position," she nevertheless generates a text from a position. This apparent contradiction becomes intelligible when one considers what "position" has come to mean today: "to have a position" no longer means to ground one's politics conceptually and theoretically, but at most to reveal one's position of enunciation by "performing" one's uncertainties and limitations ("woman-live" is depicted frequently, if not characteristically, as splutteringly and hesitantly querulous) and by insisting ultimately on one's placement outside the public representational system. Thus what interests and excites adherents of this politics is the double move of simultaneous "restriction" (limiting politics to the "micro" level [Jardine 1988, 177]) and "expansion" (proposing that alterity is "incalculable" [1988, 176] and "unknowable" [1988, 182]), and that "the other" –like the Jardine/ "woman-live" of the performance piece–occupies a "positionless position". From its post of nonintelligibility and nonrepresentability, the most that this "other" seems able to do regarding "position" is merely to index itself with that set of cultural codings by which it is marked, whatever they might be (say, black, working class, academic, lesbian, etc.). That is what "taking a position" has come to mean: (post)structuralism has transformed politics into a politics of enunciation/performance, a subversive semiotropic (meaning-unsettling) rather than a semioclastic (meaning-displacing) politics.[13] Rejecting critique as dialectics, this "new" politics embraces critique as dialogics: in the hands of its advocates, critique becomes a Baktinian carnivalesque "free-for-all" in which individual subjects "unsettle" representation by expressing their "excess," instead of becoming a practice that opens a historically determined, conceptually structured and collective space of oppositionality aimed at social transformation.

Notes

CHAPTER 1

1. See Gerald Graff, *Beyond the Culture Wars* (1992, 186–87).

2. For a sustained critique of the ways in which the recognition of *différance* has made no difference in academic practices, see Morton, "The Politics of the Margin: Theory, Pleasure, and the Postmodern *Conférance*" (1987).

CHAPTER 2

1. For more on these questions, see Zavarzadeh, *Pun(k)deconstruction and the (Post)Modern Political Imaginary* (1993).

CHAPTER 3

1. Like all concepts deployed for the analysis of culture, "(post)modernism" is not stable, but is, rather, a shifting site of social struggle. Even though one may consider certain local features of the contemporary situation as "(post)modern," (post)modernism is not an ensemble of free-floating, autointelligible lineaments. Instead, its meaning is the effect of a global frame of intelligibility in which various traces and marks are articulated. This frame of intelligibility is neither in the phenomenon itself, as empiricists propose, nor is it simply a matter of "writing," as textualists insist. It is, rather, produced

historically through social struggles, and thus there are many contesting ways of constructing it. Following Teresa L. Ebert's reading of (post)modernity (1991), we shall name as "ludic (post)modernism" the understanding of (post)modernity that makes sense of it as a problematics of "representation" and, furthermore, conceives "representation" as a rhetorical issue, a matter of signification in which the very process of signification articulates the signified. Knowledge of the "outside"—if one can mark such a zone of being—is, according to ludic theory, traversed by the rifts, slippages, and alterity that are immanent in signifying practices and above all in language. Representation, in other words, is always incommensurate with the represented since it is subject to the law of *différance*. Ludic (post)modernism, therefore, posits the "real" as an instance of "simulation" and in no sense the "origin" of the "truth" that can provide a ground for a political project. *Différance,* in ludic (post)modernism, is regarded to be the effect of the unending "playfulness" (thus the term "ludic") of the signifier in signifying practices that can no longer acquire representational authority by anchoring themselves in what Derrida has called the "transcendental signified" (*Of Grammatology* 1976, 20).

Contesting the understanding of *différance* as an effect of rhetoric, "resistance (post)modernism" articulates difference as the effect of "labor," focusing on congealed and alienated labor as private property. Labor, and not language, we argue is the frame of intelligibility that determines the regime of signification and the ensuing "representation" of the real. Language, and all other semiotic processes, are articulated by the division of labor. Difference (as opposed to *différance*), in short, is a "materialist" praxis produced through class struggle and not a "rhetorical" effect. We might add here that Ebert's reading of "resistance (post)modernism" does not emphasize "labor" in the way that we have done here because her reading of Marx's labor theory is more focused on those discourses of Marx that foreground the abstractness of labor under capitalism and thus the erasure of difference among the hetergeneous. She, in short, accents Marx's notion of capitalism as itself a form of totalization. While ludic (post)modernism seeks its own genealogy in Nietzschean texts, resistance (post)modernism is articulated in the writings of Marx.

2. For a full bibliography of the works of the Yale Critics and of commentary and criticism on them, see Wallace Martin, "Bibliography,"

in Arac et al. 1983, 203–212. The writings of Harold Bloom, who reduces (literary) history to a set of simple human relations (the anxiety of influence), is inscribed in the center of the New Humanist project for saving the subject, as are such other contemporary theoretical inquiries as reader response criticism, the New Historicism, and speech–act theory.

CHAPTER 4

1. For a rather naive, but perhaps typical, "reading" of the relationship between (post)modern theory and creative writing practices in general, see Stitt, "Writers, Theorists, and the Department of English" (1987). Stitt begins by noting that writers appear to be "alarmed [that] the 'theorists' are gradually taking over the department of English, thereby making the life of writers and writing students miserable" (1987, 1). His purpose is to comfort and support writers in their struggle with theorists, and toward this end he offers two narratives of how theory came to be: one is a "bureaucratic" narrative that sees the "birth" of theory as the product of the basic desperation of English department faculties to recover the power they had had in the 1960s when their courses were popular and English department enrollments were consequently high; the other accounts for the "birth" of theory as a result of what Stitt sees as the recent separation of critical methodology from the reading of literary texts. This was motivated by efforts of English professors to promote themselves back to their former level of power by "mystifying" students with a newfound, arcane, esoteric, and hard-to-learn knowledge (called "theory"). He ends his piece by exhorting creative writers and their students to "fight mysticism wherever you encounter it" (1987, 3), meaning of course that they should fight the new threatening "mysticism" called "theory."

2. For an interesting commentary on Lish's role as editor of *Quarterly,* see Dieckmann, "Lish Fulfillment" (1987).

3. See Voloshinov, *Marxism and the Philosophy of Language* (1986).

4. See, for example, the special issue of *Salmagundi* entitled "Nadine Gordimer: Politics and the Order of Art" (1984), esp. essays by S. Gilman, R. Boyers, and R. Smith.

5. For a more detailed development of these points, see Shoshana Felman, "Women and Madness" 1975, 2–10.

CHAPTER 6

1. In our title, we have in mind the title given to the final articulation of Syracuse University's new English and Textual Studies program: "Not a Good Idea: A New Curriculum at Syracuse." As will become clear below, the point of our title is that, far from being "not a good idea," the ideas embodied in that document are—in terms of the needs of late capitalism—"very 'good' indeed"—that is to say, they fulfill the historical function of producing subjects of labor suitable for transnational capitalism in the moment of the ludic (post)modern.

2. For a discussion of the role of empiricism and positivism, see Zavarzadeh and Morton, *Theory, (Post)Modernity, Opposition* (1991) especially Chapters 1 and 2.

3. Most of our own writing on the need for such a radical shift in the curriculum was done in the 1980s in the form of "memoranda" to the Syracuse University English Department. Next year (1993) a collection of these memoranda and the responses they provoked will be published as *The Memo Book*.

4. See Cohan et al. For further articulations of the maneuvers in the struggle between these groups, see Zavarzadeh and Morton, *Theory, (Post)Modernity, Opposition* (1991), especially Chapters 1 and 4.

5. One of the major sites of struggle over the new labor force is Paul de Man's reading of Proust in *Allegories of Reading*. For a detailed examination of the politics of de Man's putting in question metaphor and privileging metonymy as tropes of the early industrial labor force and emerging late capitalist labor force, see Zavarzadeh, "Pun(k)deconstruction" (1992b).

6. For a discussion of this exclusion, see Heller (1987).

CHAPTER 7

1. We will shortly be referring to instances of these discourses (of "pleasure" and "morals") in the media, but here we want to point to the urgency of the "ethical" for the dominant academy as expressed in books published by academic presses, as for example, Miller, *The Ethics of Reading* (1986), and Siebers, *The Ethics of Criticism* (1988).

2. On these writers, see the critique (though different from ours) of Arthur Hirsch, *The French New Left* (1981).

3. For a theoretical articulation of these issues, see Chapter 2 of this book and Zavarzadeh, *Pun(k)deconstruction and the (Post)Modern Political Imaginary* (1993).

CHAPTER 8

1. Berkhofer's lecture was the principal address for a panel titled "From Demystification to Deconstruction and Beyond: The Challenge of the New Scholarship to American Studies" which was part of the proceedings of the American Studies Association's meeting held in Miami Beach, Oct. 27–30, 1988. The title's framing of the session as a "survey" produces – as does Berkhofer's "surveying" lecture – the silent reinscription into the session's discourses of the pedagogical modality of "surveying knowledge," which is a fundamental premise of the traditional humanities disciplines. Quotations here are from a text of the lecture supplied by the author. One mark of the significance which the sponsoring organization attaches to Berkhofer's lecture is that it has made the lecture available to its members (and others) on videotape, see the *American Studies Association Newsletter,* 11.4 (December 1988): 9.

2. For an understanding of history that accepts "the linguistic turn" *and* stresses the urgency of the political, see Bennett (1987).

3. Bercovitch's passage, as quoted twice (1988, 5, 20) in full by Berkhofer, sets forth the premises presumably shared by contributors to Bercovitch's volume, *Reconstructing American Literary History* (1986):

> that race, class, and gender are formal principles of art, and therefore integral to textual analysis; that language has the capacity to break free of social restrictions and through its own dynamics to undermine the power structures it seems to reflect; that political norms are inscribed in aesthetic judgment and therefore inherent in the process of interpretation; that aesthetic structures shape the way we understand history, so that tropes and narrative devices may be said to use historians to enforce certain views of the past; that the task of literary historians is not just to show how art transcends culture, but also to identify and explore the ideological limits of their time, and then to bring these to bear upon literary analysis in such a way as to make use of the categories of culture, rather than being used by them. (viii)

4. For a further critique of Schor's work, see Morton (1989).

5. Such exemption from meaning becomes quite interesting in passages where Barthes's own situatedness with regard to sexuality is involved, as for example, here: "The alienation of sexuality is consubstantially linked to the alienation of meaning by meaning. What is difficult is not to liberate sexuality according to a more or less libertarian plan but to disengage it from meaning, including transgression as meaning" (Barthes 1985, 122). He then offers, as an exemplary instance, the interdiction of homosexuality in Arab countries, where its practice nevertheless goes on, better for never being "known": the trick is that in such a culture homosexuality remains "at the same time *interdicted and unintelligible*" (1985, 123). Thus Barthes does not urge transformation, but, remaining also quite skeptical about "transgression," seeks instead disengagement from meaning.

6. The citations in this collage come from the following sources and in the order listed here: Dick Howard (177); Bürger (7); Dick Howard (xvii–xviii); Bürger (liv); Marx *The Letters* (423); Bürger (21); Dick Howard (39); Dick Howard (xxiii); Dick Howard (54); Dick Howard (66).

7. The classic statement is of course Derrida's claim that *différance* is "neither a word nor a concept" (*Margins of Philosophy* 1984, 11); but see also the transformation of concept into "puncept" in Ulmer (1988), who—with his own notion of "fun"—in the process strongly updates and underwrites Miller's commonsensical sounding notion of the "joy of reading" (1986b).

8. See, for instance, Hoberman (1989).

9. On the deconstruction of politics, see Young (1988).

10. See also Lyotard, "Acinema" (1977–1978) and *The Libidinal Economy* (1993).

11. On the resurgence of "the political"/"the historical"/ "the material" in the American academy, see, for example, Donoghue (1989); Lehman (1988); Miller (1987); Pechter (1987); Simpson (1988).

12. What we are bringing up here is the interesting question of the relation between the writing mode of fragmentary inscription ("breaking the page" and its "coherence") and the gender of writing.

13. Jardine's work constitutes a theater in which (post)structuralist thought is clearly staged; but the semiotropic understanding of culture and politics has been so thoroughly (if largely silently) absorbed

on the American scene that it marks even the texts of many contemporary cultural critics, like Susan Sontag, who are not usually thought of as (post)structuralists. Sontag's recent texts, *Illness as Metaphor* and *AIDS and Its Metaphors* for example, make the familiar argument already outlined here that it is metaphors (and the psychological and other pressures they bring to bear on the ill) that need to be resisted. She is basically recommending a (political-seeming) resistance that takes a "private" form and ultimately diverts attention from questions of public health policy.

References

Adams, Hazard. "The Dizziness of Freedom; or, Why I Read William Blake." *College English* 48.5 (1986): 431–443.

Althusser, Louis. "Ideology and Ideological State Apparatuses." *Lenin and Philosophy and Other Essays.* New York: Monthly Review Press, 1971, 127–186.

Arac, Jonathan, ed. *The Yale Critics: Deconstruction in America.* Minneapolis: University of Minnesota Press, 1983.

Aronowitz, Stanley, and Henry A. Giroux. *Postmodern Education: Politics, Culture, and Social Critcism.* Minneapolis: University of Minnesota Press, 1991.

Atlas, James. "The Battle of the Books." *New York Times Magazine* 5 June 1988: 24.

Bakhtin, Mikhail. *Rabelais and His World.* Trans. H. Iswolsky. Cambridge, MA: MIT Press, 1968.

Barker, Frances, et al., eds. *Literature, Politics and Theory: Essays from the Essex Conferences 1976–84.* London: Methuen, 1986.

Barthes, Roland. *Critical Essays.* Trans. Richard Howard. Evanston: Northwestern University Press, 1972.

_____. *S/Z.* Trans R. Miller. New York: Farrar, Straus & Giroux, 1975.

_____. *Elements of Semiology.* New York: Farrar, Straus & Giroux, 1977.

_____. *A Lover's Discourse.* Trans. Richard Howard. New York: Hill & Wang, 1978.

_____. *A Barthes Reader.* Ed. Susan Sontag. New York: Hill & Wang, 1982.

_____. *The Grain of the Voice: Interviews 1962–1980.* Trans. Linda Coverdale. New York: Hill & Wang, 1985.

_____. *The Rustle of Language.* Trans. Richard Howard. New York: Hill & Wang, 1986.

Bate, Walter Jackson. "The Crisis in English Studies." *Harvard Magazine* September–October 1982: 46–53.

Batsleer, Janet, et al., *Rewriting English: Cultural Politics of Gender and Class.* London: Methuen, 1985

Begley, Adam. "Souped-Up Scholar." *The New York Times Magazine* 3 May 1992: 38–39, 5–52.

Bellamy, Joe David. "A Downpour of Literary Republicanism." *Mississippi Review* 40/41 (Winter 1985): 31–39.

Belsey, Catherine. "Reply to John Holloway." *Times Literary Supplement* 4 November 1983: 1217.

Bennett, Tony. *Formalism and Marxism.* London: Methuen, 1979.

_____. "Texts in History: The Determinations of Reading and Their Texts." In *Post-structuralism and the Question of History.* Ed. Derek Attridge et al. Cambridge, England: Cambridge University Press, 1987, 63–81.

Benveniste, Emile. "Subjectivity in Language." *Problems in General Linguistics.* Trans. Mary Elizabeth Meek. Coral Gables, FL: University of Miami Press, 1971, 223–230.

Bercovitch, Sacvan. *Reconstructing American Literary History.* Cambridge, MA: Harvard University Press, 1986.

Berger, Joseph. "Scholars Attack Academic 'Radicals.'" *New York Times* 15 November 1988: A22.

Berkhofer, Robert, Jr. *Poetics and Politics in and of a New American Studies.* Paper delivered at the American Studies Association Convention, Miami Beach, FL, 28 October 1988. (Videotape available from the American Studies Association)

Best, Steven, and Douglas Kellner. "(Re)Watching Television: Notes toward a Political Criticism." *diacritics* 17.2 (Summer 1987): 97–113.

Bhaskar, Roy. *Reclaiming Reality: Philosophical Underlabouring.* New York: Routledge, Chapman, & Hall, 1989.

Boumelha, Penny. *Charlotte Brontë.* Bloomington, IN: Indiana University Press, 1990.

Bové, Paul. *Intellectuals in Power: A Genealogy of Critical Humanism.* New York: Columbia University Press, 1986.

Brecht, Bertholt. *Brecht on Theatre.* Trans. J. Willett. New York: Hill & Wang, 1979.

Brooks, David. "From Western Lit to Western as Lit." *Wall Street Journal* 2 February 1988: 16.

Bruffee, Kenneth A. "Liberal Education and the Social Justification of Belief." *Liberal Education* 68 (1982): 95–114.

Bürger, Peter. *Theory of the Avant-Garde.* Trans. Michael Shaw. Minneapolis: University of Minnesota Press, 1984.

Cahalan, James M., and David B. Downing, eds. *Practicing Theory in Introductory College Literature Courses.* Urbana, IL: National Council of Teachers of English, 1991.

Carby, Hazel. "The Canon: Civil War and Reconstruction." *Michigan Quarterly Review* 28.1 (Winter 1989): 35–43.

Charbeneau, Travis. "The Information Underclass." *In These Times* 9–15 October 1991, 24.

Cohan, Steven, et al. *Not a Good Idea: A New Curriculum at Syracuse.* Syracuse, NY: Syracuse University Department of English, 1988.

Coleridge, Samuel Taylor. *Biographia Literaria.* Ed. J. Engell and W. J. Bate. 2 vols. Princeton, NJ: Princeton University Press, 1983.

Coward, Rosalind, and John Ellis. *Language and Materialism: Developments in Semiology and the Theory of the Subject.* Boston: Routledge, 1980.

de Man, Paul. *The Resistance to Theory.* Minneapolis: University of Minnesota Press, 1986.

Derrida, Jacques. *Of Grammatology.* Trans. Gayatri Spivak. Baltimore, MD: Johns Hopkins University Press, 1976.

––––––. *Writing and Difference.* Trans. Alan Bass. Chicago: University of Chicago Press, 1978.

––––––. *Spurs: Nietzsche's Styles.* Trans. Barbara Harlow. Chicago: University of Chicago Press, 1979.

––––––. *Positions.* Trans. A. Bass. Chicago: University of Chicago Press, 1981.

––––––. "The Principle of Reason: The University in the Eyes of its Pupils." Trans. Catherine Porter and Edward P. Morris. *diacritics* 13.3 (Fall 1983): 3–20.

––––––. *Margins of Philosophy.* Trans. Alan Bass. Chicago: University of Chicago Press, 1984.

––––––. *Glas.* Trans. John P. Leavy, Jr., and Richard Rand. Lincoln, NE: University of Nebraska Press, 1986.

––––––. *The Post Card: From Socrates to Freud and Beyond.* Trans. Alan Bass. Chicago: University of Chicago Press, 1987.

Dial, Tom. " 'Horses' Turns Tess to Fiction." *Syracuse Herald American Stars Magazine* 25 May 1986, 13.

Dieckmann, Katherine. "Lish Fulfillment." *Village Voice* 2 June 1987, 46.

Donoghue, Denis. "The Political Turn in Criticism." *Salmagundi* 81 (Winter 1989): 104–122.

Eagleton, Terry. [Review of R. Bhaskar's *Reclaiming Reality*]. *Textual Practice* 4.1 (1990): 469–472.

Ebert, Teresa L. "Rewriting the (Post)Modern: Resistance (Post)modernism." *Legal Studies Forum* XV (1991): 291–303.

Ellis, John M. *Against Deconstruction*. Princeton, NJ: Princeton University Press, 1989.

Felman, Shoshana. "Women and Madness: The Critical Phallacy." *diacritics* 5.4 (Winter 1975): 2–10.

Fish, Stanley. "Guest Column. No Bias, No Merit: The Case Against Blind Submission." *PMLA* 103 (1988): 739–748.

Flower, Linda, and John R. Hayes. "The Cognition of Discovery: Defining a Rhetorical Problem." *College Composition and Communication* 31.1 (February 1980): 21–32.

Foucault, Michel. *The Archaeology of Knowledge and the Discourse on Language*. Trans. A. M. Sheridan Smith. New York: Pantheon Books, 1972.

———. *The Order of Things: An Archaeology of the Human Sciences*. New York: Vintage, 1973.

———. *Language, Counter-Memory, Practice: Selected Essays and Interviews*. Ed. Donald F. Bouchard. Trans. Donald F. Bouchard and Sherry Simon. Ithaca, NY: Cornell University Press, 1977.

Fromm, Harold. *Academic Capitalism and Literary Value*. Athens, GA: University of Georgia Press, 1991.

Fynsk, Christopher. "A Decelebration of Philosophy." *diacritics* 8.2 (Summer 1978): 80–90.

Gabriel, Susan, and Isaiah Smithson, eds. *Gender in the Classroom: Power and Pedagogy*. Urbana, IL: University of Illinois Press, 1990.

Gallop, Jane. *Thinking Through the Body*. New York: Columbia University Press, 1988.

Geertz, Clifford. *Local Knowledge: Further Essays in Interpretive Anthropology*. New York: Basic Books, 1983.

Giroux, Henry A. *Postmodernism, Feminism, and Cultural Politics: Redrawing Educational Boundaries*. Albany: State University of New York Press, 1991.

———. "Post-Colonial Ruptures and Democratic Possibilities: Multiculturalism as Anti-Racist Pedagogy." *Cultural Critique* 21 (Spring 1992): 5–39.

Gless, Darryl J., and Barbara H. Smith, eds. *The Politics of Liberal Education*. Durham, NC: Duke University Press, 1991.

Gold, Arthur. "A Pox on Duke and Stanford." *New York Times* 27 June 1988, A19.

Gordimer, Nadine. *Burger's Daughter*. New York: Viking Press, 1979.

———. *July's People*. New York: Viking Press, 1981.

———. *A World of Strangers*. New York: Simon and Shuster, 1958.

Graff, Gerald. *Literature Against Itself: Literary Ideas in Modern Society*. Chicago: University of Chicago Press, 1979.

———. "Response to the Papers: 'The Cultural Wars and The Classroom.' " Modern Language Association Convention. Washington, DC, 29 December 1989.

———. "Teach the Conflicts." In *The Politics of Liberal Education*. Ed. Darryl J. Gless and Barbara H. Smith. Durham, NC: Duke University Press, 1991, 57–73.

———. *Beyond the Culture Wars: How Teaching the Conflicts Can Revitalize American Education*. New York: W. W. Norton, 1992.

Gramsci, Antonio. *Selections from the Prison Notebooks*. Trans. G. Nowell Smith. New York: International Publishers, 1976.

Hall, Donald. *Writing Well*. Boston: Little, Brown, 1979.

Hallberg, Robert von, ed. *Canons*. Chicago: University of Chicago Press, 1984.

Hardison, O. B., Jr. "The Future of the Liberal Arts: A Humanist's View." *Georgia Review* 39.3 (Fall 1985): 576–85.

Hassan, Ihab. *Paracriticisms: Seven Speculations of the Times*. Urbana, IL: University of Illinois Press, 1975.

Heller, Scott. "A Constellation of Recently Hired Professors Illuminate the English Department at Duke." *Chronicle of Higher Education* 27 May 1987, 12–14.

———. "New Curriculum at Syracuse U. Attacked by Two Marxist Professors." *The Chronicle of Higher Education* 3 August 1988, A17.

Hempel, Amy. "Captain Fiction." *Vanity Fair* December 1984, 91.

Henricksen, Bruce, and Thaïs Morgan, eds. *Reorientations: Critical Theories and Pedagogies*. Urbana, IL: University of Illinois Press, 1990.

Henriques, Julien, et al. *Changing the Subject: Psychology, Social Regulation, and Subjectivity*. London: Methuen, 1984.

Himmelfarb, Gertrude. "Stanford and Duke Undercut Classical Values." *New York Times* 25 May 1988, A31.

Hirsch, Arthur. *The French New Left: An Intellectual History from Sartre to Gorz*. Boston: South End Press, 1981.

Hoberman, J. "Lost in America: Jean Baudrillard, Extraterrestrial." *Voice Literary Supplement* March 1989, 15–16.

Howard, Dick. *The Politics of Critique*. Minneapolis: University of Minneapolis Press, 1988.

Howard, Maureen. "Can Writing Be Taught at Iowa?" *New York Times Magazine* 25 May 1986, 47.

Humphries, Jefferson. "Troping the Body: Literature and Feminism." *diacritics* 18.1 (Spring 1988): 18–28.

_____. "On the Inevitability of Theory in Southern Literary Study." *The Yale Journal of Criticism* 3.1 (Fall 1989): 175–186.

Jacobs, Karan, et al. "Theatricality of Literature, with New Works by Hélène Cixous." Special issue of *Qui Parle* 3.1 (Spring 1989).

Jardine, Alice. *Gynesis: Configurations of Woman and Modernity*. Ithaca, NY: Cornell University Press, 1985.

_____. "Opaque Texts and Transparent Contexts: The Political Difference of Julia Kristeva." In *The Poetics of Gender*. Ed. Nancy K. Miller. New York: Columbia University Press, 1986, 96–116.

_____. "in the name of the modern: feminist questions *d'après gynesis*. in five acts." In *Grafts: Feminist Cultural Criticism*. Ed. Susan Sheridan. London: Verso Press, 1988, 157–191.

Johnson, Barbara, ed. *The Pedagogical Imperative: Teaching as Literary Genre*. Yale French Studies, no. 63. New Haven, CT: Yale University Press, 1982.

Kermode, Frank. *An Appetite for Poetry*. Cambridge, MA: Harvard University Press, 1989.

Krupat, Arnold. "Criticism and the Canon: Cross-Relations." *diacritics* 17.2 (Summer 1987): 3–20.

Lacan, Jacques. *Écrits: A Selection*. Trans. Alan Sheridan. New York: Norton, 1977.

Langiulli, Nino. "Syracuse University and the Kool-Acid Curriculum." *Measure* 88 (September 1990): 5–8.

Lehman, David. "Deconstructing de Man's Life." *Newsweek* 15 February 1988, 57.

Lentricchia, Frank. *After the New Criticism*. Chicago: University of Chicago Press, 1980.

_____. "En Route to Retreat. Making It to Mepkin Abbey." *Harper's Magazine* January 1992a, 68ff.

_____. "My Kinsman, T. S. Eliot." *Raritan* 11.4 (Spring 1992b): 1–23.

Lévi-Strauss, Claude. *The Savage Mind*. Chicago: University of Chicago Press, 1983.

Lyotard, Jean-François. "Acinema." *Wide Angle* 2.3 (1977–1978): 52–59.

_____. *The Postmodern Condition: A Report on Knowledge*. Trans. Geoff

Bennington and Brian Massumi. Minneapolis: University of Minnesota Press, 1984.

———. *The Libidinal Economy*. Trans. I. H. Grant. Bloomington: Indiana University Press, 1993.

———, and Jean-Loup Thebaud. *Just Gaming*. Trans. Wlad Godzich. Minneapolis: University of Minnesota Press, 1985.

MacCannell, Dean. "Marilyn Monroe Was Not a Man." *diacritics* 17.2 (Summer 1987): 114–127.

Macherey, Pierre. *A Theory of Literary Production*. Trans. Geoffrey Wall. London: Routledge & Kegan Paul, 1978.

McIntosh, Scott. "ETS Delivers Non-Traditional Approach." *The Daily Orange* 3 February 1992, 28.

Martin, Wallace. "Bibliography." In *The Yale Critics: Deconstruction in America*. Ed. Jonathan Arac. Minneapolis: University of Minnesota Press, 1983, 203–212.

Marx, Karl. *Early Writings*. Trans. R. Livingston and G. Benton. New York: Vintage Books, 1975.

———. *The Letters of Karl Marx*. Trans. Saul K. Padover. Englewood Cliffs, NJ: Prentice-Hall, 1979.

———. *A Contribution to the Critique of Political Economy*. New York: International Publishers, 1981.

———, and Friedrich Engels. *Collected Works*, Vol. 5. New York: International Publishers, 1975. 42 vols.

———, and Friedrich Engels. *The German Ideology*. New York: International Publishers, 1988.

Miklitsch, Robert. "The Poppies of Practical Criticism: 'Rabbi, Read the Phrases of This Difference.' " *diacritics* 17.2 (Summer 1987): 23–35.

Miller, J. Hillis. *The Ethics of Reading*. New York: Columbia University Press, 1986a.

———. "The Joy of Reading." *MLA Newsletter* (Spring 1986b): 2.

———. "Presidential Address 1986. The Triumph of Theory, the Resistance to Reading, and the Question of the Material Base." *PMLA* 102 (1987): 281–291.

———. *Theory Now and Then*. Durham, NC: Duke University Press, 1991.

Modern Language Association Job Information List. October 1985. New York: Modern Language Association.

Modern language Association Job Information List. October 1989. New York: Modern Language Association.

Mohanty, S. P., ed. "Culture and Countermemory: The 'American Connection.' " Special issue of *diacritics* 17.2 (Summer 1987).

_____, and Jonathan Monroe. "John Ashbery and the Articulation of the Social." *diacritics* 17.2 (Summer 1987): 37–63.

Morson, Gary S. *Bakhtin: Essays and Dialogues on His Work.* Chicago: University of Chicago Press, 1988.

Morton, Donald. "The Politics of the Margin: Theory, Pleasure and the Postmodern *Conférance.*" *American Journal of Semiotics* 5.1 (1987): 95–114.

_____. "The Body in/and the Text: The Politics of Clitoral Theoretics" [Review of Naomi Schor's *Reading in Detail*]. *American Journal of Semiotics* 6.2/3 (1989): 299–305.

_____. "Renarrating the Postmodern" (Review of M. Zavarzadeh's *Seeing Films Politically*]. *MLN* 107.5 (December 1992): 1050–1054.

_____, and Mas'ud Zavarzadeh. *Theory/Pedagogy/Politics: Texts for Change.* Urbana, IL: University of Illinois Press, 1991.

"Nadine Gordimer: Politics and the Order of Art." Special issue of *Salmagundi* 62 (Winter 1984).

National Endowment for the Humanities. *To Reclaim a Legacy.* Washington, DC: National Endowment for the Humanities, 1971.

Nelson, Cary, ed. *Theory in the Classroom.* Urbana and Chicago: University of Illinois Press.

Norris, Christopher. *Deconstruction and the Interests of Theory.* Norman, OK: University of Oklahoma Press, 1990.

Pechter, Edward. "The New Historicism and Its Discontents: Politicizing Renaissance Drama." *PMLA* 102 (1987): 293–303.

Perloff, Marjorie. " 'Homeward Ho!' Silicon Valley Pushkin." *American Poetry Review.* November–December 1986: 37–46.

Perrin, Noel. "We Could Readmit a Little Pleasure into the Study of Literature." *The Chronicle of Higher Education* 15 June 1988, A44.

Rackham, Jeff. *From Sight to Insight.* New York: Holt, 1980.

Rajchman, John. *Michel Foucault: The Freedom of Philosophy.* New York: Columbia University Press, 1985.

Rorty, Richard. *Philosophy and the Mirror of Nature.* Princeton, NJ: Princeton University Press, 1979.

Scholes, Robert, et al. *Text Book: An Introduction to Literary Language.* New York: St. Martin's Press, 1988.

Schor, Naomi. *Breaking the Chains: Women, Theory, and French Realist Fiction.* New York: Columbia University Press, 1985.

_____. *Reading in Detail.* New York: Methuen, 1987.

Shumway, David, and Paul Smith. "Off Our Backs!" *In These Times* 18–24 November 1987, 15.

Siebers, Tobin. *The Ethics of Criticism*. Ithaca, NY: Cornell University Press, 1988.

Siegel, James. "Academic Work: The View from Cornell." *diacritics* 11.1 (Spring 1981): 68–83.

Silverman, Kaja. *The Subject of Semiotics*. New York: Oxford University Press, 1983.

Simpson, David. "Literary Criticism and the Return to 'History.' " *Critical Inquiry* 14 (1988): 721–747.

Smart, William. *Eight Modern Writers*. New York: St. Martin's Press, 1985.

Smith, Barbara Herrnstein. *Contingencies of Value: Alternative Perspectives for Critical Theory*. Cambridge, MA: Harvard University Press, 1988.

Sontag, Susan. *Illness as Metaphor*. New York: Farrar, Strauss & Giroux, 1978.

_____. *AIDS and Its Metaphors*. New York: Farrar, Strauss & Giroux, 1989.

Spanos, William. "Theory in the Undergraduage English Curriculum: Towards an Interested Pedagogy." *boundary 2* 17.2/3 (Winter/Spring, 1989): 41–70.

Spillers, Hortense. "Mama's Baby, Papa's Maybe: An American Grammar Book." *diacritics* 17.2 (Summer 1987): 65–81.

Stanislavski, K. *Stanislavski's Legacy*. Ed. and trans. E. R. Hapgood. New York: Theatre Arts Books, 1958.

Steiner, George. *Real Presences*. Chicago: University of Chicago Press, 1989.

Stitt, Peter. "Writers, Theorists, and the Department of English." *AWP Newsletter: A Publication of the Associated Writing Programs* 19.5 (September–October 1987): 1–3.

Sturrock, Jonathan. "The Linguistics of Writing: A Colloquium." *Times Literary Supplement* 11 July 1986: 769.

Suchthing, Wal. "Reflections upon Roy Bhaskar's 'Critical Relaism.' " *Radical Philosophy* 61 (Summer 1992): 23–31.

Syracuse University. Department of English. Executive Committee. Minutes 25. March 1992.

_____. *The English Newsletter* 6.1 (March 1993).

Tompkins, Jane. *West of Everything: The Inner Life of Westerns*. New York: Oxford University Press, 1992.

Ulmer, Gregory L. *Applied Grammatology: Post(e)-Pedagogy from Jacques Derrida to Joseph Beuys*. Baltimore: Johns Hopkins University Press, 1985a.

_____. "Textshop for Post(e)pedagogy." In *Writing and Reading Differently. Ed. G. Douglas Atkins and M. L. Johnson. Lawrence: University of Kansas Press, 1985b, 38–64.

_____. "The Puncept in Grammatology." In *On Puns*. Ed. Jonathan Culler. Oxford, NY: Blackwell, 1988, 164–189.

_____. *Teletheory: Grammatology in the Age of Video*. New York and London: Routledge, 1989.

Ungar, Steve. *Roland Barthes: The Professor of Desire*. Lincoln: University of Nebraska Press, 1983.

Voloshinov, V. N. *Marxism and the Philosophy of Language*. Trans. L. Matejka and I. R. Titunik. Cambridge, MA: Harvard University Press, 1986.

Walker, Charles R. *Toward the Automatic Factory*. New Haven, CT: Yale University Press, 1957.

Waller, Gary F., "Working within the Paradigm Shift: Poststructuralism and the College Curriculum." *ADE Bulletin* 81 (Fall 1985a): 6–12.

_____. "Writing, Reading, Language, History, Culture: The Structure and Principles of the English Curriculum at Carnegie-Mellon University." Manuscript circulated at a meeting of GRIP, May, 1985b.

Whitaker, Thomas. "Some Reflections on 'Text' and 'Performance.'" *Yale Journal of Criticism* 3.1 (Fall 1989): 143–161.

White, Curtis. "The War Against Theory." *American Book Review* 13.6 (Feb.–Mar. 1992): 4ff.

Widdowson, Peter, ed. *Rereading English*. London: Methuen, 1982.

Willis, Susan. "*Fantasia:* Walt Disney's Los Angeles Suite." *diacritics* 17.2 (Summer 1987): 83–96.

Worth, C. J. "Our Departments Today: New Kinds of Coherence?" *MMLA Bulletin* (Spring 1980): 29.

Yardley, Jonathan. "Paradise Tossed: The Fall of Literary Standards." *Washington Post* 10 January 1988, B12.

Young, Robert. "The Politics of 'The Politics of Literary Theory.' " *Oxford Literary Review* 10.1–10.2 (1988): 131–157.

Zavarzadeh, Mas'ud. " 'Argument' and the Politics of Laughter." *Rethinking Marxism* 4.1 (Spring 1992a): 120–130.

_____. "Pun(k)deconstruction." *Cultural Critique* 22 (Fall 1992b): 5–46.

_____. *Pun(k)deconstruction and the (Post)Modern Political Imaginary*. Washington, DC: Maisonneuve Press, 1993.

_____, and Donald Morton. "War of the Words: The Battle of (and for) English." *In These Times* 28 October–3 Novembrt 1987, 18–19.

_____, and Donald Morton. *Theory, (Post)Modernity, Opposition: An "Other" Introduction to Literary and Cultural Theory*. Washington, DC: Maisonneuve Press, 1991.

Index

249